This is
LARRY MORROW...

This is
LARRY MORROW...

My Life On and Off the Air
Stories from Four Decades in Cleveland Radio

LARRY MORROW

GRAY & COMPANY, PUBLISHERS
CLEVELAND

Gray & Company, Publishers
www.grayco.com

Library of Congress Cataloging-in-Publication Data
Morrow, Larry.
This is Larry Morrow : my life on and off the air / Larry
Morrow.
p. cm.
ISBN 978-1-59851-069-0
1. Morrow, Larry. 2. Radio broadcasters—United States—
Biography. I. Title.
PN1991.4.M585A3 2010
791.4402'8092—dc22
[B]
2010042701

Printed in the United States of America

To Rosary, the greatest gift God ever gave me,
and our three girls, Diana, Donna, and Cynthia.
And to the angel of my life, my granddaughter Lauren.
And to the thousands and thousands of Greater Cleveland-
ers, who went to bed with their transistor radios hidden
under their blankets so they could listen to WIXY 1260 deep
into the night. And to those who not only allowed me into
their homes and cars for over forty years, but who came
to the record hops, speaking engagements, and
memorable, historic Cleveland events.

Contents

WQAL

Do All the Good You Can

Introduction

From my earliest days as a factory worker in Detroit who dreamed of one day having a career in radio, to my arrival in Cleveland in the summer of 1966, Cleveland radio would weave my personal and professional strands, providing me with a remarkable, forty-year career. My relationship with the Cleveland audience extended way beyond my grandest dreams. When I decided radio would be a lifetime pursuit, I thought it would be about celebrated achievements, such as big ratings and national awards. When I finally settled in, I realized it was not about individual exploits but about a heartfelt relationship with the people of the city I served. It was my utmost desire to be their voice. The gratification from making over one hundred appearances a year, mostly for charitable concerns, is where my heart was and remains to this day.

The foundation that led to the concept of this book actually began in 2008, when I spoke to my close friend, Bill Needle, about writing a book on WIXY 1260 and my radio career. It was during our conversation that Bill coined the phrase *WIXY 1260: The Radio Station That Won't Sign Off,* an off-the-cuff but meaningful description.

History has a long memory, so it was important to me to document my radio exploits accurately. I'd like this book to be "the jewel in the crown" for the transistor radio generation—the group that stayed with me throughout the many highs and lows of my radio career, as well as the group that continues to talk about the impact WIXY 1260 had on their lives. During the past two years I have worked towards that goal by immersing myself in the labor of compiling, composing, and cutting and pasting to turn this often-talked-about project into a reality.

My goal was to assemble and produce an orderly account of the most effective promotions as well as the stirring interviews with some of the most important sports, political, and entertainment figures. I wanted to share a behind-the-scenes peek into how they came to be.

As you read through the pages of this book, you'll learn of the brilliant team of Norman Wain, Bob Weiss, and Joe Zingale, who came together equipped with a dream, determination, and a plan to make it a reality: purchase the fledgling, 5,000-watt radio station called WIXY 1260 and convert it into a ratings giant. These new owners not only transformed the once-unknown station in record time, but they made it the talk of the radio industry. The famous WIXY events you'll soon read about are certain to bring back many memories that you probably haven't thought about in years; some will make you laugh, while others may bring tears to your eyes.

After six wonderful years at WIXY, the unthinkable occurred: I would resign and leave on the same day.

In the chapters that follow the WIXY story, you'll learn about the developing trend in radio that led me to a bigger stage in growing my career. To accomplish this, I redirected my challenge to one of the top twenty-five radio signals in America: 3WE 1100. Although the call letters were new to Northeast Ohio, the station's new owner, high-flying and highly regarded local personality Nick Mileti, was not. Nick's plan was to provide a different kind of radio: an exciting, new format that Greater Clevelanders had not heard before. I was asked to not only lead this new, 50,000-watt initiative as morning host, but help sustain it over a period of years— something I personally relished.

As I was launching Phase II of my Cleveland broadcasting career, there was a cornerstone goal to rebuild our great city. My once industrial giant of a city was trying desperately to regain its footing after becoming a national embarrassment. Out of the many conflicting opinions and infinite number of possibilities on how to get Cleveland healthy again, one man emerged as a true leader and visionary. I was honored to be on his team as one of a small group of pioneers to help rebuild the city.

The decades of the '80s and '90s ushered in more change as close radio friends urged me to refocus my career and move to the FM side of the dial, WQAL 104. The young AM radio listeners from my WIXY years who once rebelled against authority, discipline, and the establishment had now blossomed into adults and quickly embraced the clearer and superior sound of hearing their favorite records played on FM. So the move allowed our journey through the years to continue and reinforced the bond between my beloved listeners and me.

Looking back, even though I couldn't articulate my feelings at the time, radio in Cleveland became a lifelong passionate pursuit. I always cared about the business side of radio because I had to, that was how I was paid. But on the other hand, I cared just as much about the relationship between my audience and my community. For the majority of my career, I was blessed to be under the tutelage of talented radio executives who felt the same. They were not only savvy but enterprising leaders who made the journey meaningful, fun, exciting, and mentally stimulating.

Time marches on, and in the radio business, that would launch a new era of younger managers. From observations of my contemporary broadcast pals, I instinctively knew that if you stay too long, someone will ask you to leave. I arrived at that point when all of the sudden a phrase coined by broadcast friend Jay Lynn became a baseline decision for me: "Larry, the kids are driving the bus." But at the end of the day, it was their time at bat. When you begin to disagree with someone's broadcast decisions that are inconsistent with yours, it's a precursor to your departure. I intuitively knew the end of my AM and FM broadcast career was near. I would have wished for a better ending, but my views and theirs were no longer compatible. My lifelong quest was always for a principled career, never for fame. Like everyone, my ultimate hope was to earn respect. And in the pages of this book, you will find that it was my sincere longing to have a meaningful life in broadcasting that carried with it an idealism of character and a distinguished professionalism that stand the test of time.

Part One

The Making of a Broadcaster

CHAPTER 1

You Will Never Make It

It's been forty years since I graduated from the prestigious Detroit School of Announcing and Speech, and I still vividly remember the day my broadcast teachers Pierre Paulin and Jim Garrett, for whom I had the utmost respect, called me into their office for what I hoped to be a departing message of wisdom, encouragement, and final advice on how to succeed in radio. I wasn't prepared for what would follow.

It was Pierre who led the discussion.

"Larry, first of all, congratulations; you have graduated from the most esteemed and influential radio and television broadcast school in America. But I must tell you, Jim Garrett and I personally believe you are *not* going to make it as a broadcaster. You've coasted through this year when you should have been working hard on your voice. You have a very nice voice and an obvious talent, but you have not learned how to use it or express it properly. In this business, if you want to be a success, you have to dedicate yourself to this process—and you have not."

I felt crushed. What Pierre said to me and what I had just heard were two different things. To me, "You will not make it as a broadcaster" meant "You will not make anything of your life." After all, my future as a broadcaster was riding on his evaluation. I was staring down at a life-changing moment. I had just spent a full year trying to hone my craft as a broadcaster in an industry where I thought I had talent.

It's very difficult to measure success against failure when

you're twenty-three years old. But this judgment placed me near the edge of self-rejection, nearly shattering my dream. Radio is a high-performance business; one has to be able to maneuver through periods of skepticism and emerge stronger and more compelling. I had been so certain I was on the right career path. Yet now my future had never seemed less clear.

CHAPTER 2

The Son of a Plumber

I was born Lawrence Dale Morrow on March 24, 1938, in Pontiac, Michigan. When I was confirmed in the Catholic church, I took on the biblical name of Joseph, after the firstborn son of Jacob and Rachel in the book of Genesis. So my full name became Lawrence Dale Joseph Morrow, making my two middle initials "DJ." How fitting. Could this have been preordained?

The official middle child of the Morrow clan, I was the third of five children until my youngest sister, Shari, came along when I was twelve. I had an older brother and sister and two younger brothers. Typical characteristics of the middle-born child include being easily hurt, feeling out of place and misunderstood, being popular with friends, and tending to avoid conflict. That's a pretty good description of me.

My father, Russell (a.k.a. Frenchy), was born in Quebec, Canada, and my mother, Katherine (Katie), in Aleppo, Syria. My father was the strongest man I ever met. He was short in stature but had muscles everywhere. We took a picture of him when he turned fifty, and his body resembled that of Charles Atlas, the famous bodybuilder. Frenchy was larger than life in many ways, but he had two traits that stood out above the rest. First of all, he was a master plumber, called the best of his ilk by many. Second, he was the funniest man I knew, always making up jokes while using his French accent for effect. Dad enjoyed making everyone around him laugh. He was gentle but firm. His "no" meant: "No, and don't ask me again."

In contrast, my mother was the tough disciplinarian. On Saturday mornings we all had household tasks to perform. It was my sisters' responsibility to clean the house, and the boys did everything else: mow the lawn, rake and bag the clippings, and clean the basement, the garage, and the front and back porches. Upon finishing our tasks, my mother, the perfectionist, would inspect everyone's work. Her inspections always included reaching up to run her finger along the window frame. If there was any remaining dust, the job had to be done all over again.

One Saturday morning during the summer before I began working, I had finished sweeping the garage and decided I was ready to play ball with my buddies. After all, everyone was waiting for me outside with their gloves, bats, and a baseball in hand. When my mom came out to inspect the dirt-floor garage I had just swept, she told the guys, "Okay, boys, run along. Larry's going to be late because the garage is not finished." My mother taught us that "good enough" never worked. It always had to be perfect.

POSTWAR, POST-DEPRESSION, THE VALUE OF A NICKEL, AND A WARM LOAF OF BREAD

Money was very tight in the '40s. Back from World War II, Dad was returning to his lifelong craft as a plumber. We lived in simple surroundings: a small, seven-room, A-frame house that had handsome gray siding. The front yard wasn't much larger than a postage stamp, but our backyard was long and narrow, just long enough for Mom to hang our clothes out on the line. One of my fondest memories is helping Mom take sheets off of the clothesline. I can still hear my mother saying, "Larry, smell the fresh air in those sheets!"

My mother, an expert gardener, loved roses so much that our backyard won several local awards for its design, upkeep, and beauty. My father kept the lawn meticulously groomed. We had the best-looking yard in our small neighborhood, which consisted of twenty homes on the block. During the summer months, almost everyone sat on the swings on their front porches and looked forward to waving and talking to whoever walked by. Our parents knew all our neighbors on a first-name basis, and we addressed them all as "Mr." and "Mrs."

The first floor of our home consisted of a living room, a dining room, where we gathered to celebrate the special holidays of Easter, Thanksgiving, and Christmas, and a kitchen that would be referred to as an efficiency by today's standards. There was a small stove, an icebox that held fifty pounds of ice, and a round, rugged kitchen table with a gray formica top and chrome trim. There was just enough space around the table to seat the eight members of my family when we met for dinner every night at 6 p.m. sharp. Dinner was mandatory, and no one was ever late. Unless my father spoke first to ask how our day went, there was very little discussion around our dinner table. My father had worked very hard during the day at his plumbing trade, and my mom was equally tired after preparing the family meals and taking care of six children. Dinner was a time for peace and quiet.

The upstairs of our house consisted of one small bathroom that was shared by the eight of us and three small bedrooms: one for my two sisters, one for my mom and dad, and a third for the four boys, who shared bunk beds.

My mother and father shopped at a large grocery store just blocks from our home. The owner, Guido, would often stand at the front of the store and greet you by name as you entered his market. I still remember when Guido arranged a six-week promotion with the Pillsbury Baking Company to bring in a rather large bag of flour and have it placed directly in the middle of the store where all of his customers could see it. The bag resembled a typical sack of flour, except that it was at least fifty times larger. Shoppers were to guess its weight, and the person who came closest to guessing the actual weight would be given the flour at the end of the promotion. My mother got very lucky and guessed the exact weight at 175 pounds.

Mom was thrilled when she received the call from Guido to tell her she was the only person who had guessed the exact weight. It took several men to carry the large sack from the delivery truck into our kitchen. I can still remember them hauling it in and placing it directly in the middle of the room, which is where it remained until the last scoop of flour was used.

My mother was a Syrian-born version of the General Mills creation, Betty Crocker, so almost as soon as the flour was delivered, she began baking large quantities of bread, coffee cakes, chocolate chip cookies, and brownies; all were her original recipes. On Fridays, the aroma of homemade bread coming from our kitchen permeated our entire small neighborhood, which was great advertising when it came time to sell the bread. When the baking was done, my two younger brothers, Bobby and Mickey, and I had the responsibility of taking the warm bread and other goodies in our wagon and knocking on doors in and around our neighborhood to sell what Mom had made.

My brother Bobby was five, Mickey was six, and I was seven. We were scared about knocking on doors, so Mom gave us our sales pitch. "Boys, hold the warm bread in your hand, knock on the door and say, 'Good afternoon, Mrs. Williams. Our mom just baked a warm loaf of bread. Would you like to buy one?'" A loaf of bread cost thirty-five cents, cookies were a dime each, and the coffee cake was sixty-five cents.

When we returned home, our wagon was always empty. Mom then took the money and put it into a large coffee can, which she kept on top of the icebox. Her homemade bread was an instant hit, and we soon began receiving weekly orders. Within a year, Mom's little bakery business made enough money to replace our icebox with our first refrigerator and buy a brand new Tappan oven. For the first time since Mom and Dad got married and started their family, they finally realized that they had left the Great Depression of 1929 behind.

It was President Herbert Hoover who encouraged America that better times were coming when he coined the phrase "a chicken in every pot and a car in every garage." It was now 1947 and people were no longer jobless; business and industry began to boom, and Mom and Dad represented the rebirth of the American dream. By the way, it took my mom over a year to use all of the Pillsbury flour. Who would have thought that an oversized sack of flour could have such a huge impact on the quality of life for one family for whom every nickel counted?

Speaking of nickels, a conversation between my mom and dad rings clear to this day. It was an early Friday morning, around 6:30 a.m., and my father was getting ready to leave for work. Mom had packed his lunch, which always consisted of a sandwich, a piece of fruit, and a homemade cookie. She also filled his thermos with hot coffee, which he sipped throughout the day. I had just awakened to get ready for school when I heard my mother raise her voice in an uncharacteristic way at Dad.

"Russ, I gave you a quarter on Monday, and it was supposed to last you all week. The quarter is for a nickel a day for a donut, but here you are, on Friday, asking for an extra nickel?"

"Yesterday I bought Tony a donut because he didn't have a nickel. That's why I need another one today," explained my dad.

"Honey, I'll do it this time, but you have to be more careful," my mother responded.

MY EARLY WORK LIFE

I began working at the tender age of nine. During the summer, my mother insisted we work rather than play all day. My older brother, Jim, was working as a caddy at a golf and country club that my parents believed was too far for me to hitchhike to, so he suggested I go to Bloomfield Hills Country Club to look for work. The next day I headed over with high hopes of obtaining my first job.

Bloomfield Hills Country Club was just outside Detroit, about five miles from home. It was the most prestigious golf and country club in the area. The members consisted of the "Who's Who" of the auto industry: the Henry Ford family; the Fishers, makers of the Fisher Body car frames; heirs to the Chrysler fortune; and a number of Detroit's old-money families. These men and women, revered by many, dressed and acted as conquerors of the business and social world. They were Detroit's wealthy and powerful members of high society. While most of America was struggling from the effects of the war, and although the auto industry was pulling itself up by the bootstraps, prosperity seemed to be everywhere at Bloomfield Hills Country Club.

When I arrived at the club, I entered through the servants' entrance and was greeted by a giant of a man.

"Hello, I'm Danny," he said. I had never met a black man and was impressed by his kindness and soft-spoken demeanor.

"Hi, my name is Larry Morrow, and I'm looking for a job. Is there anything I can do here?"

Danny gently put his arm around me and said, "Son, you've come to the right place at the right time. We could use your help. Have you ever worked in a shoeshine department before?"

"No sir," I replied enthusiastically, "but I can learn fast."

"We don't pay much, but how's twenty-five cents an hour suit you? The club is closed on Mondays, but otherwise we'll need you eight hours a day, six days a week. Some days the tips are better than others, and when we have a good day, we'll share the tips with you. When the day is done, you'll sweep up and put all the polish back where it belongs. Is that okay with you, Larry?" I ecstatically accepted his offer. I had my very first job.

Danny then gave me a tour of the area where all male permanent help slept, showered, and ate their meals. The women shared similar quarters on the other side of the club. There were no white servants in those days; everyone he introduced me to was black. All servants lived in the lower level of the club; their private quarters ran along the side of the boilers and furnaces. Each bedroom consisted of four small cots, a small dresser, and a lamp at each bedside. They also shared one large bathroom with a large shower, similar to what you would see in a men's locker room. There were no windows in the bottom level. It may sound like I'm describing a dungeon, but to me it was paradise.

At the end of our tour was the shoeshine room. "This is where we make our living," Danny said. It was a large room with high walls and a bathroom. There were three buffers where they would put the finishing touches on the members' shoes. I was awestruck by the large wall behind the shoeshine buffers that consisted of stacks and stacks of Kiwi polish in every color that you could imagine. The aroma of shoe polish permeated the air.

Danny went on to explain that many of the shoes for the special members, such as Lee Iacocca and Walter Chrysler Jr., were not to touch the buffer to avoid burning the expensive leather. These shoes were individually shined with a soft cloth instead. This basement would be my summer home for the next several years. To this day, each time I polish my shoes, I take a whiff of the Kiwi polish, and it takes me all the way back to those memorable days spent in the shoeshine room.

I was instructed by Danny that when I arrive for work, always enter the club through the servants' entrance; never use the front entrance. The front entrance was exclusively for members, who would arrive in their brand new Fords, Chryslers, and Cadillacs, and drive around a beautiful circular drive to the main entrance. Members were greeted by a black valet dressed in a black suit, white shirt and tie, and white gloves. "Good morning, Mrs. Ford," the valet would say. "Are you having lunch today? Have a wonderful day." He would then park her car while she walked to the tall double doors to the grand living room in the center of the club. Another servant with the same uniform, including the white gloves, stood at the front door. He would greet her by her formal name, open the huge double doors, and wish her a great day as she passed by. It was common for every helper, whether you were a waiter, busboy, shoeshine boy, or parking attendant, to know every member by name. That was the beginning of my memorization of names—an early-learned skill that became a lifelong pursuit.

I remember being very excited as I got ready for my first day of work. Dressed in a T-shirt, Levis jeans, and ankle-high sneakers, I left home at the crack of dawn and walked a mile to the main street of Woodward Avenue. For the next leg of my journey, I hitchhiked four miles to the club.

Upon my arrival, Danny sat me down at the shoeshine table and said, "Larry, this is what you will do on a daily basis. Just above us is the main locker room where the golfers change into their golf clothes, leave their unpolished shoes in front of their locker, and go play golf. The locker room attendant will pick up the members' shoes and bring them to the door located at the top of the stairs, which I will show you in a minute. He will then ring a bell that can be heard in this room to signal us that shoes are waiting to be shined. You will then go to the top of the stairs just adjacent to the shoeshine room, open the door to the locker room, and pick up the shoes. Now, this is very important, Larry. Club policy prohibits us from entering the members' locker room, so you are never to go in there without my permission. At times there will be five or six pairs of shoes waiting for you to pick up. Let me show you how to stack five pairs of shoes on your arm."

You can imagine how amazed I was to witness the art of carrying so many shoes at one time without dropping one or having the leather rub against another shoe. Danny informed me that each pair of shoes was to be treated as precious cargo.

After the shoes were shined, I would carefully take them back upstairs, open the door, and gently place the perfectly shined shoes on the carpet. This process was later repeated with the members' golf shoes following their day on the golf course.

After two years of working with Danny, my responsibilities expanded as he now trusted me (after a lot of practice) to polish and buff the golfers' shoes. He respectfully gave me the title of "assistant shoeshine boy." I was only allowed to polish and buff the black or dark brown shoes; tan shoes needed to be carefully buffed, and that was left to the experts. At the end of the day, as promised, when the tips were really good, the guys would give me a small portion of their bounty. I can remember one day bringing home two dollars. These men, who clearly faced discrimination, taught me many admirable traits, including self-respect.

My ultimate desire at the club was to be a caddy. In my youthful opinion, that's where the big money was being made. So, with five years under my belt, at the age of fourteen, I was thrilled to finally reach my goal. As a caddy, I would wait in line just outside the pro shop where the golfers assembled until I was assigned a loop (carry a golf bag) for eighteen holes. Walking the holes and carrying the bag for the member golfer would take around four-and-a-half hours. That was enough for a young guy. I earned $1.50 for a day's work and, most of the time, a tip that ranged from $1 to $1.50; if I was really good in finding a member's lost ball, I would be given an additional dollar. Most days, I went home with three to four dollars, which doubled my shoeshine wages. When I arrived home for dinner at the end of the day, I gave all the money I earned to my mother to use for whatever she thought necessary.

Of all my memories from Bloomfield Hills Country Club, my one claim to fame happened when was I was chosen out of a group of caddies to carry the bag for Sam Snead, who at that time was the world's greatest golfer. Sam was also known as being very frugal, but to a teen with a limited vocabulary who didn't understand the meaning of frugal, I was extremely disappointed when I didn't receive a tip from him.

SCARRED FOR LIFE

Another vivid memory from my days at Bloomfield Hills took place at an event where I saw numerous stars of a different type. While waiting for a loop, the caddies often played baseball behind what was known as the caddie shack. I was in the batter's box, waiting my turn at bat, when the batter let the bat slip from his sweaty hands. It flew through the air and hit me directly in the mouth. I was rushed to the hospital with a gash on my upper lip and eight broken teeth. Twenty stitches later I returned home. I have worn a mustache for almost my entire broadcast career to cover up the scar.

I continued to work at the club six days a week until I was sixteen. I then moved up to busboy (carrying dishes), where I remained until I graduated from high school. My father assumed I would follow in his footsteps and become a plumber. He had the connections to get me enrolled in plumbing school, and it made perfect sense to everyone that I would naturally follow my dad, as well as my older brother, Jim, who had already gone that route and was now working in the plumbing industry.

As for my plans, I was eighteen years old and at an awkward stage of life. I was not brave enough to turn down my father's request, and I certainly did not want to disappoint him. As confused as I was, this much I knew: I had a deep love and respect for my dad, but I lacked the fire in my gut to become a master plumber like him. I also knew I had to hustle to make my own decision on what to do with my life because if I vacillated, my dad would make the decision for me.

As I continued to sift through the options, my thoughts drifted towards the military, which was something I had always been drawn to. When Dad returned from Saipan, Japan, following the war, he not only brought back his uniforms, but several Navy and Army stripes. So whenever my two younger brothers and I would play war games, one of us would try and grab my dad's Navy jacket or pin the old military stripes on our shirts.

Another factor that played heavily into my decision was that in the 1950s, all young men were required to serve in the military. For me, it was a logical conclusion that it would be best to get my military obligations over with sooner so it would not interrupt my life later. I began talking to good buddies from high school about my possible plan.

Once the decision was finally made, I was eager to put my

plan in motion. I woke up early one Saturday morning, rolled out of bed, and immediately headed for downtown Pontiac, Michigan, to the military recruiting offices. Upon my arrival, I proceeded to visit all the branches of service: Navy, Army, Air Force, Coast Guard, and Marines. My first thought was that I'd enlist in the Navy, as my father had been a Navy Seabee in WWII, and my older brother, Jim, followed in his footsteps and had completed four years of duty as well. But when I saw the Marine sergeant in his impressive dress blues with that famous leatherlike neck and red stripe down the outside of his dress pant, my heart began to beat faster. I knew that was it: I wanted to be a Marine. What further solidified my decision was their buddy plan. The buddy system was founded on the premise that it was much easier to get integrated into the Marines if you had a buddy to go through it with you. So in the end, my decision broke my family's Navy tradition. I signed my enlistment papers and was thrilled with my choice.

CHAPTER 3

My Very First Interview:
Elvis Presley

I became a United States Marine in June 1956. With that decision, I would soon leave my boyhood home for boot camp at the Marine Corps Recruit Depot in San Diego. I was to report to the Detroit military departure office and leave on July 7. When I went home and told my parents of my decision to enlist, Dad was not very happy, but Mom was supportive.

When the day finally came for me to leave home, my dad said he would drive me to Detroit. I could see the sadness in his eyes, and I'm sure he could sense the same in mine. The trip took about forty minutes. We didn't talk much, but I could tell that, despite his sadness, he was supportive. We didn't hug in those days, but my dad had some imperative parting words for me as he dropped me off: "Good luck, son. Don't forget to write your mother." The plane left Detroit filled with Marine recruits.

We stopped in Chicago for a brief layover. A few of us went into a bar to get a soft drink. I was a huge fan of rock and roll then, so I was very aware of all its top stars. Sitting at the bar with a few members of his band was the newest superstar, Elvis Presley, who had the number-one record in the country: "Heartbreak Hotel." I said to the guys, "Look, there's Elvis Presley." We couldn't believe our eyes. His picture had been in all the music magazines. His music was being played on *American Bandstand*, and I had just read that he would be performing on the very popular Ed Sullivan TV variety show in September. That appearance would be his breakthrough performance.

I suggested to the guys that we go over and say hello. They were afraid so they said, "You go first and we'll follow." I was quite nervous, too, but sitting at the bar just a few feet away was America's new musical sensation. We could not pass up this opportunity. Can you imagine a group of Marine recruits ready to do battle for their country with rifles, bayonets, and machine guns, yet fearful of approaching a guy with a guitar?

What a story we would tell our parents and friends: *We met Elvis Presley!* When we approached him, he was quietly sitting, having a soft drink. I said, "Please forgive me, but we're Marine recruits on our way to boot camp in San Diego, California. Is it possible we could have your autograph?"

Elvis could not have been more engaging. He inquired where we were from and then congratulated us on serving our country. None of us had paper, so he signed his name on a little bar napkin. What we didn't know then was that in six months, in early 1957, Elvis would become one of us and serve his country in the U.S. Army.

I have no idea what became of my napkin. In retrospect, I believe that meeting with Elvis was my destiny. I would leave the Marines in a few years, become a DJ, and end up playing almost every hit single he ever recorded. Now I can proudly say, "My very first interview in entertainment was with Elvis Presley."

We left Chicago shortly thereafter and flew straight to San Diego. There were around seventy recruits on the plane. Prior to this, not one of us had ever been this far away from home. I won't go into all the "interesting" details on what happens to recruits once you are in the hands of the Marines, but know that it was intimidating, demanding, and incredibly scary. Through it all, I was excited about being in California and, above all, being a United States Marine. There was a tremendous distinction among the military services. Being a Marine meant you were called on to be the best and the toughest.

Compared to the weather in Pontiac, San Diego was heaven. Each morning would begin as a beautiful, crystal-clear, sunny day. The temperature would rise to 75 to 80 degrees every day and drop to a very comfortable temperature at night. Although boot camp was true drudgery, it didn't matter. It was during this time that I decided I would never leave California.

SEMPER FIDELIS PUT TO THE TEST

When I enlisted under the buddy plan, my close friend, David Jones from St. Fred's High School in Pontiac, joined up as well. To my best recollection, David was the only black student in my class. St. Fred's was a small Catholic school, with a total of seven hundred students enrolled from first through twelfth grades. There were fifty-six students in my graduating class of 1956.

David and I were in the same class together, from first grade all the way through grade twelve. We were also teammates on St. Fred's football, basketball, and baseball teams. He wore a perpetual smile, and because everyone had such deep love and respect for him, he was elected as one of the officers of our graduating class. Because we lived on separate sides of town, I don't recall ever being at David's house or him being at mine. But there were so many social activities going on at St. Fred's that we got to know everyone's parents in our class. I remember David's mom had the face of an angel and, like her son, wore a smile from ear to ear.

During our boot camp training, David's mom died suddenly. As his buddy, we left San Diego to travel home for the funeral. We had very little money; we were paid only eighty-four dollars a month, so we had to find the least expensive way home. The cheapest transportation was a train that carried cattle. The train would pick up cows and bulls and deliver them to different cities across America with the final stop in Detroit, just outside our hometown. David and I sat and slept on hard board seats the entire way. The accommodations weren't plush, but the fare was inexpensive and the only way we could afford to get home. The trip took us six days.

Following the sad funeral and burial of David's mom, we had to find a different way back to our base in California. My mother saw an ad in the newspaper where a man in California needed to have a car driven from Pontiac to his house in San Diego. We contacted him, and he agreed to let us drive his car if David and I would pay for the gas and our meals. That was the extent of our expenses. Two eighteen-year-olds would now travel twenty-six hundred miles across America for the very first time.

We mapped out our strategy for the trip and headed west to Chicago, where we picked up Route 66 in a brand new 1956 Cadillac, at that time, the most expensive American-made car. There was a very popular song from the '50s, "Route 66":

> If you ever plan to motor west,
> Travel my way, take the highway that is best.
> Get your kicks on Route 66!

The modern turnpike and interstate highway systems made Route 66 obsolete. In 1956, it was the most direct route to travel from Chicago to Los Angeles, crossing through the Great Plains and southwest.

David and I traveled in our green Marine fatigues, which is casual military gear that you still see soldiers wearing today. Before leaving Michigan, our families stocked our coolers with enough food to last us for a few days.

In central Missouri, we were detoured and ended up traveling as far south as Jackson, Mississippi, before we could pick up Route 66 in Oklahoma. Around noontime we decided to take a break and grab a quick bite to eat. As we walked into a small restaurant just off the main highway, I noticed that there were a few huge eighteen-wheel trucks parked outside as well. When we opened the door to the restaurant, we were stopped by a rather large man who stood just inside the entrance. He looked straight at me and said, "Look guys, I can serve you but not the nigger."

During this time, racial clashes between blacks and whites were making headlines, especially in Mississippi. I was familiar with the N- word, but up to this point in my life I had *never* heard anyone use it. What an incredible shock this was to both of us.

I firmly blurted back, "Hey, we're Marines. We serve our country so you can live in a peaceful America. We are both very hungry. Can't you just give us a sandwich and a Coke and we'll be on our way?" With a little more firmness in his voice he repeated, "I can serve you, but not the nigger." We left immediately.

The same, shocking scenario played out in a second restaurant a few miles away. At our third stop, we were again stopped at the door. This time, a white man sitting nearby saw the terrible situation that was before us and came to our rescue. He took us outside and said, "I, too, was in the Marines. Tell me what you want to eat. I'll buy it for you and then it will be best for you both to get the hell out of Mississippi."

Making our situation particularly scary, we were traveling through a state that had put its stamp of approval on a murder: Two white men had killed a fourteen-year-old black boy named Emmett Till. Both men were acquitted, which writer Amos Dixon explained in the February 1956 edition of the *California Eagle:* "Their acquittal would weaken the written law; their conviction would strike a blow at the unwritten law, which is far more sacred in the South. The unwritten law rests on the premise that the law for Negroes is whatever the dominant whites of the community say it is. Under the unwritten law, Negroes can be, and are, denied all manner of rights and privileges supposedly guaranteed under state and federal constitutions and laws." Although progress and change would come slowly, the tragedy of the legal racial segregation that existed then no longer exists today.

I could not have felt worse for David. I was so angry I wanted to take on the guy in the restaurant right there and then. After all, I was just out of Marine boot camp and felt I could make mush of him. David took it all in stride as if he knew something like this might happen. Once we finally got our food, I realized that what had been drummed into our heads in boot camp was true: We were a band of brothers. Semper fidelis: always faithful.

David and I could hardly wait to get out of Mississippi. We never encountered racial prejudice again. Our six-day, disastrous train ride, where we slept sitting straight up on hard boards, was a little different. Our three-day, luxurious ride in the comfort of the best from General Motors took us safely back to California, where we arrived well rested.

FOOTBALL

I was fortunate to have some athletic ability as a youngster. Like a lot of kids, I sometimes daydreamed of becoming a professional athlete. In each of my four years in high school at St. Fred's in Pontiac I lettered in football, basketball, and baseball. Football was my favorite.

I had joined the school football team in fifth grade, and for four years we won almost every game in our division. Then, in high school I made the team as a freshman—and we *lost* every game for four straight years. When we played against the best teams in our division, we lost by one point. The same was true when we played the worst teams. We lost by one or two points. In my junior year, despite all of our losses, I was voted to the second team All-Catholic squad as quarterback. But I never knew what it was like to win a high school football game.

In the Marine Corps, after boot camp and infantry training, I went out for the Camp Pendleton football team. There were 40,000 Marines at Camp Pendleton. The base was made up of the 1st, 5th, 7th and 11th Marine divisions, each with its own football team. My division, the 11th Marines, were called the

"Cannon Cockers." (We fired the 105 and 155 howitzers, which could take out a small tank division at 500 yards. We also fired four-deuce mortar shells, designed to blow up smaller units, such as tanks and personnel.) Three hundred men showed up for the first day of practice. Some of them had played college football, I was told. I had never seen guys that big. While playing at St. Fred's, the biggest guy I ever competed against was at best six-foot-three and maybe 220 pounds. Some of these guys were giants—six-foot-five, 250 pounds and up.

We lined up for our first exercise, two lines stretched from one end zone to the other, standing five yards across from each other. At the coach's whistle, one side would tackle the other. I was in the line that had to tackle first. The whistle blew, and I hit the guy across from me as hard as I could. The twenty-five coaches present for that exercise went down the line judging players on their tackling ability.

A coach came to me and said, "Morrow, you're out." I thought that meant for this particular drill. So I dropped back and waited for the next drill. After all, this was going to be a long day of practice. I hadn't touched a football yet. I knew as soon as I got a football in my hands, I'd show them what I could do. But I never got the chance. A few minutes later, a coach yelled out, "All those who were told 'you're out,' head for the locker room, take off your uniform, shower, and get back to your unit. You're finished. You're not tough enough to play for the Marine Corps."

Needless to say, I was crushed. Four years of failure in high school and now this. I thought that was a weak judgment on my ability. After all, I wasn't a lineman; I was a quarterback.

The entire next year I worked almost daily to get ready.

When the tryouts began the next season, I was ready to line up and kill the guy across from me. Well, they never did that exercise. The coach said, "All linemen over here, quarterbacks over there . . ." I made the team and was the starting quarterback for the 11th Marines Cannon Cockers. We won the base championship and were invited to play San Diego State College (we beat them handily). So I wrapped up my football career once again undefeated. (After leaving the Marines, I considered going out for the team at the University of California, Berkeley. But after seeing how big and fast their quarterbacks were, I decided my football career was over. At five-foot-ten inches tall and 175 pounds, I was much too small to compete at that level.)

MARINE CORPS BOOT CAMP

My Hawaiian drill instructor (DI), who was also the head of our platoon, would assemble us at the end of every day. I can still hear him shout out, "Platoon 1016 on the road." We would run from our billets, forming two long lines of forty-three each. While we all stood at attention, he would shout out, "My wife, Kaleena, in Oahu, Hawaii, is waiting to hear you all say, 'Good night, Kaleena.'" In unison, we would reply, "Good night, Kaleena." The DI would then shout back, "She can't hear you." This would go on and on until he was satisfied. Before hitting the sack every night, I would take a few moments to stare at the starlit sky, watch the light breeze tip the tops of the palm trees, and dream of my future, wondering where in California I would settle after my time in the Marines.

While serving in the corps, I learned how to protect myself and my platoon in wartime. However, in the tradition of my father and three brothers, the privilege of serving my country meant more to me than anything. To this day, when I walk onto my front porch, I swell with pride as I see the American flag next to my Marine Corps flag. Semper fidelis, always faithful, was not negotiable. It was a way a life for all of us who wore the uniform.

AFTER THE MARINES: THE NEXT PHASE

In July 1958, at the age of twenty, I was honorably discharged from the Marines. I then went to live and work with a friend from Pontiac, whom I'll call Andy, whose family owned a tire recap service in Berkeley, California, located on Telegraph Road, just down the street from the University of California. My job was to pick up tires from companies that wanted their clients' tires recapped—a process where the old tire is buffed down and resurfaced with new rubber. We serviced the local clients in and around Berkeley, as well as in San Francisco. The entire recap process took about an hour for four tires, followed by another hour to cool down. After the cool down was completed, the tires were ready for delivery. We had several machines, which meant I could take up to twenty tires at a time.

I was following my dream, which was to remain in California, graduate from U.C. Berkeley, and begin my new life in the bright, warm sunshine of northern California. I frequently reconfirmed the decision I had made while in boot camp to never go back to Pontiac. I had found my paradise on earth.

MOVING UP, MOVING OUT, MOVING BACK

While I was busy putting down roots in California, my older brother, Jim, five years my senior, got married, had three children, and was living in Virginia Beach, Virginia. My two younger brothers, Mickey, one year younger, and Bobby, two years younger, were both serving in the Marines (a new tradition for the Morrow boys). My two sisters, Sandy and Shari, were building their own families at home in Michigan.

CHAPTER 4

Leaving California Behind

February 1960 would begin a new series of events that changed the course of my life. My mother called with devastating news: "You'd better pack up everything and head home. Dad is sick and in the hospital, and you're the only son available to help the family." Although I was primarily concerned about my father, I admit that I was crushed by the thought of having to leave my dream in California.

Yet, when I look back, it was surely the hand of God directing me away from what would have sadly become a catastrophic lifestyle of emptiness, destruction, and unfulfilled expectations. Why? By the time I had finished my term in the Marines, I had picked up a bad habit: what began as casual drinking in California would become a daily routine of sharing a fifth of gin a day with Andy.

RECKLESS LIFESTYLE

For Andy and me, our morning routines began in a similar fashion, with Andy going to classes at a local college while I roamed the campus of U.C. Berkeley. Later in the afternoon, Andy and I would meet up at his father's business.

When our work day was finished, we returned to his family's beautiful home snuggled in the scenic hills of Orinda. I lived with Andy's family for a short while before moving one block from the university. In lieu of paying rent, my daily duty was to feed their two thoroughbred horses every evening following dinner.

IT'S PARTY TIME

After all our daily duties were done, it was time for the night-life to begin. Our first stop was the liquor store, where we would pick up a fifth of gin and party at the home of one of Andy's friends. As I recall, there was a party going on almost every evening. On the rare nights when there was no party, we would drive through Walnut Creek to the highest peak between Orinda and Oakland and view the popular bridges—the Golden Gate, the San Raphael, and the Oakland Bay bridges—and drink. Some nights, our goal was to finish the fifth. Afterward, we would drive around the mountains of Oakland and San Francisco like it was the Daytona 500, many times on two wheels.

We never consumed alcohol during the work day, but our reckless behavior continued. One day we had to deliver two tires to Los Angeles, several hours south of San Francisco. While driving Andy's 1958 Corvette south on famous Highway 1 along the Pacific Ocean, he opened it up. The speedometer was pinned at 160 mph, and he left it there for a few miles. We were frightened but thrilled at the same time. On one hand, it was the buzz of my life. I could feel my heart pounding in my chest, almost as though it were racing to compete with the speed of the Corvette. On the other hand, as I smelled the burning of rubber on our rear tires, my common sense kicked in. With the objects outside of my window moving by too fast for me to focus on anything, I knew that in one quick, foolish moment, we could easily become airborne and launch into eternity.

The feeling of going 160 mph also brought back raging memories of my first, and absolute worst, roller coaster ride. I was seven years old when my older brother Jim prodded me to join him on the ride. First of all, I didn't want to, and second, my brother insisted that we sit in the front car. He reassured me, "You'll love it, Larry!" When we hit the first, long hill, my brother threw his hands up and asked me to do the same. I was so petrified that I thought the hot dog I had eaten for lunch was about to make a quick exit from my stomach. That was the good news. The bad news was the ride operators couldn't stop the roller coaster because it was raining. The coaster sped out of control around the track seven times before we could come to a stop. For a seven-year-old, it was the scariest moment of my life. To this day, I have never been on another roller coaster.

Now here I was again, this time going 160 mph down Highway 1 in a Corvette made of fiberglass that wasn't much stronger than a potato chip. Once Andy backed off of 160 mph, we both took deep breaths and decided right then and there that there would be no more of that kind of dangerous silliness.

CHAPTER 5

From Trainee to President

Well, I quickly did as Mom asked. I sold my car and what little furniture I had and returned home within a few days of her call. My father had spoken to the Pipe Fitters Union and secured a job for me as a ditch digger. In just one week, I was removed from heaven in California and found myself in hell in Detroit, using a thirty-pound jackhammer to grind through fourteen inches of frozen tundra in ten-degree weather so the pipe fitters could lay their pipe. Talk about a shattered dream.

Around the same time, Chevrolet began building the new four-door Corvair and was hiring several thousand employees. I applied and got a job putting on sill plates, which are the chrome plates that hold the carpet down along the front and back doors. I was soon transferred to the water-test department and later promoted to assistant foreman.

In the initial phases of a car's production, it moves along the assembly line with only the body and the windows in place. The engine, wheels, seats, and everything else would be assembled further down the line. My job was to climb into the car, close the doors, and ride in it through a water tunnel for about two minutes. In my left hand was a flashlight so I could look for leaks. In my right hand, I held a diagram of the inside of the car. When I spotted a leak, I would jot it down on the diagram and pass it on to the inspection department to be fixed further down the line. I mastered my job, received adulation from my department's upper management, and was now dreaming of one day becoming the president of General Motors. Indeed, General Motors played a major role in shaping my future, but it was not to be as president of the corporation.

As a youngster, I often whistled tunes unfamiliar to my mother. She once remarked to me that perhaps I could become a music writer when I grew up. In 1952, when I was fourteen, my mother saw an article in the paper about a jingle company that wrote musical slogans for advertisers. She encouraged me to take the Woodward Avenue bus to the jingle-making studio in Detroit. The bus fare each way was a nickel, and it was a forty-minute ride from Pontiac.

When I entered the studio, the owner asked me why I was there. I told him my mother thought I was creative and suggested that one day I could be a jingle writer. Knowing that I had traveled a long distance, the owner wanted to encourage me, so he told me, "Well, Larry, here's what we do. We write slogans for our clients. Do you know what a slogan is?" I told him I did. He then asked if I played a musical instrument. I responded, "No, but I can come up with an original tune." He then excused himself from our meeting, telling me, "I'll be right back." A few moments later he returned with a few slogans and a tape recorder. One of the slogans he left for me to sing was, "GM Mark of Excellence," the famous logo for General Motors. He then turned on the tape recorder and left the studio.

I sang a few original tunes to each slogan. The owner came back a few minutes later, listened to what I had sung, and indicated that he liked the GM slogan. He told me that they paid their writers fifteen dollars for every original piece of music used. And since he was convinced that they were going to use this jingle, he paid me. As I hopped on the bus for the return trip home, I felt jubilant. Then, when the bus stopped in Pontiac, I ran the entire two blocks home because I couldn't wait to show my mother and father the money I had earned. The jingle, *GM Mark of Excellence*, ran for almost twenty years with my music. This experience marked the beginning of a long and successful jingle-writing career.

Since I had already written the musical theme to the GM slogan, I asked myself, "Could it be my destiny to one day become the president of GM?" I did all the right things to put myself on this path: After studying engineering at the Detroit School of Technology, I enrolled at GM Tech in Flint, Michigan, and began my new career path in the auto industry. Sadly enough, I never stayed in one school or in one city for more than a year, which meant I never finished either of these educational opportunities.

A BRIEF DEPARTURE TO STARDOM

Before my youngest brother, Bobby, joined the Marines, he formed a singing group, the Originals, with two of his closest friends, Bob and Jerry Rigonan, who were young, talented brothers from a Filipino family in our neighborhood. Since Bobby was the lead singer of the group, he asked me to take good care of the Originals until he returned home for good. I was a bass singer in St. Fred's church choir, and I had a singing group while in the Marines, so I began meeting with Bob and Jerry to practice background vocals in preparation for becoming part of my brother's backup singing group when he returned from the Marines. Bob, Jerry, and I met almost nightly to practice.

We picked out some of the vocal styles of the "doo wop" groups behind superstar singers like Elvis Presley and his backup group, the Jordanairs. We also liked the group that sang backup for local sensation Jack Scott, who had a few hit records under his belt. Jack lived close by, just outside of Detroit in Hazel Park. We practiced singing the background to all of Jack's well-known hits and thought we were actually better than his original singing group, the Chantones.

I read that Jack owned a little entertainment club in Hazel Park, called Jack Scott's Barn Dance, and that he would be performing there on the upcoming Saturday night. It was late winter of 1958 when I suggested to Bob and Jerry that we go down there and see Jack, meet him, and tell him of our desire to sing backup. If he liked us then he might help us get our start with another singer.

When we arrived at the club, we saw a stage and dance floor that resembled that of Dick Clark's *American Bandstand*. Only this time Jack Scott, not Dick Clark, was the central figure. After we paid the one-dollar admission fee, the ticket-taker informed us that Jack was on a break but would return in twenty minutes. As we continued our conversation, I mentioned our desire to meet Jack and was very excited when he told me he would talk with him. I also said, "Tell Jack that we're a singing group and that we think we're as good, if not better than, his current backup group. Also, tell Jack that we know the background vocals to all of his songs." What we did not know at the time was that Jack was having issues with his current group and was thinking of making a change.

Within a few minutes, the ticket-taker returned to where we were waiting and told us Jack wanted to meet with us in his dressing room. It happened so fast we didn't even have time to get nervous. He was there when we walked in—the embodiment of a young Canadian guy who had settled in Detroit and followed his dream to become an international sensation.

As soon as we introduced ourselves, Jack got right to the point. He picked up his guitar and said, "Okay, let me hear what you know." He went right into his biggest hit, "My True Love." Without hesitation, we hit all the vocals perfectly. I could tell he was pleased by the giant smile on his face. He stopped in the middle of the song and said, "Let's try another." In just a few minutes we went over four songs. He then said the most incredible phrase I could ever expect to hear: "All right, let's go out and do it." We then joined Jack on stage for his next set; at that moment, we became Jack's new backup group. Following the success of our unofficial debut, Jack said he was going to record four new songs on a new record label, Top Rank, and he would like to use us for the recording session. "Can you guys make a rehearsal at my home tomorrow? The whole band is coming," Jack said. When we arrived at Jack's house, he had a brand new 1958 red Cadillac sitting in his driveway. We were awestruck. We were about to walk into a house that was owned by a guy whose voice and name were heard on radio stations all across America.

Jack's home was not overly ostentatious, but for us it was a castle. We rang the doorbell, and when the door opened, Jack was there to greet us with a giant smile. "Come on in, guys, and meet the band." When we walked in, Jack introduced us to each band member. The group was set up and ready to go into a large room just off the living room. There was a lead guitarist, a drummer, a piano player, and a bassist. Jack played rhythm guitar. He sat on a chair in the middle of the band and told us to stand close to him and sing. Jack taught us the songs, and we created our own vocal set-ups. The rehearsal went well, and the following Tuesday we recorded four songs with Jack at United Sound Studios in Detroit.

We had never been in a recording studio before, so when we walked in, it was as though we were in Hollywood. The studio was very large, with individual microphones set up for the musicians, one for us and one for Jack. Hanging just above a long window where the producer and engineer could see through to the recording studio was a huge playback speaker about five feet long and three feet high.

The engineer said, "Okay, Jack, whenever you're ready." That was the signal for Jack to begin counting down in rhythm, *a-one-and-a-two-and-a-three-and-a-four*. When Jack began singing, in my mind I had just been launched into stardom. Somehow, as we were singing "What in the World's Come Over You," I knew it was going to be a hit. When Jack was happy with the take, he asked the engineer to play it back for us. It was too much to wish for, a kid from a small city singing with an international superstar and feeling something big was about to unfold. These kinds of things only happened to someone else, surely not to three guys from Pontiac, Michigan, whose fathers were laborers and working-class men.

When the two-hour recording session was over, we had recorded four of Jack's original songs. We left the studio feeling on top of the world. Jack thanked us and said we would hear from him as soon as Top Rank decided which song would be released first. Within a few months, Jack called and said the song "What in the World's Come Over You" would be released in the summer. When we heard the recorded song played on the radio, we told our family and all of our friends to listen because it was the three of us singing background with Jack. In a short period of time we were local superstars. And just as we had dreamed and hoped, *the song* climbed the music charts and became the nation's number-one song in the fall of 1958. We were each paid six hundred dollars for our efforts. The other three songs we recorded with Jack were mediocre hits and never achieved Top Five status. It didn't matter, though, because we were now small-town celebrities and continued to be the talk of our little neighborhood.

For the next phase of Jack's career, he went on to record a different style of country music without the use of a backup group, so the three of us never recorded with him again. Throughout the time we sang backup with Jack. I have always felt bad about the fact that my brother, Bobby, was tied up in the Marines and couldn't enjoy the celebrity. After all, the Originals were his group. When my brother got out of the Marines, it was time for me to move on. However, Bob and Jerry rejoined his group, but stardom was not in the cards.

GOODBYE GM . . . HELLO RADIO!

It was a sunny day in the summer of 1960, and I had just left my afternoon shift at the Corvair plant. I was zipping along

Michigan Avenue in my sporty-looking, new 1960 MGA with the top down. My radio was cranked up while I was listening to my favorite radio station in Detroit, WXYZ, which they called "the living end of the alphabet," and to my favorite DJ, Joel Sebastian, "The Singing Spaniard." Joel mentioned that he was broadcasting from their satellite studio on Michigan Avenue. I thought to myself, "Hey, it's only a few miles out of my way. I think I'll drive by to see what he looks like!"

I arrived just moments later and spotted Joel broadcasting from his studio. I was now almost face-to-face with a real live celebrity. Boy, was I surprised! I expected the Singing Spaniard to be about five-feet-ten, with dark hair and dark eyes. Much to my surprise, when Joel stood up, he was tall, had blond hair and blue eyes! It didn't matter because the moment I saw him, lightning had struck. I suddenly knew *what I wanted to do for the rest of my life.*

That encounter led me to explore options for broadcast schools. I decided on the nationally known and respected Detroit School of Announcing and Speech. It was here that I would be taught by two well-known broadcast icons in Detroit radio, Jim Garrett and Pierre Paulin. Jim was a newsman at one of the nation's most popular radio stations, WJR. Pierre was news director of another powerhouse in Detroit, WWJ, at that time owned and operated by Detroit's afternoon newspaper, *The Detroit News.* These two men were more than popular; they represented what all young broadcasters should aspire to accomplish: a trained voice, masterful articulation, and a reputation that propels you into major-market radio in America.

In my mind, learning to be a broadcaster would be a breeze. However, this was coming from someone who had been a quick learner but a bad student. In other words, a fast starter and a bad finisher. Up to now, this had been my modus operandi.

After spending a year at the school learning how to run a broadcast board, mastering the use of the microphone, reading and interpreting news and commercial copy, I was ready for my first job. So when Pierre and Jim gave me the devastating news that I would never make it as a broadcaster, my mind quickly raced back to my dream in California. Having left educational opportunities in Berkeley to move back home to Detroit to become a ditch digger, I was now faced with the unfathomable reality of becoming a potential failure in the radio business.

THE HAUNTING FEELING OF FAILURE

In life, there is a time for confidence and a time to learn. I was born with the former, but fiddled around with the latter. Moving around from one place to another as I did, I was haunted by the idea of failure. My trajectory was moving downward.

Yet, even in the face of defeat, I reassured myself, *Look, you're young, reasonably intelligent, and ambitious, so go get it!* I needed to become a success in a family where failure was not an option. After all, my father was the most respected and sought-after master plumber in the area; my older brother Jim followed in my dad's footsteps and jumped one rung higher by teaching master plumbing and psychology at the University of Indiana. My two younger brothers, Mickey and Bobby, would, too, become successes: Mickey as a prestigious businessman, and Bobby as a decorated lifetime police officer. My two sisters, Sandy and Shari, were each successful in business and family rearing.

CAREER PATH

In retrospect, if you look at the ending rather than the beginning, what Pierre did jolted me into reality. I hung in there with the belief that nothing would stop me from making it. At that moment I was keenly aware that my calling was radio. I had finally found the inspiration and the deep desire to become successful. The obvious place for me to start my radio career would be in my hometown of Pontiac, which only had one AM radio station, WPON.

I was still young, impressionable, vulnerable, and very nervous when I walked into WPON looking for a job. It was a small, 5,000-watt radio station that covered most of Pontiac, Flint, and the surrounding areas. It was surely Pontiac's most listened to radio station. Wanting to make a good first impression, I dressed for the interview like Jay Gatsby, from F. Scott Fitzgerald's *The Great Gatsby*, minus the ascot. It was probably unnecessary to dress like that, but I wanted to achieve a good first impression and I thought this was the way to do it. I carried with me an attaché case. Tucked in one of the pockets was one small piece of paper, my degree from the Detroit School of Announcing and Speech. Actually, it was the only piece of paper in the case.

"Mr. Morrow, our general manager, Mr. McLeod, will be right with you." Don McLeod was a famous radio personality in Detroit who had moved up to general manager. You can imagine how surprised I was when Don personally came out to greet me with a big, "Welcome to WPON." On the way back to his glass-walled office, we passed by little recording studios where the radio commercials were produced. Then he took me directly to the main broadcast studio, and that's where my adrenalin began to pump. I was launched to cloud nine. Suddenly I visualized myself sitting in the announcer's chair, talking into the microphone to an audience in my hometown where my family and friends could hear me. Don continued to show me around as he explained to me how the station worked. We then went directly to his office.

Don's office resembled a miniature version of Detroit's Radio Hall of Fame. He had worked with all the early legends of Detroit radio, and the pictures on his wall reflected that. Don questioned me about why I wanted to get into radio and what unique qualities I thought I could bring to the industry. At first, I didn't have a clue how to answer him. I sat quietly for a few seconds, and then it came to me. As green as I was, as nervous as I was, I did know one thing: I wanted to be in one of those frames hanging in his lobby.

I told Don that I thought I would be very good at this job because I love people and wanted to use radio as a communications tool to make their lives richer. After that response, Don said, "Well, Larry, this is a very good place to start. I cannot offer you an on-air position because you have no on-air experience, but I can offer you a position recording the DJs doing commercials, running the broadcast board when one of the announcers is on location, and, from time to time I will take you on sales calls so you can learn everything there is to know about how a radio station operates from top to bottom. I'll pay you one dollar an hour. And finally, Larry, if you learn well and truly believe in your ultimate goal, one day your picture too will hang in the lobby of WPON."

His perspective on motivating me could not have been more compelling. It helped me begin to shed my earlier fears of *You'll never make it, Larry*. Don's concluding remarks, although simple and sincere, captured everything I wanted for my broadcast life. I quickly accepted his generous offer, and we signed our deal with a gentlemen's handshake.

When I returned home and told my parents about what had happened, my mother asked, "How do you plan on getting to work? We live five miles from the radio station. We don't have a car, buses don't run out this far, and your father drives the company truck back and forth to work." Despite my mother's concern, nothing was going to prevent me from getting to work. I woke the next day and ran five miles to work and back. This would be my routine for several months, through rain and sunshine. It was actually enjoyable because it was reminiscent of my boot camp training in the Marines. We walked and ran for miles everywhere we went. The experience of running to the radio station actually awakened my desire to become a long-distance runner. After a few months, I was able to save enough to afford a 1954 Desoto.

Once I had a year under my belt of learning everything about a radio station, it was time to get a job as an announcer. Don told me of an opening for an evening DJ at WKHM AM in Jackson, Michigan. Jackson, located about two hours north of Detroit, had one of the most famous prisons in Michigan. It was also the home of Jackson Junior College. What an irony that a higher-education establishment and a prison were located in the same small town.

I called WKHM (more commonly referred to as KHM) and spoke with the general manager. I told him I worked for the widely known and respected Don McLeod, and would love to interview for the night-announcer position. He asked if I could come the very next day. With Don's permission, I drove to Jackson and arrived at 10 a.m. for the interview.

In small towns like Jackson, radio stations are generally located in old houses, and KHM was no exception. It was located in a quaint, two-story house. As I rang the bell and waited for someone to answer the door, I remember thinking how the house reflected the warmth of a small college town. The general manager answered the door. I introduced myself, and he invited me in. We walked directly into what must have once been the living room but was now the news studio with a huge grand piano right in the middle. Next to the piano was a microphone hanging from the ceiling with a small table under it for the news director to read the news. What looked as if it once had been the kitchen was now the main studio where the DJs did their shows. The only other room on the first floor that hadn't been transformed was the bathroom. All of the offices were upstairs.

I was mildly tense about the interview, but I was extremely nervous about a live audition. The last live audition had been my exit broadcast from radio school, which I thought was a disaster. In those days, rather than bring a tape of your work, most managers wanted to hear you live.

Following a brief interview about my desire to work in Jackson, the GM then said, "Okay, Larry, let's see what you've got." He placed me in front of the microphone in the main studio by the piano and said, "Why don't you begin talking? I'll be upstairs getting a level on your voice." I asked him what he would like me to talk about. He said, "It doesn't matter. Just tell me everything about you and your family. I'll be right back, and we'll begin taping you."

I began talking and talking and talking. He was gone for about five minutes, which I thought to be a long time to get a level on my voice. (Normally, it would take about thirty seconds.) When he returned from upstairs, he walked up to me with his hands behind his back. He apologized for being so long then said, "The whole time you were talking, I was listening to every word you had to say. This was your live audition." He then took his hands from behind his back; nestled in his hand was a wad of recording tape all tangled up in a ball. As he handed it to me, he said, "Here's your audition."

I was stunned. With a rather blank look on my face, memories of Pierre Paulin's devastating comment came flooding back. For a split second I began to feel devastated. He must have noticed the look of panic on my face because he began to laugh. He shook my hand and said, "Larry, I didn't mean to frighten you, but I'm a prankster and I love to tease people. This is my humorous way of saying we'd love to have you become part of our announcer staff at KHM."

He continued, "How would you like to be our night-time DJ? Your shift will be from 7 p.m. to 1 a.m., six days a week. Your show will be called, *Evenings With Larry Morrow*. We'll pay you a dollar an hour. What do you think? Do we have a deal?" The sudden rush of relief combined with the thought of being hired for my very first on-air job hit me all at once. I almost broke down in tears as I quickly replied, "Yes, I'm thrilled for the opportunity." It would also give me a chance to continue my education at Jackson Junior College.

During my very first show at WKHM, a member of the night-time clean-up crew walked into my studio while a song was playing. She introduced herself as Loraine. I'll never forget Loraine or our conversation. "Welcome to KHM, Larry. I hope you do as well as some who have come before you." With equal importance she said, "If you have anything on the ball you won't be here very long." I was intrigued by her comment and asked, "Why is that?" She went on to say that every successful broadcast person who came to KHM never worked there longer than one year. She rattled off the names of about five famous announcers in Detroit radio who worked at KHM but left after one year. Her observation of what had become Detroit radio's farm system, if you will, motivated me to be out of Jackson in one year.

I worked very hard on the air and learned my craft well. I also attended Jackson Junior College. Still, my father was not very happy with my choice to pursue radio instead of plumbing. It didn't bode well for me the day when, with no food in my apartment and not a penny in my pocket, I called him. "Dad, could you wire me ten dollars until payday, which is just a few days away? I haven't eaten in twenty-four hours and don't have any money for food. I can pay you back next week." My dad was never someone who held back his words, so based on the silence, I could sense that he was biting his tongue to contain his sadness for me.

I knew my situation brought back memories from his childhood, when he had left home at the age of fourteen after his father's death. Dad reminded me what it was like to be hungry. At one time, he too had worked all day shoveling coal from railroad boxcars and his foreman had refused to pay his wages, a dime a day, until the next day. So he had to wait to eat. He gladly wired me fifteen dollars. By the way, my first day at WKHM was July 1, 1962. I left the station on June 30, 1963, one day shy of one year, just as Loraine had predicted.

GOT THAT? YES, SIR, I GOT IT

With a year of DJ experience under my belt, I was now ready to move up to a larger market and hopefully a bigger paycheck.

While at WKHM, I had struck up a close relationship with another DJ, Bill Hennes, also from Detroit, who worked opposite
me at a noncompeting station in Jackson. Following our nightly
shifts, we would go out every morning at 1:30 for breakfast and
break down our day. When Bill accepted a job at WTRX in Flint,
a Top 40 radio station, he called and told me of an opening for
mornings, 5:30–10 a.m. The station was about thirty minutes
north of where my parents now resided in Waterford. If I got
the job, I could move back home and save a little money. This
thought was very appealing since I was living just a hair above
the poverty level in Jackson.

As Bill suggested, I called Eddie Clark, the program director (PD) at WTRX, and asked him about the opening. A PD is
responsible for every single piece of information that goes on
the air. He indicated that he was looking to fill a position on
the afternoon shift. We agreed on a time to meet. As soon as we
hung up, I hopped into my car and drove to Flint with a tape
copy of my air work.

WTRX was different than WKHM. It was housed in a building just outside of the main part of the city of Flint. Flint was a
much larger radio market than Jackson. It was actually ranked
number 65 in America, which would be a giant leap for my career, if I were to get the job.

When I drove up to the WTRX building, it looked much
more like the larger radio stations in major markets—a real radio station, rather than a radio station located in a house. There
were large glass windows, a spacious main studio, engineering
facilities, sales offices, and large offices for management. The
offices were set up so all employees had personal contact with
each other, including the main broadcast studio. I wanted to
work there in the worst way. It would be a move up in market
size, and I would be just a step away from Detroit radio, which
in the opinion of the broadcast industry was the epitome of big-
time radio.

When I arrived at WTRX, I sat down with Eddie Clark for

the interview. He must have sensed my strong desire to interview for the job, as only a few hours had passed since our initial telephone conversation. Eddie was truly a character. Dressed in green pants, a green shirt, a green tie, and green alligator shoes, he also smoked continuously. I later learned that Eddie was a one-color-a-day guy. It was common to see Eddie dressed from head to toe in a block of color: black on Monday, blue on Tuesday. I met him on green Wednesday. Eddie not only looked different, he was colorfully unique. He sat me down and said, "Look, kid, around here they call me Fast Eddie because I talk fast. So when I talk, you need to listen, got that?"

"Yes, sir, I got it," I responded. Eddie puffed on his cigarette incessantly while speaking to me with machine-gun quickness. This would be the trademark of our conversation. Each time Fast Eddie took another puff of his cigarette, he would say, "You got that?" And each time my response was "Yes, sir, I got it." He listened to my ten-minute presentation while continuing to take puffs from his cigarette, crossing and recrossing his legs. It made me nervous just watching his unusual routine. Each puff from his cigarette triggered another leg change. I was mesmerized with his demeanor, and I couldn't help but love the guy.

After listening to my tape, he turned to me with rapid fire and said, "Look, kid, you've got some talent, you got that?"

"Yes, sir, I got it."

"You've got real potential, and under my tutelage, one day you can be a radio star. You got that?"

"Yes, sir, I got it."

Fast Eddie asked me how much I was making. I told him a dollar an hour. He said, "Well, we pay much better than that. This is your next step to major market radio, got that?"

"Yes, sir, I got it."

"How's $100 a week sound to you? You'll get a raise to $120 a week in six months if I think you've improved and if I like you. You got that?"

"Yes, sir, I got it."

"So when can you start?"

It was the middle of June 1964, and I told Fast Eddie that I wanted to give WKHM two weeks' notice.

"Can you start July 1?" asked Eddie.

"Yes, I can, and thank you for this great opportunity, Mr. Clark."

"Don't mention it, kid. And by the way," with one final puff on his cigarette and one more crossing of his legs, he reached out his hand to shake my hand, "from here forward, call me Fast Eddie. Got that?"

With a giant smile on my face, I gently replied, "Thank you, Fast Eddie, and yes, sir, I got that." I left WTRX and immediately climbed into my car. Driving down the long driveway, I let out a loud scream, then thanked my Lord for this incredible opportunity.

My shift at WTRX was morning drive, 5:30 to 10. When I arrived for my first day of work I met and became friends with the about-to-become-famous Terry Knight. At WTRX, the DJs were called "the Jones Boys" after the popular '50's song, "The Whole Town's Talking About the Jones Boy." This song became the theme song for the radio station, and all of our names had a Jones theme to them:

5–10 a.m.: John Paul Jones, the Captain of the Ship (Larry Morrow)

10 a.m.–3 p.m.: Tom Jones, the Lover (Jack Mindy)

3–7 p.m.: Casey Jones, the Conductor of the Train (Terry Knight)

7 p.m.–midnight: Davey Jones' Locker, the Bottom of the Ocean (Bill Hennes)

All night: Lonesome Jones (Les Root)

Over the years I taught myself to play the guitar, piano, and bass for the jingles I wanted to write. These skills came in handy while working at WTRX in Flint. Terry Knight (Richard Ter-

rance Knapp) and I teamed up to play guitars together, performing at noonday lunches at business offices around town for
twenty-five dollars apiece. As I mentioned, Terry's broadcast
name was Casey Jones, Conductor of the Train. It must have
been destiny. Terry never forgot his role as the conductor, as he
would later go on to form a million-dollar group whose name
referenced a train theme. It all started when he was a DJ at
record hops in Flint and met a group called the Jazz Masters,
which consisted of Don Brewer on drums, Al Pippins playing
guitar, Bob Caldwell on keyboards and Herb Jackson playing
bass guitar. When Herb was drafted into the military, he was
replaced by Mark Farner.

Terry Knight left WTRX for the popular 50,000-watt powerhouse in Windsor, Ontario, CKLW 800 AM, "The Big 8." While
there, Terry solely promoted a new British group to America,
the Rolling Stones. He had become a huge star at CKLW (7
p.m.–midnight) when he made the decision to leave after one
year to launch his own music career with Terry Knight and the
Pack.

Terry Knight and the Pack had a hit record called "I Who
Have Nothing." After a few additional changes in the band, Terry
dropped out to become its manager, and the band changed its
name to Grand Funk Railroad, inspired by a Michigan landmark, The Grand Trunk Western Railroad. With Grand Funk
Railroad, Terry soon reached a level of international fame and
success, nearly achieving legendary status.

I still fondly remember the day I called Terry after I had
made the move to Cleveland. During our conversation, he told
me, "I owe you one for promoting my record and partnering
with me in Flint, Michigan, for our entertaining guitar lunches,
for which I was always grateful." Later, Terry brought the Pack
to Cleveland and performed at one of my record hops at Byzan-
tine High School in Parma in 1968.

Sadly, we lost Terry in 2004 at the age of sixty-one.

FROM OBSCURITY TO MEGA STARS

One Saturday morning (we all worked six days then) near the end of my show, a very popular Detroit DJ, Lee Alan, who worked the night show at WXYZ, showed up at the radio station with a very young and talented black singer who was only fourteen at the time. Lee Alan had become very friendly with this dynamic young man whom he met through his good friend, Berry Gordy, and he wanted to help him get his record exposed. He explained that he had just been signed by Motown records and this was his very first release. Without hesitation, I agreed to play the song. As I listened to it, I couldn't believe how good it was. He went by the name Little Stevie Wonder, and the name of the song was "Fingertips." It was obvious to me that he was destined for stardom.

Shortly after I arrived at WTRX, my friend and program director, Fast Eddie Clark, left for New York. He was replaced by George Brewer, a young, creative program director whom the station hired out of Buffalo. George was the antithesis of Fast Eddie; he spoke slowly and concisely, and he was quick-witted.

He arrived with an abundance of ideas that would help separate TRX from our major competitor, WTAK, which played the same Top 40 music. George possessed an extremely high IQ and an abundance of innovative ideas. Upon his arrival, he plunged right into leaving an indelible mark on WTRX.

George came up with a brilliant idea for the official kick-off to the first day of hunting season, which was a major fall and winter event in Michigan. The day also happened to be the date scheduled for the Division I championship football game between two very popular Flint high school football teams. George said, "Larry, let's do something radical to get the radio station front-page attention." As George explained his outrageous idea of strapping a hunter to the fender of his convertible Corvair with me wearing a deer's head while driving the car, I knew it would be a major success and a giant coup for WTRX. I said, "Bingo! Let's do it!"

We went directly to a costume store and rented a deer head, a mannequin, and red and black plaid clothing that resembled what hunters wore: a jacket, pants, a hat, and boots. On the day of the big game, we strapped the mannequin dressed in hunter's attire to the fender of the Corvair, prominently displayed the WTRX call letters on each side of the car, put the deer head on me, and, at noon, drove to the stadium. As several thousand people were entering the stadium, I drove around and around watching people break out in laughter upon seeing the bizarre role reversal of a deer driving a car with a hunter tied to the fender. George's instinct was right. The next day a picture of the event appeared on the front page of Flint's daily newspaper. George's spectacular promotion received as much attention as the game itself. It was George's off-the-wall ideas and creativity mind that catapulted WTRX into the number-one position in the market.

While at WTRX (TRX 13 for short), I met several new stars in the record business, including Johnny and the Hurricanes and Freddie "Boom Boom" Cannon. I also met several record promotion men who would visit the radio station to bring in their new records to be auditioned, and hopefully chosen, for our Top 40 list. I had become best friends with Pete Gidion and was best man at his wedding. At that time, Pete was the Michigan promotion manager for Decca. All of us at WTRX were captivated by The Who, a unique new group on Decca's European label, Brunswick, and their new song, "I Can't Explain."

Since the British invasion was just starting to take hold in 1963, we wanted to play "I Can't Explain" from this brand new band. According to Pete, I was the first person in America to play this song, which would soon prove to be a benchmark in my career. Later, while at WIXY in Cleveland, I would introduce The Who at Public Hall.

GREETINGS DUKER, WELCOME TO MAJOR MARKET RADIO

When Terry Knight departed CKLW for his music career, the station looked for someone to replace him. Terry recommended me for the job, but management decided on the more seasoned Tom Shannon as his replacement. After two interviews, I was hired for the midnight–6 a.m. shift. I was so excited to be going on the air in a major market. To illustrate the magnitude of the difference in radio markets, Flint was ranked the sixty-fifth radio market in America. CKLW was fifth.

There was an article in Detroit's number one newspaper, the *Detroit Free Press*, in the popular Bettelou Peterson's "DJ of the Week" column, with the headline, *Meet Duke Windsor (Once a Jones Boy)*.

CKLW had given me the name Duke Windsor, "Duker" for short. I was quite disturbed by the changing of my name because I had told everyone I knew about my new show. They would be listening for their friend Larry Morrow, not Duke Windsor.

The evening before going on the air, Tom Shannon, who had already established himself as a radio and television star in Detroit, said to me, "Duker, you'll be fine. Welcome to big-time radio." That comment relaxed me and gave me the vote of confidence that I needed. Here I was, after only two years of being on the air, working in a market that requires a minimum of ten years' experience. Pierre Paulin's comment from my days spent at Detroit School of Announcing and Speech continued to echo through my head: "I personally believe you are *not* going to make it as a broadcaster."

When I arrived at CKLW in July 1965, I was ready for prime-time—but humbly ready. My present circumstances were puzzling even to me. Nevertheless, I was sure of this much: I was the new guy on the block, and I couldn't shine the shoes of 90 percent of those on the air in the Detroit/Windsor metropolitan area, one of the most revered markets in America for radio DJs and television personalities.

When I went on the air, the all-night show had very few sponsors. My entrepreneurial side kicked in and then got the best of me. I met an advertising fellow and told him of my desire to have more commercials on my show. At that time he was advertising for the top fifteen Buick dealers in the Detroit area. Wanting to surprise our general manager, Bob Buss, as well as the CKLW sales staff, I went with my friend to visit all fifteen dealers and became their spokesperson. We agreed the show would be "brought to you by the Greater Detroit/Windsor Buick Dealers Association" (GDWBDA). The radio portion of the buy would cost the association $50,000. They also bought a five-minute TV show on TV Channel 9, also owned by CKLW, and used me as the host.

TV Channel 9 was located in the same building as CKLW, which made it easy for me to leave the TV studio, walk down the hall and into my radio studio. The on-camera show was the daily wrap-up version of *Entertainment Tonight*, again, brought to you by GDWBDA. At the conclusion of the show, I would say, "Please join me now on my radio show on CKLW for the next six hours, brought to you by the Greater Detroit/Windsor Buick Dealers Association." They also gave me a new Buick convertible to drive. The car was painted with *Detroit/Windsor for Buick* on the doors and *CKLW-Radio 80* on the side rear panels. An advertisement with a picture of me in the car appeared in the *Detroit News* on October 25, 1965: "Right people among the night people . . . Do listen to Duke . . . Duke Windsor, that is, on Giant CK, midnight to 6 a.m.!"

Following the hoopla of getting me started with all the Buick sponsors, I had settled into a nice rhythm in doing their commercials. Then, something happened that was so bizarre that, to this day, I still cannot understand it. The general manager, Bob Buss, came to me and belittled me for going out and getting the show sponsored without his knowledge or the knowledge of the radio/TV sales managers.

I was shocked. I would have thought that since the sales staff personnel did not go out and sell commercials for my show, at the very least my efforts would not only be appreciated but management would be grateful. The new sponsorship also paid my salary of $20,000, but the profit would net an additional $30,000 of revenue for both radio and television for CKLW. It didn't seem to matter because, from that day forward, I would remain on Mr. Buss's list of least favorite people.

Tom Shannon, who held the 7–midnight spot, was not only the best-looking celebrity in Detroit, but, in my opinion, the best DJ of his kind in America, as well as my good friend. Tom was doing a call-in show called *Bear Skin Rug*. Program director Alden Deal had another opinion: He believed the 7–midnight slot would be best suited with a fast-paced rock and roll show. He then asked me to go on the air at midnight and demonstrate what I thought that might sound like. To my surprise, he moved me to 7–midnight. Tom was moved to afternoons.

After a short time on that show, the ratings went to number two in Detroit against the evening giants in radio. I was now a player in a Top 5 radio market in America after only three years on the air. Even with all that adulation, I knew I still had not professionally arrived. All I had to do was listen to the personalities around me, not only on my radio station but through the rest of Detroit, to know how far I had to go.

THE DUKER MEETS MOTOWN–HITSVILLE USA

Among the musical experiences that transpired during my short time in Detroit, several stand out. Berry Gordy, who was in his early days of building Motown, would often send his talent out to our record hops for exposure. He once sent Edwin "Double O Soul" Starr to my record hop at Notre Dame High School. Berry would also often invite DJs to come over to his studio on West Grand Boulevard, which is famously known as "Hitsville USA," where all the songs were recorded. Sometimes the invitations were just to chat; other times they involved sitting in on a recording session downstairs.

One day Berry introduced me to a new, young female talent

by the name of Diana Ross. He had a dartboard in his office, so while he conducted business on the phone, I joined Diana in a game of darts. After Berry got off the phone, he took us across the street to the studio where all the Motown talent learned their dance steps.

BOB SEGER BEFORE HE BECAME "BOB SEGER"

While at CKLW, I was spinning 45s at a very special record hop in Windsor, Ontario, when a young man came up to me and said he played guitar and piano. I asked to hear him play; after listening to him briefly, I was amazed at his talent. I told him, "I have a good idea. I'll spin records for a half hour and you play for a half-hour. We'll do that for three hours and I'll split my $50 fee with you." He agreed. His name was Bob Seger.

Years later, while working at WIXY, I would introduce Bob in Cleveland. He had a hit record at the time called *"Ramblin' Gamblin' Man."* As I stood on the stage, I told the story of the Windsor record hop and said, "There is something wrong here. I'm still being paid $50 to introduce Bob Seger while he's getting $50,000." We had a good laugh.

A SONG, A FRIENDSHIP, A LAKE

Another significant CKLW memory was the Capitol Records recording of "Time Won't Let Me" by Cleveland's new rock group, The Outsiders, featuring gifted lead singer Sonny Geraci. I had heard the record just after its release in 1965 and began playing it on my 7–midnight shift, believing that it was going to be a smash hit. By the middle of 1966, "Time Won't Let Me" reached number five on *Billboard Magazine's* Top 100. I also knew that I had a large Cleveland audience, so I would often speak fondly of Sonny, the group, and their song.

When my career brought me to Cleveland, I became friends with Sonny and The Outsiders. Later I became partners with

Tom Baker, the trumpet player responsible for the group's horn and string arrangements, in The Cleveland Jingle Company, which produced several national jingles including one for Sea World. To this day, Sonny continues to give me credit for the national launch of their first hit record.

While I worked at CKLW, Sonny and I lived across the lake from each other: a giant lake called Erie that stretched from Windsor to Cleveland. Today we remain good friends separated by a lake—a much smaller version of Lake Erie, located just east of Chagrin Falls, that keeps us five minutes from each other.

A YOUNG DJ—A YOUNG RELATIONSHIP

While at CKLW, I was introduced to promotion director Pam Conn. Pam was tall and incredibly intelligent—her IQ was over 150. At first glance she looked like the cover girl for a glamour magazine. We started dating shortly after I started working at the station and were married in the summer of 1965. Our compatibility made the relationship special. Like me, Pam desired a life of jingle- and song-writing. My major in college was political science. Pam loved politics and wanted to change the world. So off we went—Pam, in promotions and writing, and me, behind the microphone. Together we carved out a short life together, becoming nationally recognized jingle writers for Kentucky Fried Chicken and B.F. Goodrich. Unfortunately, we were not as successful as hit song writers. We came close to releasing songs on national labels. Close, as they say, but no cigar.

REACHED THE TOP AND FIRED AT THE TOP

In a Detroit teen poll I was voted "Detroit's Most Popular DJ." I truly believed that angered Mr. Buss because he felt my lack of major-market experience made me too young for this level of success. It seemed the more popular I became at CKLW and in the Detroit area, and the more aggressive I was at going out and working in the community (for which CKLW got the credit), the more he resented me. What made it so strange, though, is that I worked for him. In the end, I think his resentment of me consumed him. I was fired by Bob Buss in 1966, after fewer than two years at CKLW.

The law of cause and effect says that for every effect in your life there is a precise cause. A good subtitle would be, "everything happens for a reason." The effect of me being fired would bring good news. My night show at CKLW covered half of Canada, most of Michigan, Indiana, and most important, Cleveland. It was the number-one rated evening show in Cleveland from 7–midnight, which obviously caught the attention of Norman Wain, owner of the newly formed WIXY 1260.

Part Two

WIXY

CHAPTER 6

Welcome to Cleveland, Duker

In radio and television, you want to move up to larger markets
with each new job. I was waiting for calls from New York (#1),
Los Angeles (#2), or Chicago (#3)—the big three, as I called
them, but I never heard from any of them. I did receive an offer
from WXYZ, a very popular Detroit radio station, that wanted
Duke Windsor to come to their station. I told them CKLW
owned that name; I would have to use my real name. With that
critical piece of information, the deal was off. I had officially lost
my identity. No one knew the name "Larry Morrow." It was as if I
had never worked a day in radio and was starting all over again.
They wanted "The Duker," Duke Windsor. So, sadly enough, I
had to leave the market, my family, and my friends.

After a few months of being unemployed from CKLW, I received a call from Norman Wain in Cleveland. He indicated
that he had heard my show on CKLW and was interested in me
coming to his new radio station, WIXY 1260. He had an opening from 7–midnight to replace a talented-but-rambunctious,
hard-to-manage Jack Armstrong, and wanted to know if I was
interested. I said yes. Norm replied, "I'll call you in a few days
and we'll work out the details of you coming to Cleveland for an
interview."

Well, Norm kept his promise and did call me, but for a different reason: "I'm sorry and embarrassed, Duker [Norm did
not know my real name at this time], but we've decided to keep
Jack." At the time I wasn't disappointed. In fact, it didn't matter

much to me at all because Cleveland was a much smaller market than Detroit. Cleveland was ranked number eight.

Almost one month had gone by and, other than smaller-market offers, I had not received a single call from the big three. I was getting more than a little worried; I wanted to get back on the air.

As good fortune would have it, my next call came from Norm Wain. "Duker, we just had our midmorning man, Johnny Walters, leave. I know it's not evenings, but would you be interested in our 9–noon shift?" I promptly said, "Yes." Phase one of my early career had come to a close. Phase two was about to begin, and it would carve out many of the happiest days of my life in Cleveland. Neither Norm nor I had any idea it would shape a life for me and my family that would continue to this very day, more than forty years later.

I arrived in Cleveland on July 18, 1966, to sign the contract to begin working at WIXY 1260 in September. I was picked up at Hopkins Airport by our young music director, Eric Stevens. I was amazed that this teenager was so musically wise beyond his years. It was no surprise that Eric would become one of the cornerstones in the foundation of WIXY.

After Eric dropped me off at my hotel, I turned on the television. It appeared that the same movie was showing on TV 3 (NBC), TV 5 (ABC), and TV 8 (CBS). Suddenly it dawned on me that it wasn't a movie. There were serious outbreaks of civil disorder in the Hough area, and all three Cleveland television stations were carrying it live. I was minutes away from the epicenter.

Racial turmoil was something that concerned me and saddened me deeply. My heart sank as I compared Cleveland to Los Angeles. People were killed and dozens injured, and it took a week for the National Guard to restore order. My nerves got the better of me. I began thinking, *This is not a place for me. Cleveland's too small a radio market anyway.*

Also, I rationalized that I didn't like my drive along I-77;

there were all those ugly smokestacks, and I hated the smell of sulfur. I kept telling myself, *That's okay. I'll stay for just a little while. New York, Los Angeles, Chicago, or Boston; that's where I'm headed.* But I knew I had to bite the bullet and stay put for a while. I had been on the air less than five years, worked at three radio stations, and was fired from my last. At this time, the worst thing that could happen to a radio personality is to be known as a "floater"—one who never stays in one place very long. No one wanted to hire a floater.

WIXY 1260: THE JOURNEY BEGINS

You are about to experience the story of three visionaries who had a dream, formulated their plan, and made it a reality. WIXY 1260 was made for a certain moment in time, and I was fortunate to be there when it happened and to become part of its success.

Despite my wanting to move to a larger radio market, I was excited to be in Cleveland. During my high school days I was anchored in sports and had pictures of Otto Graham and Dante Lavelli of the Cleveland Browns taped to my bedroom wall. Now I could actually visit the stadium they played in. The other reason for my excitement was that WIXY had just brought the Beatles to Cleveland.

I received a call from Jane Scott, the entertainment writer for Ohio's largest newspaper, *The Plain Dealer*, with a request for an interview. When Jane and I spoke, I had not yet been on the air. She was familiar with my work at CKLW and thought it was a major coup on WIXY's part to bring Duke Windsor to Cleveland. The interview went well, and the following Friday, September 21, my picture appeared on the front page of the entertainment section with the headline, *WIXY Makes Duke Theirs*. In the interview, Jane asked if I would be using my real name rather than Duke Windsor. I told her that CKLW owned the name Duke Windsor, but The Duker was mine and I would use it as a nickname with my real name. I wanted Cleveland to know me as The Duker, Larry Morrow.

My first day on WIXY 1260 was September 23, 1966. Norm Wain was going out of town and expressed disappointment that he would miss my debut. In Norm's absence, program director Johnny Canton asked me what name I would be using. Everyone just assumed I would be using Duke Windsor; after all, that's why I was hired. I then told Johnny that since CKLW owned the name "Duke Windsor," and since Jane Scott printed my real name in *The Plain Dealer* article, let's go with The Duker, Larry Morrow.

GOOD FORTUNE

Norm was driving back from his three-day business trip in Pittsburgh and was anxious to get within range of his 5,000-watt radio station. By this time I had been on the air for almost a week, and Norm was looking forward to hearing his new hire, Duke Windsor from CKLW. Poor Norm, he was about to get the surprise of his life. When he tuned in to his WIXY 1260, instead of hearing Duke Windsor on the air, he heard a name he had never heard before: Larry Morrow. I would have loved being in the car when Norm heard the then-unknown Larry Morrow doing an impersonation of Duke Windsor. Ouch!

WHO IN THE HELL IS LARRY MORROW?

After all, Norm Wain's whole purpose for bringing me to Cleveland was to capitalize on the name of the guy who already owned the number-one evening ratings in Cleveland. And that guy was The Duker, CKLW's Duke Windsor. Norm must have been thinking that whoever made that decision to use the name Larry Morrow just screwed up his entire strategy. He continued to steam as he drove directly to the radio station in Seven Hills. He promptly walked into the studio and blew up at me.

With his voice raised and veins popping out of his neck, he said, "Who in the hell is Larry Morrow? You're supposed to be Duke Windsor!"

There are certain experiences that forever change your life, and this was one of them. Nervous and red-faced, I responded, "CKLW owned that name, so we had to use my real name." Norm was powerless; the situation was non-negotiable.

Following Norm's unexpected tirade, he never raised his voice at me again. I would use my birth name forever. In addition, thanks to the convincing power of WIXY and Norm Wain's ingenuity, he never had to ask me again, "Who in the hell is Larry Morrow?"

LARRY, LARRY, WHAT'S IN THE BOX? WHAT'S COOKIN'?

My shift on WIXY was 9 a.m.–noon. I followed our very funny morning man, Al Gates, who had a sidekick named Feathers. Al could carry on an imaginary conversation between himself and that bird that would keep you laughing for the rest of the day. Unfortunately, Al left WIXY to accept a position in Boston. Within a few months, the arrival of Mike Reineri, Lou Kirby, and Dick Kemp would round out our new staff, thus forming the foundation for which WIXY would build number-one ratings.

We created two new games for my show: one called "Larry, Larry, What's in the Box," and another known as "What's Cooking?"

At 10 a.m., when I began my air shift, I would start by announcing the ingredients to a certain recipe. Depending on how long the recipe was, I would reveal one or two ingredients and then play two records, so on and so forth. Each listener call began with: "What's Cooking?" At the end of the hour I would then take calls on what I was cooking. The winner won two loaves of Wonder Bread and a twenty-five dollar gift certificate to a grocery store.

The other game, "Larry, Larry, What's in the Box," started right after "What's Cooking?" I would begin the game by giving my audience clues, such as, "What I have in the WIXY box today is bigger than your coffee cup and smaller than your sink. What is it?" After revealing the first clues, I began taking calls by answering the phone with "Larry, Larry, What's in the Box?" The answer to "What's in the Box?" could be any variety of items, ranging from a toaster to a basketball. As for the prize, it would vary from a popular album, to tickets to a concert, to dinner for four at a popular restaurant. Both games remained staples and ratings giants throughout my six-year stay at WIXY. I continued to play them at all my appearances as well.

Speaking of ratings, I was recently told by a radio archivist that I hold the record for a 70 percent share during one rating period. That means 70 percent of people listening to the radio were tuning into my show. Following that rating period, in which I had slipped back to a 50 percent share, I received a comical note from Norm Wain that read, "Duker, we will no longer put up with this kind of slippage."

CHAPTER 7

A Team of Retreads

Jim Collins, in his number-one bestseller, *Good to Great*, wrote, "To build a superior executive team, get the right people on the bus, get the wrong people off the bus, put the right people in the right seats and then determine where you want to drive."

That's exactly what Norm Wain did. It took about eighteen months to establish the right mix of people. They were: program director George Brewer; promotion directors Candy Forest and Linda Scott; music directors Eric Stevens and Marge Bush; and on-air personalities Mike Reineri, Larry Morrow ("The Duker"), Jerry Brooke ("Brookeberger") Lou "King" Kirby, Dick Kemp (the "Wilde Childe"), and Bobby Magic ("Magic Man").

Now the right people were in the right seats, under the uncanny leadership of bus drivers Norm Wain and George Brewer. *Look out, Cleveland, the WIXY bus is on its way.*

I convinced Norm to hire George at WIXY to help assemble a new on-air staff. George Brewer was brilliant at plotting and scheming to control ratings. He did it at WTRX, and I believed would do it here. He obviously did not disappoint. Even though we resembled a bunch of young retreads, George knew it would work. Mike ("I eat nails for breakfast") Reineri had been *fired* from a 50,000-watt station in Florida; Lou "King" Kirby *fired* from the number-one station in Dallas; Dick "Wilde Childe" Kemp, *fired* from the largest station in Chicago, and Larry "the Duker" Morrow, *fired* from one of the most prestigious stations in the Detroit/Windsor market, CKLW. So we all had major market experience. We represented a new generation of young rock and roll disc jockeys and brought with us a culture that would turn Cleveland on its ear.

We all loved George Brewer. We believed in him and lined up behind him while he taught us how to harness this new energy and fine-tune our on-air presentation. George and Norm would give us the keys for what we wanted out of life: to be successful broadcasters.

SUPERMEN ARRIVE FLYING HIGH

The eclectic group of DJs had arrived at the precipice of a changing culture and unveiled the new rock model: *More Music, More Often*. George's goal was to play eighteen songs each hour. At this moment, we were all of the conviction that there was no other radio station in the market but WIXY 1260. Equally valid was the response from the marketplace.

Norm and George set benchmarks for us to accomplish. The first goal was to defeat the 50,000-watt powerhouse, WKYC radio, whose DJs were staples in the market. The second goal was to dethrone WHK, which had brought the Beatles to town before WIXY. It, too, had well-known and established DJs with a long history. The task was formidable. Norm called his new on-air staff "the WIXY Supermen."

DON'T MESS WITH THE MUSIC

Many of the songs in the '60s were less than three minutes long. We would play the Top 40 songs in America over and over again. Eric Stevens and Marge Bush would stack up forty songs in the WIXY studio. It was Eric who mandated that all the DJs adhere to the following procedure for playing the records: (1) Always take a record from the top of the stack. (2) Play the song on the turntable. (3) Remove the record from the turntable when finished. (4) Return the 45 to the bottom of the stack. The goal was to repeat the most popular songs every two hours. Eric and Marge had an effective and winning system, and we were to never violate it. If you ever played one of those songs out of rotation, young Eric Stevens would chop off your head. Due to Eric's uncanny musical knowledge and his gut feeling for what Cleveland wanted to hear, you could sense the market shifting. It would only be a matter of time before the new format and exciting DJs caught on. Even though many of us were educated, we brought with us street language that somehow went right along with the culture of the music. *I'm here to put some glide in your stride and some slip in your hip.* It was different, exciting, clean, and fun.

WIXY CULTURE

During the runaway decade of the '60s, the DJs at WIXY 1260 not only chronicled the cultural change, we led it. We helped integrate the ideals of the time. We were right in the middle of the rebellion, surrounded by social injustice. Bob Dylan's "Blowin' in the Wind" ("Yes, how many years can some people exist before they're allowed to be free?") was an accurate representation of the civil rights movement, which was now in full swing. As our culture continued to unravel, Dylan again quickly reflected on those changes with the release of "The Times They Are a-Changin'" ("There's a battle outside/And it is ragin'/It'll soon shake your windows/And rattle your walls/For the times they are a-changin'").

The Vietnam War became the voice of the new counterculture. Technology had evolved to a point where my friends and neighbors, along with the rest of America, were now watching our beloved newscaster, Walter Cronkite, the most trusted man in television news, bringing us nightly visions from the battlefield. His newscasts became a double-edged sword. We hung on his every word. Many in America were now wearing POW-MIA bracelets: Prisoner of War/Missing in Action bracelets with the name of the serviceman on it. At the same time, we witnessed the terrible bloodshed just moments after it happened because it had been video recorded and instantly sent back to the television stations in America.

Due to this depressing exposure, negative attitudes about the war had gained momentum. Even talking about it now, I can vividly remember seeing Clevelanders carrying antiwar posters around Public Square that read, "Hey, Hey, LBJ, how many kids have you killed today?" This was a reference to President Johnson's authorization to double our efforts in Vietnam and send an additional 45,000 American troops, bringing the total to over 100,000, which, in the eyes of the protestors, brought us no closer to winning the war.

Timothy Leary, a renowned professor at Harvard University, became another new and distinctive voice on the American landscape. He was an early advocate of LSD experimentation. Leary believed in the spiritual, emotional, and therapeutic benefits of psychedelic drug use. He coined the catchphrase, "Turn on, tune in, drop out," which became the anthem for his new religion. This generation of fifteen- to twenty-five-year-olds who believed in him rejected their parents' ideals, and many became social outcasts.

As a WIXY DJ, on one of the most popular and influential rock stations in the nation, I watched a young America coming apart at the seams. Many, specifically in Washington, D.C., were wondering where in the world the glue would come from to reassemble the missing parts.

Many popular rock groups had taken a detour from typical contemporary music and headed directly to the new counterculture genre, Jefferson Airplane and the Grateful Dead, to name two. I can still remember playing the Byrds's "Eight Miles High," and wondering, "Are they talking about being high?" The entire psychedelic experience had a tremendous influence on Cleveland youth, and WIXY 1260 was a central figure in all of it. Our WIXY 1260 Top 40 list was sprinkled with psychedelic rock.

It was well known in the music industry that Beach Boy Brian Wilson had experimented with LSD. When I first heard "Good Vibrations," I truly wondered if he was on some hallucinating journey while writing it. I happen to love the song and, to this day, still think of where he may have been when he wrote it. When the hippie movement began in San Francisco, I saw it swiftly travel eastward as the new hippie generation became a radical society of its own. Although I was young—twenty-eight years old—and was personally caught up in the emotion of the movement, I was not part of the rebellious aspect of the generation. While I began greeting friends with a peace sign, rather than a handshake, others in the counterculture began wearing flowers in their hair. Scott McKenzie wrote the song "San Francisco (Be Sure To Wear Flowers In Your Hair)," and it symbolized the movement.

During this time, my fellow DJs poked fun at me for the way I dressed. It was their continuous comical criticism that drove me to visit Man Talk, the hippest men's clothing store in Cleveland, located at Severance Shopping Center in Cleveland Heights. I knew the owner, Chuck Abner, and asked him for a complete clothing makeover. This was to be phase I of my transformation.

Chuck replaced my conservatively striped, three-button suits with a hipper look that was straight out of the men's fashion magazines. I first put on a mod, oversized dress shirt with billowing sleeves and a flashy looking pair of corduroy bell-bottom pants. I also tossed out my once-beloved wing-tip shoes for Beatle boots. When Chuck finished dressing me, I looked in one of those three-way mirrors and broke out in laughter. Chuck said, "Well, what do you think, Duker?"

"It's innovative, all right," I said, "but it's such a radical departure from what's going on inside of me." For phase II of my complete makeover, I grew out my preppy, Princeton haircut for shoulder-length hair. I already had a mustache, but I let it grow out to a thick Fu Manchu.

It was 1969, shortly after my new makeover, when I walked out on to the Public Hall stage all decked out in my new look in front of 10,000 screaming fans. I was introducing the WIXY/Belkin presentation of Gary Puckett and the Union Gap, one of the nation's most popular singing groups. As I walked to the microphone the audience began to laugh. Of course, I went with it and said, "Okay, blame it on Man Talk." To this day, I am convinced they saw me as one going to a hippie costume party. Even though I wanted to represent the culture of the times, it felt more like I was the person in the room wearing a fake fur. In time, your friends will know it's not the real deal and you will be thought of as a phony. I was never comfortable with the extreme look, so within a few months, I exchanged the hippie look for a more moderate look.

Another part of the counterculture was the new sensation from Britain, Twiggy, a teenage model. Many young British and American teenagers ran parallel to their feelings about Twiggy. Eager to look just like her, they copied her makeup, long eyelashes, very thin build, and wore miniskirts. On its own, the miniskirt became a permanent fixture of the era.

In a very depressing way, stories about the wild actions of popular musical artists who reflected this culture started to pop up everywhere: Jimi Hendrix, Jim Morrison, Janis Joplin, Keith Moon, Brian Jones, and others. Collectively, they electrified a new attitude in America. Sadly enough, their reckless lifestyle would rob the world of their exceptional talents. When Bob Dylan wrote the song "Like a Rolling Stone," it became the prevailing musical view of the times. The haunting chorus, "How does it feel/ To be on your own/ With no direction home/ Like a complete unknown/ Like a rolling stone" summed up the counterculture of the '60s.

Along with all of the WIXY DJs, I was part of a transitional time in both American and British history. I could hardly wait for the decade to end. The combined ugliness of the Vietnam War, the assassinations of President John F. Kennedy, civil rights leader Dr. Martin Luther King, Jr., and United States senator Robert F. Kennedy was almost too much to bear. Even though Senator Edward "Ted" Kennedy used these words to eulogize his brother Bobby at his funeral in St. Patrick's Cathedral in New York, I feel it represents what all three of these dedicated Americans tried to do. I have purposefully and respectfully changed Senator Ted Kennedy's words around to better describe the three men rather than just Bobby Kennedy. "They saw wrong and tried to right it, saw suffering and tried to heal it, and saw war and tried to stop it." The emergence of these men and the counterculture of the decade spawned violence, controversy, and ultimately deep sadness. As the musical piece of the '60s came to an end, I thought it fleshed out all that was bad about the radical movement of sex, drugs, and rock and roll that lasted almost an entire decade.

CHAPTER 8

Radio Juggernaut

WIXY 1260 was now unstoppable. We had all embraced George Brewer's encouraging opinion that we were the newest and the best. Judging from the ratings, the Greater Cleveland marketplace clearly agreed.

THE ECLECTIC WIXY SUPERMEN

The core group of the WIXY Supermen did not represent the majesty of speech like our predecessors, Bill Randle and Phil McLean, who were both intellectuals and had been in the Cleveland market for a long time. While we were not academically vacuous, we were out to have fun and were marching to a beat of a different drummer.

George made sure the WIXY Supermen were always a unified team. Even though we were all as different as a dog from a cat, George coached, taught, and guided us in our on-air deliveries and assured us the response from our listeners would ultimately crush our competition. George also kept us within ourselves and our individual personalities. If we caused uncharacteristic mistakes on the air, like talking over the vocal of a song, he immediately called us on it and helped us through it. George always reminded us of who we now were: *simply the best.* Our current successes left us confident, and we knew we could beat our competition by following his plan.

Because of our enormously different broadcast styles, there was very little competition between the WIXY Supermen. You would think that with all these uniquely different ego-driven personalities there would be chaos, but the opposite was true. In retrospect, it was surprising to me that there was never a power struggle for fame among us. We all threw in our lots for the betterment of WIXY 1260, maintaining a delicate balance among one another.

There was also the unswerving loyalty to George. In the early development stage of WIXY, we partied often at George's home near the radio station in Seven Hills, with his wife, Cathy, who made sure we were all well fed. When we were together, we referred to each other by our nicknames. We called Dick Kemp, Childe; Lou Kirby, My King; Jerry Brooke, Brookeberger; Bobby Magic, Magic Man; and I was simply, Duker. Oddly, we did not have a nickname for Mike Reineri.

THE IMPISH MIKE REINERI

I can distinctively remember two of Mike Reineri's very funny Duker put-downs. While driving into the studio to replace Mike at 10 a.m., I heard him say, "The Duker has just arrived. By that I mean his nose is here; the rest of his body will be here in ten minutes." Another memorable Duker put-down happened during one of our daily changeovers at 10 a.m. It was the first day of spring, and I was fashionably dressed in light green pants with a dark green shirt, a green and white striped tie, a green and white seersucker sport coat, and white, patent-leather shoes. When Mike introduced me he said, "You look like the president of a lizard factory." I still laugh whenever I think about Mike's quick-witted humor.

LOU "KING" KIRBY

Lou Kirby, our King, bought a long Cadillac limousine, painted it black, and had a kingly looking WIXY crest painted on the sides in gold. He wore a red velvet cape and a king's crown. He always made sure he had a beautiful female chauffer him around town and to his record hops while he sat in the back seat. This was before the days of cell phones, so he carried a fake phone in his limo. I can remember riding with him; whenever we stopped at a red light, people couldn't help but stare at this unusual site. Lou would then make the phone ring and say to the person looking on, "It's for you."

DICK "WILDE CHILDE" KEMP

I thought Dick Kemp the most extraordinary and entertaining nighttime personality I had ever heard—definitely one of a kind both on and off the air. He owned nighttime radio in Cleveland. One of his favorite lines was: "I'm the Wilde Childe. I live in the woods; I know all the trees by their first name." The Wilde Childe was paradoxically different. He was both disarmingly charming and dangerously playful. One night when I dropped by the radio station to pick up my mail, I thought I'd peek in the studio just to say hi to the Childe. There he was with his headphones on, singing to the music, stark naked!

Another memorable episode with Childe occurred when Norm Wain called a WIXY staff meeting to meet our national sales reps from New York. Attendance was mandatory, which not only meant that we all had to be there, but we had to be dressed for the occasion. When the meeting began, the only one missing was Childe. Halfway through the meeting, you could hear and see in the distance the Childe riding his motorcycle down our 100-yard dirt driveway, wearing just his Bermudas and no shirt. When he arrived, Norm said, "Childe, you're late. Why didn't you call?" Dick Kemp responded, "I didn't have a dime," which drew a burst of laughter from all of us, including Norm. Dick Kemp was, by all admissions, our most unique entertainer and the most talked-about WIXY personality by teenagers. And the ratings reflected it. Dick was the Wilde Childe in every sense of the word.

There was a radical on-air distinction between our different

approaches to the audience. For example, I was known around
the radio station as "Mother Morrow" because of the time of my
shift, when most women were home during the day. Remember,
this was the mid-'60s, just before women's liberation gained momentum and women began leaving home for the workplace.

We also had phrases that our audience knew and loved. I've
given you some of Dick Kemp's. Mine were:

> *I'm here to get your heart to quivil and your liver to bivil.*
> *Ain't nothin' cookin' but the peas in the pot, and they wouldn't*
>   *be cookin' if the water wasn't hot.*
> *Ain't nothing shakin' but the leaves on the trees, and they*
>   *wouldn't shakin' if it wasn't for the breeze.*
> *I'm here to put a little glide in your stride and some slip in*
>   *your hip.*
> *I'm jam up, jelly tight, and peanut butter right.*

I knew these catch-phrases had caught on when people
would come up to me and repeat one of them, or every once in
awhile, all of them with the same funk and rock style that they
were delivered.

CHILDE GOES PLATINUM?

At this time, I was married to Pam Conn, and we wrote a
song for the Wilde Childe on the new CLE-Town label called
"Wilde Childe Freakout." The hook was from Tommy Roe's 1970
hit, "Jam Up Jelly Tight." I'm still not sure who added the phrase
"peanut butter right." The song immediately sold 10,000 copies,
with all the profits going to charity. After Dick Kemp left for our
McKeesport, Pennsylvania, station, the phrase was so popular
at WIXY that I began using it from time-to-time. To this day,
many WIXY 1260 listeners give me credit for that phrase. Although we wrote part of it for him, the Childe made it quite
popular.

RAMPING IT UP

During my first two years at WIXY, we were building our station unlike anything the market had ever seen and has not seen since. All of us were appearing at three to five record hops a week. I can vividly remember asking Norm if I could have one hundred pictures made of myself. I told him my plan was to visit shopping centers on the weekends and introduce myself to as many people as possible. I gave a picture to each person I met and asked them to listen to me on WIXY 1260. I wouldn't leave the plaza until all the pictures were gone. Just eighteen months later, due to WIXY's explosive growth, the appearance of a WIXY DJ at a shopping center would draw a crowd of two thousand.

Norm encouraged me to begin calling people from the White Pages every day before my air shift. As I made each call, I would cross off the name of the person I spoke to so I would never make a duplicate call. In the early days of WIXY, when we weren't that popular, I would spend an entire hour trying to get ten people to agree to listen to me. During my first two years of making those calls at 9 a.m., I called between fifty and sixty people because so many hung up on me. When they picked up the phone, I would say, "Hi, Mrs. Williams, I'm Larry Morrow, and I work at this new radio station called WIXY 1260. If you'll listen to me today I will mention your name."

Starting year three, when the station finally caught on, almost every person I called listened to WIXY. In my sixth year at WIXY, I would begin calling at 9 a.m., and by 9:15, I had spoken to ten people and they all said they would listen for their names. The one souvenir of my six years at WIXY was the phone book; it had the names of over 17,000 people whom I had spoken to and had crossed off when they told me they listened to the station.

CHAPTER 9

The Genius of Norm Wain

Behind the WIXY 1260 success was the intellect and brilliance of owner and general manager Norman Wain, who designed the character and purpose of the station. Under his leadership, the entire WIXY team dominated the Cleveland ratings. Norm created WIXY to be made up of a very well-planned and executed troika: sales, promotions, and ratings. Sales were directly related to ratings and, due to high-flying promotions and carefully produced programming, great ratings began to come in bunches. Norm not only knew how to pick talent, he knew how to draw crowds—really big crowds.

Because Norm valued people so much, it was natural for him to encourage everyone's development. He also empowered all of us as individuals to understand his vision and make it a reality. He created conditions that would spawn superstars, and he helped each one of us to not only get on the bus but to get in the right seats. He then determined where we would drive.

I am not sure about the others, but Norm accelerated my career beyond my grandest dreams. My instincts of going to the community were sharpened by his support. Norm pushed for all of us to get involved—from record hops to speaking engagements, from high school events to parades. Behind his leadership and creative mind we would climb and reach the summit together. We had all become extensions of his entrepreneurial spirit.

Norm could not have assembled a more varied group of DJs.

We were all successes in major-market radio that, for one reason or another, had left their market. On paper, it would never
have worked. The WIXY Supermen were the sum of many parts.
We all had different looks, diverse personalities, and distinctive
styles. Although there were fundamental similarities and dis-
tinguishing differences in our on- and off-the-air styles, Norm's
mantra of "No one DJ can carry a radio station" affected all of
us. I worked with that original staff for almost four years and
never felt that anyone was ever on the verge of idolatry.

PUTTING AIR UNDER OUR WINGS

Up to this point, I had worked for GMs who kept a low profile,
but Norm came out of radio as a celebrity himself. Early in his
radio career, he was known as the "Big Chief" on WDOK. Norm
understood a radio personality's thirst for success because he
was one of us, and he was a very good personality, at that.

Had Norm decided to be a head coach, he would have been
immensely successful simply because he understood the value
of teamwork. Behind him, we would not only fly on the wings of
an eagle but learn how to fly on our own. His goal was to focus
on the whole view of WIXY, not just one personality.

There was also a constant effort inside WIXY to deflate any
notion that we wouldn't become the leading radio station in the
market. We ultimately did because of Norm: The combination
of his business savvy, his flair for promotion, and his programming acumen would prove to be dynamite. Had Norm been created as a fish, he would have been a shark.

SHARK NORM SMELLS BLOOD IN THE WATER

WIXY began to open up a wide gap in the ratings between
the two powerhouses in the market, WKYC and WHK. It was
the new radio versus the old, and for stations that were behind
the times, the clock was ticking. The new WIXY 1260 proto-

type of "More Music–More Often," eighteen-songs-an-hour format, coupled with the duality of slick, fast-talking DJs and flashy promotions, moved through the community like a hungry shark. We had touched the lives and emotions of every part of Greater Cleveland.

It was now absolutely certain: WIXY 1260 was about to become the new giant in town. We were sprouting up everywhere: concerts, parades, school functions, advertising agency promotions, and record hops. Television cameras followed what was happening at the station, and much of it ended up on the nightly news, giving us additional exposure. We had reached critical mass, and the Cleveland radio market was about to validate the goal set by Norm and George.

The familiar sound of Cleveland radio had now taken a back seat to WIXY "Six-Packs," "Triple Plays," Top 40 countdowns, and rock concerts, and teenagers and adults tuned in regularly. Enormously popular personalities such as Bill Randle, Phil McLean, Johnny Holiday, and Jack Reynolds, among others, were lost in the frenzy.

When I arrived at WIXY, I asked Norm who I had to beat. I can still visualize Norm standing in front of me as he said, "The guy you need to beat, Duker, is Bill Randle on WERE." Known as one of the most intellectual personalities on the air in America, Bill was solely responsible for bringing Elvis Presley, along with Bill Haley and the Comets, to Brooklyn High School in 1955, cementing his status as a local icon. He also owned the midday ratings in Cleveland.

Up to this point, radio stations were built around one or two single, talented personalities, such as Bill Randle and Phil McLean. Norm's innovative model built WIXY around multiple personalities. Although stations of the past had remained in the hearts and minds of their loyal followers, the constant bombardment of this new entertainment template had all but obliterated what had come before.

The "More Music–More Often" format was so swift and

powerful, it began to sweep through Top 40 stations in America like a tidal wave. It also cast a glaring spotlight on the British Invasion, Psychedelic Rock, Motown, and the new contemporary country. As the broad set of musical styles was changing, WIXY 1260 was at the forefront in Cleveland. The cultural and social change evoked a new sense of awakening in America, and WIXY gave a full voice to the youth culture.

It had become clear that our competition was on the chopping block. The new WIXY kids in town were about to sculpt out their own place in Cleveland radio history. We wanted to be remembered as a group of DJs who were part of something exciting and unique. We were a cohesive unit, and the two words that best described us were *unity* and *bond*.

Having said that, to this day I don't feel we'll ever find a historical comparison to earlier luminaries such as Phil McLean and Jack Reynolds. I worked with them both in later years and will never forget the joy and companionship we shared. They helped solidify a place for me in Cleveland radio history. I loved and respected them both.

VIRTUE BECOMES OUR REWARD

It was early 1968, just a few years after Norm had assembled all the pieces of WIXY, when he called the staff together to give us the great news: WIXY had just beaten the powerhouse WHK Good Guys and made them change their format to Easy Listening. What made the victory so gratifying was that WHK was the first radio station on the air in Ohio, preceding WIXY with fast-talking DJs, such as Johnny Holiday and Joe Mayer. It also had the most respected "Action Central" newsroom in Cleveland. And it didn't hurt that, at one time, all three WIXY owners—Wain, Weiss, and Zingale—had been WHK salesmen.

WHK also brought the Beatles to Cleveland in 1964 for their first North American tour. On the cover of the Beatles' *Sgt. Pepper* album is a doll wearing a sweater emblazoned with "Welcome the Rolling Stones" and "Good Guys." "Good Guys" was an unofficial reference to the WHK Good Guys. We were now at the halfway point of reaching our goal. Next to fall in the ratings battle would be the giant, 50,000-watt WKYC 1100. In a short period of two and one-half years, we had cast a compelling shadow over the Greater Cleveland listening audience. WIXY 1260 had not only arrived; it was here to stay.

CHAPTER 10

Masters of Promotion

During the early years, WIXY had promotions unlike anything Cleveland had seen before. They really got the community involved. One of the people responsible was the young but incredibly talented Candy Forest, our first promotion director.

Candy worked closely with Norm, and together they dreamed up new ways to build WIXY's image. One of their biggest ideas was the first WIXY Christmas parade in 1965.

As Candy tells, it, one day in September Norm came to her and said, "Candy, I've got a great project for you. We're going to do a Christmas parade with the May Company; you know, like Macy's does in New York!" Candy immediately felt a wave of panic.

"Norm," she said, "it's September already. Macy's probably starts working on their parade in January. You're talking about pulling this together in eight weeks?"

"It's easy," Norm replied. "I'll get you the floats and some celebrities and you get the bands and the Boy Scouts." That was Norm. He wasn't going to take "no" for an answer.

"Somehow, I conjured up a parade complete with Santa Claus," Candy said later. "Our grand marshal was Tim Conway, riding on an antique fire engine from my hometown fire department in Painesville."

The parade, televised on WJW-TV, was conceived, planned, and executed in only two months. Candy and Norm worked fast.

WIXY APPRECIATION DAY

Constant promotions helped us climb the ratings ladder quickly. For another promotion, Norm wanted to thank all who had supported us over the past few years. He called it WIXY Appreciation Day. As always, he challenged Candy to find the best venue for the event, a place that would hold over 25,000 fans. And, as always, Candy found it: Chippewa Lake Amusement Park, which had been around since 1878.

Our music director notified record labels of the importance of the event and requested each to send some of its biggest rock stars to appear for free. The record companies quickly responded with an enthusiastic, "Yes." It would be great exposure for the artist, the song, and the record label. After all, WIXY was playing their songs. What we didn't know is that we were about to launch a spring/summer tradition for WIXY.

In the late '60s we didn't have limousines at our disposal, so Norm sent me out to the airport in my own car to pick up one of our performers, a relative newcomer to the music industry, but one with a West Coast hit that had started to cross over into Top 40. The artist's name was Neil Diamond, and his hit song was "Solitary Man." At the time I was driving a Chevy station wagon, stylishly equipped with wooden paneling on the sides and a big luggage rack on the top. The good news was the car could seat up to eight people, depending on their size, because in those days, you could still seat three in the front.

To this day I don't know how we did it, but stacked in my wagon was a drum set, two guitars, and one bass guitar. Neil sat up front with me and my wife, Pam, with his guitar case sprawled out over their laps. His four band members all squeezed into the back seat. Neither the van nor the sport utility vehicles that are so popular today had been invented yet, so my loaded-down station wagon must have been an amazing sight to see as we made the trip from the airport to Chippewa Lake Park.

We arrived at the park right on time, and to my surprise and that of everyone else at WIXY, especially Norm, over 100,000 excited fans had been pouring into the park. On the WIXY ticket was: Tommy James and the Shondells, Cleveland's Outsiders with Sonny Geraci, Music Explosion, Paul Revere and the Raiders, Gary Lewis and the Playboys, The Left Banke, Creedence Clearwater Revival, and, of course, Neil Diamond. The WIXY DJs took turns introducing each act. We were all dressed alike: blue jeans and our famous dark blue WIXY Supermen short-sleeved sweatshirts.

The entire event was very fast-paced. Three hours after it began, our very first WIXY Appreciation Day was in the bag and a tremendous success. The fans experienced great music, a fun time, and shoulder-to-shoulder interaction with the WIXY Supermen. Many left with the autographs of future superstars.

When I took Neil back to the airport, Pam came along with us. She was once again seated in the middle of the front seat between Neil and me. Neil, who was living on the West Coast, brought up that he had recently met the legendary actor John Wayne. Pam then went on to give Neil her impression of John Wayne, which, by the way, sounded just like him. Neil got such a kick out of that impersonation that he never let me forget it.

Following that event and a few telephone interviews for my show, Neil and I became long-distance pals for awhile. At this point, he was an established rock star. When Neil was scheduled to return to Cleveland to perform at the Public Hall, he called me ahead of time and asked if I would pick him up at the airport. The day before his arrival, he called and said he wanted to ride the rapid downtown. He asked if I would pick him up there instead.

The evening of his show, I remember vividly that Neil was quite nervous. First, he had just performed on the big screen as Yussel, the young Jewish cantor in the remake of the 1927 film, *The Jazz Singer.* Due to his enormously successful performance, the CBS crew followed him everywhere, filming his every move. We asked them to turn off their cameras so I could interview him. They declined, so we were forced to retreat to a sacred place: the men's restroom behind the stage at Public Hall Auditorium. It was here that we finally conducted the interview in peace and quiet, just before I introduced him to 10,000 fans.

The reason for Neil's nervousness was that this would be the first time that he would perform in front of 10,000 people in a closed-in venue. The last time I saw Neil was with my wife, Rosary, in the early '70s, when he performed at the sold-out Coliseum.

EXIT CANDY, ENTER LINDA

When Candy got burned out and decided to leave WIXY after two years, Norm found a very capable replacement in Linda Scott.

Linda was also young and bright, with a creative energy, and she learned quickly—at Norm's urging—to do everything she could to get the WIXY call letters or our DJs' names in the paper. She told me, "Norman's standing orders were clear: 'Always keep the call letters in front of the public. Do whatever it takes to get us constant coverage and print.'"

Linda's office was right next to mine. One day she came bouncing into my office laughing out loud. I asked her what was so funny. She asked me if I could cook. I responded with a loud "No!" Laughing hysterically, Linda said, "You'd better learn quickly because I just spoke with the food editor of *The Cleveland Press*, and told her you were a great Lebanese/Syrian cook. The food editor then said, 'Great. Larry can cook me a meal at his home. I'll photograph it and do a story on him.'"

Linda scored a real coup in 1970 when she signed up David Cassidy, Susan Dey, and Danny Bonaduce as grand marshals for the WIXY Christmas parade. Linda had seen a preview of their TV show, *The Partridge Family*, and thought it would be a hit. But because the show had not yet aired, the actors were still unknown, and she got them for a bargain. By the time of the parade, *The Partridge Family* was Number 1 in the Neilsen ratings, and David, Susan, and Danny were stars. The crowd for our parade nearly doubled in size.

One of the most unusual WIXY promotions Linda organized was WIXY's Crusade to Save the Miniskirt. "A few hours after we announced the promotion," she said, "a crowd of 10,000— mostly men—showed up on Public Square to see young girls dressed in very trendy, very short miniskirts." There was some negative feedback, but the event made the five o'clock news on TV.

Norm would come up with an idea, and his first words were, "Linda, get in here!" Then she would have to figure out how to get the job done. Like the time he told her, "Linda, I want to bring back the Edsel!"

"You want to bring back the *what?*" Linda replied. The Edsel, of course, was the car that became the Ford Motor Company's biggest failure. The promotion would be called "WIXY Brings Back the Edsel," and now Linda had to make it work.

She managed to find a 1958 Ford Edsel, and on the evening of the promotion, the car was to appear in the front lobby of the Loew's Ohio Theatre on Euclid Avenue. Cleveland Mayor Carl Stokes was on his way to cut the ribbon, and just minutes before the crowd was allowed to come in, a major problem arose. No one had thought to measure the width of the car. The fins of the 1958 sedan would not fit through the metal frames of the theatre doors.

"Linda, get a blowtorch," Norm said.

"He actually wanted to cut holes in the doorframes," Linda told me later.

They didn't have to damage the historic theater, but some-how they got the car inside. The result: more newspaper and TV coverage for WIXY.

One of Linda's favorite promotions was WIXY's Salute to the Vietnam Veterans Talent Show, in 1970. Linda got a call from a young woman at the Veterans Administration Hospital asking if they could bring some of their patients to one of our WIXY rock concerts. Unfortunately, the venues we used for the concerts couldn't accommodate wheelchairs. So Linda suggested that WIXY bring the show to them. This time it was Linda bringing a bold idea to Norm. When she pitched it to him, she could tell right away he liked it by the big smile on his face.

"With Norman, there was no such thing as lukewarm," she said. Linda organized tryouts and selected a variety of acts to put on a great show for the veterans. "As I looked around at the room filled with wheelchairs, crutches, and veterans lying in beds, tears were falling from everyone's eyes. My heart was pumping with so much joy."

WIXY OPENS BLOSSOM MUSIC CENTER

Blossom Music Center, forever the summer home of the Cleveland Orchestra, opened in the summer of 1968. The orchestra performed at the venue's grand opening. Blood, Sweat and Tears (BST) performed the following evening at Blossom's first rock concert, which happened to be sponsored by WIXY 1260.

For the most part, not many knew where Blossom was located. It was hidden somewhere in Cuyahoga Falls between Cleveland and Akron. I was chosen as master of ceremonies for the concert. The opening act was John Denver, who was mainly known for writing the hit song, "Leaving on a Jet Plane," for Peter, Paul and Mary. He had not yet had a hit of his own.

After receiving a very welcoming response, John performed a forty-minute set. Following a twenty-minute break, I was to introduce BST. Blossom Music Center seats 6,500 in the closed-in amphitheatre and another 13,500 on the lawn. When John went on, we had around 8,000 in attendance. That meant another 12,000 were stuck in traffic, including BST. Backstage, we all became very worried. This was long before cell phones, so we communicated through walkie-talkies. It was our only way of knowing what was happening.

We were in constant contact with the Cuyahoga Falls police,

who were trying to manage the chaos. To help stall for time, we asked John if he would go back out and sing until BST arrived. He quickly answered, "Sure!"

Looking back, we could not have written a sadder script. The news that BST was stuck in traffic and that John Denver would be the entertainment until they arrived was not well received. You could feel the uneasiness of the audience.

A few minutes after John began to perform, the audience started to boo him and throw things on stage. Anxiety was mounting, and I was told to get John off the stage. The producers of the show needed a few minutes to figure out what to do next. Luckily, Bobby Colomby, the drummer for BST, showed up. He went on stage with me, and the swelling crowd welcomed him with a thunderous applause. Bobby said, "I'm sorry for the delay. We got stuck in traffic, but the rest of the group will be arriving soon by helicopter. We'll play until the last person goes home." The band arrived within fifteen minutes and, as promised, played until the early morning.

Following the concert, I had a few people over to my apartment. I knew John Denver was distraught, so I asked him if he'd like to come over for awhile with my friends. We could wind down, and then I would take him back to his hotel. To this day I still feel very bad about what happened next. John began playing his guitar in my living room and, once again, a scenario similar to that at Blossom played out: although they didn't throw anything, my friends stopped listening and turned away. I knew what they all were feeling: How much more of this country stuff can we listen to?

Adding more insult to injury, John had taken to our female promotion director, also at my party. Around 3:30 a.m., tired from the long day, she excused herself and went home. John had her phone number, called, and began to play more music over the phone. It wasn't long before I saw John walk back into my living room with a long face. I found out the next day that she had actually fallen asleep listening to him, and he knew it.

A few years later, after several hit records, John was a major musical sensation. As I was getting ready to introduce him to a sold-out Coliseum crowd, John and I laughed as we reminisced about that sorry evening.

It no longer mattered because John now had several number-one songs, played in front of standing-room-only audiences, had hosted the Grammy Awards on national television, starred in two movies, was married, and was now loved by many.

Another memorable promotion that stands out involves Billy Bass. It was in the summer of 1969 and WIXY sponsored a concert at Public Hall Auditorium in Cleveland. Cleveland's own James Gang would open the concert. James Taylor ("JT"), who only had one hit record at the time, would follow them, and The Who would headline.

There was serious concern from the WIXY jocks whether brothers Mike and Jules Belkin had made the right decision by putting James Taylor, who was for the most part a ballad singer, between two hard-rock bands. Earlier that evening I had dinner with my good friend from the Detroit days, Pete Gidion, who was the promotional manager for Decca, Coral, and Brunswick Records. The Who wanted personally to thank me for being the first DJ in America to play their hit song "I Can't Explain," which was released on the Brunswick record label. I remember the band being very funny, kind, and in control, unlike their stage persona of being wild and out of control.

Needless to say, the concert was fabulous, and JT was a showstopper. To this day I can't believe I stood behind the curtain, just ten feet from lead guitarist Peter Townsend, and watched that unbelievable band do what they did. What would follow would be a night to remember.

BILLY BASS BRINGS JT HOME

Following the concert, Billy Bass, who knew JT, asked him if he'd like to come over to his house along with a few of Billy's friends. JT agreed, and we ended up at Billy's for a free concert. James Taylor was riding on his number-one hit, "Sweet Baby

James," a name he decided to use for the title of his second album on Warner Brothers Records. Carole King would play piano on the album. Other than the title hit, the public had not heard the album, and we were about to get an exclusive. There were only about twenty of us at Billy's that evening, so it was a warm, personal setting, sort of how Billy always liked it: quiet, intimate, and very cool.

JT sat on the steps to Billy's upstairs. Back then, JT had long, shoulder-length hair, in contrast to his bald, bespectacled look today. In addition, he was dressed in the same clothing that he wore for the concert. He was very hip and casual looking in a white long-sleeved shirt with a vest, casual pants, and the oh-so-popular Beatle boots.

We all gathered around Billy's steps as JT began playing. He previewed for us his entire not-yet-released album, which spawned the monster hits "Fire and Rain," "Country Road," and "You've Got a Friend." When he sang "You've Got a Friend," which was written by Carole King, tears came to our eyes, all of us very aware of his earlier struggles with drugs. It was well known that JT had personal problems with heroin and was able to write about them. None of us wanted the evening to end.

What I find so interesting about several of the performers I've written about is that in the beginning, my relationship with them made me feel as if we were pals. Once they achieved superstar status and became widely known, the relationship slowed to a trickle and, in most cases, ended. Although my relationship with Neil Diamond and a few others lasted over fifteen years, once they became prominent and successful, their managers, "image-makers," and promotional agents were very choosy about who they let in. I can remember calling Neil's office several times only to be met with, "We'll get back to you." I was sure Neil never got the message. It took a while for me to realize that maintaining close contact with men of that stature was virtually impossible. I learned to back off and bask in the reflected glory of their success.

CHAPTER 11

The Breakup of That
Old Gang of Mine

We now had four years under our belts. Ratings continued to soar, and those radio stations that once mattered to us were now distant competitors. Norm and his partners decided to invest in their success and bought another Top 40 radio station in Mc-Keesport, Pennsylvania, just outside of Pittsburgh, and called it WIXZ, which sounded just like WIXY. To ensure that the same successful format would work there, George Brewer, Mike Reineri, and Dick Kemp were sent to launch the new station.

George was replaced by Bill Sherard, another very smart and engaging Top 40 program director. Over a period of a few years, original team members Mike Reineri, Dick "Wilde Childe" Kemp, and Lou "King" Kirby would leave WIXY for WIXZ in Pittsburgh. New arrivals were the legendary Joe Finan, "Music Professor" Jim Labarbra, Billy Bass, Chuck Knapp, and Chuck Dunaway. In spite of all the major changes, we didn't lose a beat. The replacements caught on, and the ratings continued to swell.

Chuck Dunaway had worked at WABC, New York, and brought with him a Top 40 style that was as good as you would hear anywhere in America. I was partial to Chuck's voice and talent. As a youngster, I loved listening to the likes of "Cousin Brucie" Morrow (no relation) on WABC, and Chuck Dunaway was the epitome of New York Top 40 greatness.

Popular, talented DJs started popping up on WIXY and continued to add diamonds to its crown: Steve Hunter and Chip Hobart from CKLW, "Truckin" Tom Kent; Bobby Knight, and many more over a period of years.

WIXY CROSSES THE CHASM

Despite all of the departures, WIXY continued to roll on. Our new program director, Bill Sherard, had different skills from George Brewer. His knowledge of the marketplace and unique insights into Top 40 radio continued to propel WIXY upward. In addition, he would create a new paradigm that would extend the current bridge into previously unexplored boundaries. The cumulative effect would keep Clevelanders listening and talking about WIXY more than ever before. WIXY would become the new prototype for Top 40 radio stations across America.

I'm not sure whether Norm Wain ever played the game of chess, but his mind worked like a seasoned chess player. Good chess players like to take risks. They play the most unpredictable moves and somehow know the outcome . . . checkmate! Unpredictability is most often the tactic of a master, and Norm Wain was a master at picking talent. In my opinion, his move to bring on Billy Bass was masterful. Billy, a fixture in Cleveland radio with the underground at WMMS, held your attention with his low, mellow voice. Billy had the most unusual approach of any of the WIXY Supermen. He never tried to win you over or court your affection. Billy's style reminded me of a hunter, always knowing how to capture his prey. Norm knew instinctively that Billy would score, and for that reason he brought him to WIXY.

The FM market had yet to take off when we had a chance to pick up Billy Bass. He began his career at WIXY doing overnights and later moved to evenings. It would be a scary move. First of all, Billy was African American and had a smooth and sexy voice, but that's what made him extraordinary. The combination of the these attributes gave him a mysterious and exotic persona.

Second, his style was uniquely different from the Childe's. Billy was slow and intimate when compared to the Wilde Childe's machine-gun approach to the music. I wondered at the time how Clevelanders would react to such a drastic change on WIXY's number-one rated evening show. As good as Billy was, and there was no one more different in the marketplace, Clevelanders had been roaring for WIXY 1260 for three years. Due to our programming consistency, all the incremental changes would only help catapult us higher in the ratings.

It was 1969 and Cleveland was still staggering from the riots of '66 and '68. Race relations had begun to improve, but some attitudes had not, and Billy was black. Billy had slowly climbed his career ladder, and it was now time for his star to shine. His shift on WIXY was 7–midnight, which had the highest ratings in the Greater Cleveland radio market. Billy adapted quickly, and Clevelanders became acquainted with his distinguished style and loved it. On the flip side, Billy began wondering why all the WIXY DJs were being promoted outside of the radio station but not him. I spoke to Billy recently about the frank conversation he had with Norm Wain. Although it sounds crude and unbelievable in today's society, what follows is Billy's stinging yet friendly, word-for-word confrontation with Norman Wain. He sat down with Norm and said, "All the WIXY jocks are being promoted on the radio station, in the newspapers, in promotional pieces for advertising agencies, and given promotional pictures for listeners, and I'm being excluded from all of that? Norman, it appears to me as if you are trying to hide me. I never get to go anywhere. What goes?"

Norm Wain had to reveal his intentions. He looked at Billy, and with firmness in his voice he said, "Billy, are you stupid or something? You're black." Billy then retorted with, "So?" "They'll murder you," said Norm. "You're black and our audience does not know that. I'm not trying to hold you back, Billy; I'm trying to protect you." That conversation was the cord that bound Norman Wain and Billy Bass for over forty years. To this day Billy says, "I love Norman Wain; he was my father protector."

AN ABRUPT DETOUR

When Pam and I married a few years earlier, we talked about a family and a home with a white picket fence. We had been married three years and the possibility of achieving that dream began to dwindle. After a long discussion about settling down, having children and other things that were once important to both of us, it was clear that Pam, too, wanted a career in music. The morning after our heart-to-heart discussion, she decided to move back home to Detroit. It was painful for both of us because we were close friends who had achieved so much together.

We continued to work on many projects, but as time went on, and as agonizing as it was, we divorced within a year. Pam went on to achieve her dream, becoming a distinguished author, composer, and playwright, and winning an Oscar for her 1988 short documentary film, *Young at Heart.*

CHAPTER 12

The WIXY All Stars

I was so absorbed in WIXY that I wanted to form a basketball team to play area high schools and raise money for charity. Norm Wain and George Brewer encouraged me to go out and find basketball players who could put on a great show. Our new team was called the Larry Morrow WIXY All Stars. Having the likes of Chuck Knapp and Billy Bass on board was a bonus; they were gifted radio performers and outstanding athletes. Their athleticism made our WIXY sports team competitive.

When I challenged the high schools to a basketball game with the WIXY All Stars, the understanding was all the proceeds would go back to the schools to be used as needed. The high schools had teachers who could really play ball. On the other hand, the WIXY All Stars were great talk jocks, but not talented sports jocks, excluding Billy and Chuck. If we were going to be competitive, I would need ringers. I had struck up a close relationship with NFL Hall of Fame and Super Bowl wide receiver Paul Warfield, who at that time was with the Miami Dolphins but still lived in Cleveland. Cleveland loved Paul with a capital L-O-V-E. Paul helped bring other players to me from the Cleveland Browns.

I received a call requesting the WIXY All Stars come to Lakewood High School. Lakewood insisted, "You must bring Billy Bass." It was obvious that Billy had amassed a significant and loyal following. This was no surprise to the WIXY jocks because Billy was the real deal and we all knew it. With the recent assas-

sination of Dr. Martin Luther King, Jr., whites and blacks across
America were obviously confused over what was going on. With
the racial imbalance, and because Lakewood was a noninte-
grated city, I too became concerned about Billy's welfare.

Before the start of each game, I would introduce the team.
When it came time to introduce Billy, the sold-out Lakewood
gym erupted with cheers, and he received a standing ovation
that went on for over two minutes. Enough said about the concern. Billy scored 38 points that evening and was elevated to cult
status. Chuck Knapp was also very good and consistently scored
in the upper 20s. One evening against Parma High School, he
dropped in 38 points.

After each game, we all stayed and signed autographs until
the last person went home. My job was to schedule the games,
make arrangements with my guys, practice once in awhile,
make sure the uniforms were cleaned, and introduce the players. Even though I was a former basketball player, I could not
play at the same level as Billy and Chuck.

The WIXY All Stars also played the Cleveland Browns at
Chagrin Falls High School. Big, strong Walter Johnson of the
Browns took the game very seriously, and for the very first time
we had trouble controlling someone's behavior. I thought for
sure the game would be suspended, but in the end, the WIXY
All Stars prevailed. A good time was had by all.

One of our big draws was the day we played the TV 8 All
Stars: Big Chuck and Hoolihan and Dick Goddard. At the time
the three of them were the most familiar and famous faces in
Cleveland television.

In my entire six years with the WIXY All Stars, we never lost
a game other than when we played the internationally famous
Harlem Globetrotters in the old Cleveland Arena on Euclid Avenue.

Following that success, Candy Forest arranged for the WIXY
All Stars to play TV 5 in a football game. It would be a match-
up between the number one TV station in town and the num-

ber one radio station, along with all of their well-known stars. From TV 5: John Hambrick, Don Webster, Nev Chandler, and Gib Shanley. The game was at St. Edward High School. Even though the temperature was in the teens that day, the game was sold out. John Hambrick kicked off with his bare right foot and kicked a field goal the same way. The WIXY All Stars reigned again in a close game. Afterward we all stayed and signed autographs in the freezing temperatures. Weatherman Don Webster and I, to this day, continue to talk about that game.

One day I received a call from Cleveland Browns NFL Hall of Fame fullback Marion Motley. Marion had formed and was coaching a Cleveland women's national professional football team called the USA Dare Devils. They were a group of very talented players.

The WIXY All Stars played the USA Dare Devils on Sunday, November 12, 1967, in front of 7,000 spectators at Cloverleaf Speedway. Before the start of the game, Marion told me, "No grabbing and no foul language—after all, these are women." I was our quarterback, and the first time I was hit, I was shocked: I'd never heard such foul language from a woman. That's saying something from a guy who played QB for the 11th Marine Division at Camp Pendleton.

Over a period of six years the WIXY All Stars raised thousands of dollars for schools through our sports efforts.

WIXY AND BELKIN FORM A RELATIONSHIP

WIXY 1260 formed a close bond with Mike and Jules Belkin (Belkin Productions). The two brothers were making a name for themselves by promoting concerts of national and international acts. Mike Belkin also managed a number of major acts, including Joe Walsh, The James Gang, Wild Cherry, and others. The relationship with the Belkins spawned a series of concerts over my six years at WIXY. These concerts further catapulted 1260 as the undisputed entertainment leader in Greater Cleveland. Together, we sold out almost every concert at Public Hall with groups such as the Who, the Rolling Stones, Herman's Hermits, the Monkees, Neil Diamond, Crosby, Stills, Nash and Young, and the soulful Motown Review, which consisted of the Miracles, Diana Ross and the Supremes, Temptations, Stevie Wonder, Marvin Gaye, the Marvelettes, and Martha Reeves and the Vandellas.

The tickets for these concerts were four dollars in advance and five dollars at the door. The WIXY DJs were present at every concert. The catalytic effect of 10,000 screaming fans and the exposure of the WIXY Supermen on stage for every concert could not have been greater. The result was a larger listening audience, which resulted in higher ratings and greater revenue for the radio station. The music may have reigned supreme at WIXY, but the station itself was the underlying force. It was like a magnet, purposefully designed to drag you in, constantly driven by the quest to raise the bar and establish new industry standards.

Due to a succession of one promotion after another, our collective strengths were all wrapped up in one man: Superman. The WIXY Supermen's lives were changing faster than a speeding bullet. As for me, mine was about to reach the stratosphere.

PROGRAMMING YOUR MIND FOR SUCCESS

In the entertainment industry, it is very natural to want as much attention focused on you as possible because your paycheck is directly tied to your popularity and your ability to attract an audience. I was unaccustomed to chasing celebrity because I was uncomfortable with personal adulation. However, my friend Pete Dangerfield, then general manager of Stouffer's Inn on the Square Hotel, once told me, "Larry, if I don't have people waiting in line for an hour for brunch, I don't have a successful restaurant. If you don't have listeners bugging you for your autograph and tugging at your clothes, you don't have a career."

Yet, there was something outside of radio that brought me both satisfaction and the long-term reward I was craving: the use of my voice in commercials, along with writing and producing music. To this day my wife, Rosary, continues to remind me, "It is your voice that will carry you the distance."

Up to this point, it had been WIXY that applied the foundation to my life. My loyalty to the station ran deep. This fact was further solidified by my eighteen-hour workdays days, which had given many the impression that WIXY was the only thing that mattered to me. Nothing could have been farther from the truth.

I always knew that God had given me other talents. Up to this point, they had been a sleeping lion within me that was about to be awakened. Although I had been working diligently with WIXY appearances, I had also immersed myself in a tireless effort of recording commercials and writing jingles for clients. By itself, radio was a wonderful and satisfying career. However, another side of me craved fulfillment that would satisfy my heart.

JINGLE AND VOICEOVER WORK

If I were to use my voice and jingle-writing skills outside of radio, I would need to do some serious bridge-building. My vision to succeed in this arena meant I would compete for voice-over commercials and jingle-writing opportunities for companies at the highest level, such as Disney and Universal Films. When I met with Wain, Weiss, and Zingale to ask to be introduced to key people at the agency level, each wholeheartedly supported my effort and immediately began to introduce me to several of the most productive advertising agencies in town.

Those introductions opened a door for me. I would actually walk into advertising agencies with three reels of tape: my jingle reel, my voice reel, and my creative reel. For the most part, I always met with the creative director of the advertising agency. I hardly ever went directly to a client. When it came to jingles, the creative director would give me a client's slogan, and I would go home, sit at my piano, and write a sixty-second song around that slogan. If the creative director liked it, he would then take it to his client for approval. Once he received the client's approval, I would arrange the music and hire the musicians and singers for the recording session. I normally recorded a sixty-second version that could also be broken down into thirty- and ten-second versions. Being in radio helped me write jingles. I believed jingles were no more that one-minute hit songs.

Over a period of four years, I was fortunate to become the local and national spokesperson for national brands such as BF Goodrich, which included an on-camera Super Bowl appearance. My jingle company, Morrow's Music Machine, had garnered the same kind of positive response. Much to my surprise, I was asked by Wyse Advertising, Cleveland's largest agency as well as a national legend, to write a jingle for Smucker's. When the Smucker's campaign was launched on the NBC Today/ Tonight Show package, the result would be a CLIO award—the advertisers' equivalent to an Oscar—for writing and producing the musical jingle, "With a name like Smucker's, it has to be good."

CHAPTER 13

WIXY Brings the Boys Home for Thanksgiving

WIXY 1260 had created a buzz on the streets and earned top ratings thanks to great leadership, visionary program directors, highly regarded music directors, and hard-working and determined promotions directors. Now were were going to put that popularity to work in a very special promotion that was one of the most personally rewarding projects I ever worked on.

By the fall of 1969, the Vietnam War was out of control. The hostilities had already claimed over 48,000 lives, and there was no end in sight. For the first time ever, a war could be seen on television while Americans gathered in their family rooms to watch the evening news. It had become an emotionally charged situation for everyone.

One Friday afternoon I was called into Bill Sherard's office, with our promotions director, Linda Scott, present. Bill said, "Linda has an idea for a promotion that will set a new tone for WIXY and will also set WIXY apart from the entire media in Cleveland. It will be called 'WIXY Brings the Boys Home for Thanksgiving.'"

With a smile from ear-to-ear, Linda said, "Larry, we're going to send you to Vietnam to interview all the Cleveland-area troops there." She intuitively knew how to connect listeners to WIXY, and this promotion would create an emotional response never experienced before, one that would ultimately turn out to be the most important building block WIXY ever created.

A JAW-DROPPING HONOR

At first I was puzzled. Then I said, "Are you guys out of your minds?" But once I caught my breath and we further discussed the plan, I got very excited. Wow! It only took a few minutes for me to realize what a privilege it would be to represent my radio station and my community. I gladly accepted the challenge, and the wheels went in motion the following day. Linda contacted our congressman, Charles Vanik, who was popular in Washington, to act on our behalf.

Because the war had escalated and the danger factor was very high, it would take extraordinary measures to secure permission for me to enter South Vietnam. From my perspective, it was incredible to think about interviewing Clevelanders and experiencing first-hand how excited they would be to see one of their radio personalities from back home. On top of that, the opportunity to play those interviews over WIXY 1260 for all their loved ones to hear over Thanksgiving and Christmas was spine-chilling.

It was also my desire for the society at large to view this WIXY event as one of honor. In addition to my deep personal thoughts about the mission, I had professional questions as well, such as whether WIXY would move up the ladder in the minds of many and gain the respect that a few Cleveland writers thought it needed? Would the new WIXY, so to speak, now represent a symbol of distinction as a radio station that cared deeply not only for its listeners but its beloved community? Only time would tell.

From my prior Marine experience, I was familiar with terms like *ground forces, guerilla warfare, artillery, fire power, search and destroy,* and *air strik*es. I had not experienced combat during my active duty since my time in the Marines occurred mostly during peacetime. This time would be vastly different, as I would be in the heart of the action interviewing our Cleveland troops.

If Linda could get permission from the State Department, the mission was a go. There was a part of me that doubted the plans would become a reality because of the constant reports of some of the bloodiest episodes going on in Vietnam, Laos, and Cambodia. My fears became a reality when we received a letter in October from Mr. Vanik's administrative assistant denying our request.

Just when all hope had been dashed, I received a surprise phone call from Colonel Melton, head of the armed forces in Vietnam, at the Pentagon. He said he had talked with Mr. Vanik and assured me my orders would be forthcoming. When I told him I was skeptical that the call was legitimate, he responded by reciting my serial number, which had been assigned to me when I enlisted in the Marines. It is part of your official designation and, except as indicated, will ordinarily appear in every military record in which your name appears, including every letter, telegram, order, report, and payroll document. Once you have served in the military, you never forget your serial number. As we continued our conversation, part of me remained unconvinced that the call was legitimate, so I told him I would like to call him back for verification. When I called the number he gave me, the Pentagon answered and I was transferred to his office.

I immediately passed on the good news to Linda and Bill, and as I remember, we were all excited, especially Linda. My confidential materials arrived the next day. I was to report to Major Key, USAF, in Saigon on October 25, 1969.

Finally, it hit me. I realized the Vietnam mission was a go.

MAJOR LAWRENCE D. MORROW, UNITED STATES MARINE

My itinerary would have me leave Cleveland on October 23 and return November 17. After receiving twenty-one inoculations and my instructions, I was declared ready to travel. I packed two tape recorders, several cassettes, a suit, one white shirt, and one pair of shoes. When I arrived in Vietnam I would receive all my Marine military gear, which included everything from field boots to underwear. I carried an identification card that gave me the rank of major, USMC.

When I left the Marines in 1958, I was discharged as a corporal, so it would be an adjustment for me to get used to officers saluting me as a major. Being promoted to major from corporal was the equivalent of a secretary being promoted to president of the company. The reason for the promotion was to give me the ability to go anywhere I wanted to complete my mission. I would fly from base to base on C130s, troop carriers for the military.

My United Airlines flight left Cleveland as planned. The trip took six hours to reach Los Angeles. My next flight to Hawaii took seven hours, and I stayed overnight at the Eli Kai. The following morning I flew out of Honolulu on Pan Am Airlines to Guam, then on to Manila, crossed the International Dateline, and finally arrived in Saigon on October 25—a twenty-five-hour flight. Surprisingly, when we were about twenty miles outside of Saigon, two American F105 Phantom jets came out of nowhere and flanked both sides of the plane just before we landed. It was something right out of a movie.

We were told they would safely usher our plane to the Air Force base in Vietnam. Once the Pan Am jumbo jet landed, an American army jeep with a heavy 50-caliber machine gun on its turret arrived to take the passengers into the airport. Up to this point, the most intriguing part of the trip was the jets escorting us in to the airport and the arrival of the army jeep. But what surprised me the most was how we traveled from the Air Force base into the city of Saigon. I assumed a military vehicle would transport me to John W. Key, Jr., Major, USAF, in Saigon. To my disbelief, what greeted me and a few other military passengers was a dirty, bullet-ridden bus with no windows. On top of that, it was monsoon season in Vietnam so the temperature was over one hundred and the air extremely humid. Of course, I was wearing a suit.

The trip from the airport into Saigon took about thirty minutes, and nothing could have prepared me for what I saw along the way. I witnessed poorly constructed shacks supported by stilts in about three feet of water. The families who lived in these huts threw their garbage into the water. The stench was overwhelming. It depressed me because I never imagined such deplorable conditions.

Once I arrived in Saigon, I expected to see a giant metropolis of tall buildings and historic architecture. There was only one hotel, the Caravelle Hotel Saigon, and it would be my temporary home for one night before joining our troops in the field the next day.

The Caravelle Hotel Saigon was a famous ten-story hotel where many dignitaries stayed, such as Alabama governor George Wallace a few years earlier, in 1967. The interior of the hotel was historic and beautifully decorated—a stark contrast between the serenity inside and the scary ugliness on the outside.

Just beyond the front doors was a fifty-foot-tall aluminum statue of a military man holding a rifle. I was puzzled by it and asked many, but no one could tell me why the statue had been erected.

On every street corner I would witness something that in all my time in the Marines I had not seen before. There were sandbag forts, roughly six feet tall and six feet wide, with peephole openings on all four sides. Each fort was occupied by a friendly Vietnamese soldier with his machine gun, an instant reminder that the war was all around me.

"DON'T WORRY, THEY'RE HARMLESS"

I had never seen anything like my hotel room. It was truly magnificent and educational at the same time. First, the sixteen-foot ceilings were splendid, with fans in every room. There was no air-conditioning, so the fans helped cool the temperature and humidity. Second, I'm from Pontiac, Michigan, where we had one bathroom for a family of six. And now I'm faced with two commodes next to each other. I called downstairs to the concierge to ask about the use of the second commode. After some embarrassing laughter, I was told it was a *bidet*, a French word that refers to a cleansing fixture common in many foreign countries.

I was exhausted from the long, wearisome, and unnerving trip and wanted nothing more than to go straight to bed. Unfortunately for me, the constant running of motorbikes around the square kept me awake for much of the night. When the noise woke me in the middle of the night, I decided to get up and take a look outside. Before returning to bed, I went to the bathroom. While there, the movement of something caught my attention. It was a huge lizard that appeared to be the size of an American squirrel climbing to the top of the ceiling to make a quick exit. I immediately called downstairs to the concierge, who again laughed. "Don't worry, they're harmless," said the voice at the other end of the telephone. I got off the phone thinking, *Maybe in your life, pal, but not mine!*

I would not sleep well the rest of the night, and daylight could not come fast enough. I wanted to head for the "bush," a military term used to describe where the troops lived and fought. From my military experience, I knew I would be very comfortable there.

The next morning I reported to Major Key's office and received my orders. He presented me with a complete list of Cleveland personnel, the bases where they were stationed, and some important "dos and don'ts." For example, *do* only drink water from the military water tanks and *don't* stray from the base because it is dangerous. I had travel privileges on any military vehicle or plane, with the exception of the tanks and F105 Phantom fighter jets. I mostly traveled from one city to another on C130s.

PENTAGON ORDERS SECRET MISSION

I was given orders from the Pentagon that for every interview I conducted, with both enlisted personnel and officers, I was to ask how they felt about the war. I would do as commanded: conduct the interviews, complete my confidential report, and hand it over to Colonel Melton's office before departing Saigon. During my interviews, I found it fascinating that the officers who knew the details about the American strategy felt the war was useless and that we should not be there. The enlisted men and women felt just the opposite.

At the beginning of my mission, I was asked if I wanted to carry a weapon. I originally thought I did but was advised not to. If I were captured by the enemy, because of my officer ranking and not carrying a weapon, my life might be spared. Although I was a registered marksman in the Marines with the M1 rifle and an expert with the 45-pistol, I decided not to carry one.

Taking into account that all I had with me was a map of South Vietnam and a list of the two hundred names and locations of the Cleveland service personnel, it was going to be a daunting task. Not knowing the country and the danger involved, you might think I would be discouraged; the opposite was true. I was confident, excited by both the assignment and the opportunity to meet each and every one of our Cleveland military.

I was also excited about how Cleveland would react to hearing these wonderfully moving messages from their loved ones. Even those who did not have a family member in Vietnam or in the military would appreciate and be inspired by the WIXY mission of bringing the voices of sons, daughters, and friends home for the holidays.

The trip would take me north from Saigon, then up the China Sea to where North and South Vietnam split, or what in military terms is called the Demilitarized Zone (DMZ). I would then work my way back down to Saigon. The trip would take no more than ten days. Whenever I arrived on a base and met a Clevelander, the first remark was, "Wow, look who's here! It's the Duker from WIXY. What in the hell are you doing here?" Or, "The Duker's here from the 'world.' What's going on back home in the world?" ("The world" was a slang military term for those back home.)

A BRIDGE BETWEEN TWO WORLDS

I would spend precious time with our troops, giving updates on what was happening back home on WIXY, the latest show-biz buzz, and the newest Top 40 songs. In many cases it was as though I were Santa talking to an excited child at Christmas. I brought with me WIXY 1260 stickers for their racks (beds), helmets, jeeps, tanks, or wherever they wanted to put them. I also brought several WIXY Supermen sweatshirts.

As small a token as it was, it was reminder gift of a little slice of home. It carried with it wonderful memories, treasures at this point in your life. The interviews took place at all hours of the day. I would start each interview with their name, rank, branch of service, job classification, and the city they lived in, followed by the question, "Would you like to send a message back home to Mom, Dad, or a loved one for Thanksgiving and Christmas?" Not all did, but the fifty-five who recorded messages with me brought tears from both of us. After all, I knew what it was to be away from home serving your country; it's also lonesome for those whom you love and miss so much, especially during the holidays.

FORTY YEARS LATER AND THE MEMORIES ARE STILL VIVID

The most dangerous mission of the trip came near the end of my three-week stay. I needed to get to Cam Rahn Bay Hospital, located near the east coast of the China Sea, where several of our young men from Cleveland were hospitalized. Just before I boarded a small, four-seater plane, a military doctor ran to the plane. He and another soldier carried a wounded, high-ranking officer to the plane. The officer's head was heavily bandaged from a serious wound caused by a piece of shrapnel.

The plane immediately took off with just the pilot, the doctor, the wounded soldier, and me. It was raining heavily with blustery winds. Once we were in the air, the plane was tossed around like fruit in a blender. I thought this was the end for all of us, as there was no way this small plane could make it in this weather. The wounded officer was moaning loudly, and the doctor was doing his best to keep him comfortable. The trip to the hospital took about thirty minutes, but when we arrived at Cam Rahn Bay, I thought it had taken at least an hour. Up to this point in my life, I don't ever recall being so frightened.

Once we landed, I headed to the field hospital where I would meet the five injured Cleveland boys. To enter the hospital, I had to first walk through a set of green doors. Each door had a red cross in the middle, similar to what you saw night after night on the popular '70s television show, *M*A*S*H*. As I recall, I gently pushed the doors open and took about ten steps into a room that was filled with twenty-five beds before I made a quick exit. I was neither mentally nor emotionally ready for what was before me. Unknowingly, I had missed the sign to the right of the swinging green doors that read Amputee Section. After taking a few minutes outside to compose myself, I walked back through the green doors to meet our boys.

Upon returning to the room, a loud yell came from the soldier in the second bed off to my left, who was obviously a Clevelander. I once again heard the familiar, loving words that had been shouted at me often during the trip whenever I was recognized by someone from back home: "Hey, you guys, the Duker from WIXY 1260 is here from the world." He was enthusiastically waiving to me with his good arm. As I approached him, I saw the bandaged remnant of his other arm that, not long ago, had also been healthy. This particular young man was so excited and surprised to see a familiar face from back home, the next

words out of his mouth were, "Duker, what are you doing here?"
We chatted for a few minutes and I explained the purpose of my
trip. When I began my interview with him, his first comment to
me was, "Larry, I'll do the interview, but not a word about the
loss of my arm. When I get home I want to surprise my family
with my new prosthetic arm." I found it amazing that this same
story was echoed by almost every soldier in that hospital amputee unit.

Throughout my visit at Cam Rahn Bay Hospital, I continued to feel more and more devastated by what I saw. I began
to feel very guilty that I had never been involved in any serious military conflict. Once again a flood of emotions hit me as I
thought about how these brave young men were America's most
effective weapon: no glory, no credit, just doing their job for the
country they loved so deeply.

ANOTHER VERY SCARY MOMENT

Throughout my stay in Vietnam, I was very much taken by
the scenes of the raging war. I witnessed everything from the
big war guns dropping bombs close to where I was stationed,
to visiting wounded soldiers in military hospitals. At one very
tentative time, I was in a C130 troop carrier on the way to my
next stop. The plane was filled with friendly South Vietnamese
ARVN (meaning Army of Vietnam; pronounced *ARVON*), who
looked a lot like the Viet Cong, our enemy. Well, on this day I
sat directly across from several ARVN, who had machine guns
in their hands and grenades draped around their necks.

Before I boarded the plane, I was told by a lieutenant that a
Viet Cong had recently gotten on a C130 and pulled the pin on a
grenade, causing the plane to blow up. All were lost. Following
that flight, I was petrified to travel on C130s. My options were
limited, though, because early on I had ruled out helicopters—
my only other option for travel—because I was petrified to fly in
them. This fear originated in Saigon when I spotted what ap-

peared to be a forty-foot-high pile of twisted metal of about half a football field in length. I inquired only to find out it had been named the Helicopter Graveyard. Each downed helicopter represented American lives lost. Enough said. I was out of options. From that day forward, like it or not, I traveled from base to base on C130s.

GOING HOME?

My last day in Vietnam was unnerving in more ways than one. I had just returned from the bush, and the plan was to spend my final day near the U.S. headquarters before beginning my long journey back to Cleveland. While I was resting in my hotel room in Saigon, I received a call from Colonel Melton's office with an imperative message: "Get all of your gear together because you're leaving Saigon immediately!" I was told they were expecting serious conflict in Saigon, and the colonel wanted me, along with all other nonmilitary personnel, out of there *now*. I scooped up my gear and within fifteen minutes was on my way to Tan Son Nhut Air Force Base, where I would board the Pan Am jet that would transport us out of the country and the impending danger.

As I recall, it was evening when we boarded the Pan Am jet to Guam. Not counting the pilots, there were fewer than fifteen people aboard. We were in the aircraft less than an hour when the pilot came back and informed us that we had lost the use of one of the engines. He went on to explain, "We may have to ditch. If we do, here is what will happen." He then proceeded to give us the unpleasant details on the dangerous and gut-wrenching evacuation procedure.

I can still vividly remember my prayers: "Look, Lord, how could you have me travel safely to this most troubled spot in the world, risk my life to some degree, trek throughout the dangerous areas of South Vietnam, record all of these important conversations from our brave Cleveland military for their families back home, only to have this plane go down and lose it all?"

It was two hours later when the pilot relayed the message, "Stand by, we'll be landing in Guam in just a few minutes." Once we safely touched down, I realized that we had been flying in the protective hands of our Lord. His answer to my deep-seated prayer was, "Okay, Larry, not yet."

MISSION ACCOMPLISHED

Landing in Cleveland officially marked my having traveled halfway around the world. Throughout the return trip, I reflected over how many times I had repeated the same phrase to every soldier I interviewed: "The entire city of Cleveland is pulling for you and praying for you every step of the way." The stakes were high and they all knew it. I also wondered how the Pentagon would use my report. I don't remember how many officers or soldiers were against the war, but the one constant was how they supported each other. Imagine over two hundred brave Cleveland warriors all telling the same story: how they loved America; how they loved their jobs; and how deeply they loved those back home in the world. Their stories were played over WIXY 1260 on Thanksgiving and Christmas. In addition, a cassette of each interview was mailed to the soldier's parents. WIXY and I received a thank-you letter from every parent who received a cassette.

At the conclusion of each interview, I made an agreement with each soldier: *Upon your return to Cleveland, please call me and let me take you to lunch.* Not all called, but many did, and I did treat a few to lunch. Sadly enough, some of those lunches were at the Cleveland Veterans Hospital. I was devastated to later learn that a few boys whom I interviewed never made it home for our lunch date.

"WIXY Brings the Boys Home for Thanksgiving" stirred my heart. What lay at the very core of my task was that I was living between two worlds. In one world, I was bringing to our beloved and brave Cleveland soldiers an updated picture of their home. In the other world, WIXY represented the emotional bridge between the war and those whom they loved and missed back home. Even though Vietnam was a terrible war, it was part of daily life. My emotions were driven by the hope of nourishing their souls—even for just a little while. It was this promotion that cemented my relationship with Clevelanders, as they felt I had risked my life to bring a message home from their sons and daughters.

THIRTEEN YEARS LATER

Rosary and I visited the Vietnam Veterans Memorial in Washington, D.C., on the day it opened, November 13, 1982. Walking along the wall and viewing the names was sobering. I looked up some of the names of those soldiers I knew who never made it back home . . . and wept.

Even now, I continue to think of Linda Scott's creation and the indelible mark she left on our community. There is an old saying, "People don't care how much you know until they know how much you care." Clevelanders now knew how much WIXY cared about them and their families. Some adventures cannot be put into words. To this day, my Vietnam trip remains the most rewarding experience of my broadcast life.

CHAPTER 14

Going Out on Top

The Vietnam promotion spawned a new market for us: adults. Up until this time we were mired in the teenage market. But now all those moms and dads who heard their sons' and daughters' messages over WIXY had now begun to listen to us. We also got very lucky because we were about to experience the second wave of the British Invasion.

Tom Jones wore tight pants and billowing shirts, and the ladies loved it. His sexiness attracted an older female audience, which not only fit my persona perfectly since I played to that demographic on my midmorning show, but it also improved the older demographic of my ratings. He had several hits in the '60s, including "It's Not Unusual," "What's New, Pussycat," "Delilah," "Green Green Grass of Home," "She's a Lady," and "Help Yourself."

Engelbert Humperdinck (real name: Arnold George Dorsey) was tall, sexy, and handsome. He was less energetic than Tom, although he, too, filled the charts with hit songs: "Release Me," "The Last Waltz," and "There Goes My Everything." Historically, WIXY's ratings had been top-heavy with teenagers. When Tom and Engelbert became popular, WIXY began to attract an older, mature female audience.

I was approached by a group of ladies who insisted I become the president of the Greater Cleveland Tom Jones Fan Club. I agreed to attend monthly lunch meetings at local restaurants where we would discuss my perspective on Tom Jones. In exchange, I was given proprietary information to use on my show.

They shared with me all the inside information that came directly from the national office of the fan club, including an itinerary of Tom's and Engelbert's comings and goings. The girls would often visit me at the WIXY studios, taking pictures and bringing cakes, cookies, and an assortment of goodies, which I loved. The same scenario was played out with Engelbert. At one time I was the official WIXY poster boy for both of their fan clubs. This ultimately helped me build a wonderful, long-lasting, and loyal female base.

THE DUKER, KING OF THE DJS

In 1972, *The Cleveland Press*, Cleveland's afternoon newspaper, ran a contest to crown Greater Cleveland's favorite DJ. At the time there were seventy-two radio signals on AM and FM that got into Cleveland, including WJR (760 AM) in Detroit, Michigan, and CKLW (Radio 8) in Windsor, Ontario, Canada. I had been on the air on WIXY 1260 for almost five years when the three-week poll began. Bill Barrett, the radio and television writer for the newspaper, ran weekly full-page stories, with pictures, on how the DJs were doing. At this particular time, WIXY had already established itself with ratings never accomplished by any Cleveland radio station, so you would have thought all of our DJs were front-runners in the contest. That was not the case. Cleveland had always been very loyal to its celebrities, no matter where you worked, and many of them had established careers much longer than my five years: Bill Randle, Jack Reynolds, Phil McLean, and many more.

Upon completion of the contest, Bill Barrett called program director Bill Sherard at 10 a.m., the start time of my show. Bill Barrett was live and on the air. Bill Sherard knew the outcome of the contest. I did not, although I began to get very excited because I questioned why this conversation would be going on in my studio during my air shift.

In his conversation with Barrett, Sherard asked, "Now that the contest is over, how did our WIXY DJs do?" Barrett let us know that votes were cast for seventy-three DJs and twenty-three radio stations. He then said, "The winner comes from you folks. It's the Duker, Larry Morrow, the winner of *The Cleveland Press* Favorite DJ contest." It was just another huge win for WIXY, which not only owned the ratings but the town itself. I was humbled and flattered at the same time. And of course, the sharp-witted and laser-tongued Mike Reineri went on the air the next day during our 10 a.m. exchange and said, "So, if I understand it correctly, Duker, you stuffed the entry box."

There was a full-page spread on the cover of the Friday edition of *The Cleveland Press*, along with a picture of me receiving a copy of the article. Rather than running a picture of me, *The Press*'s graphic artist drew a caricature instead, which I thought was flattering in a fun way. With caricatures, the artist takes one part of the body, whether it's your head, ears, or belly, and overemphasizes that part. Mine happened to be my nose. (My opinion of my nose has always been that God gave me this nose, and I believe it fits my face just fine.)

My parents in Michigan were excited I won, so I sent the article home.

Upon receiving a copy of the caricature, my mother immediately wanted to kill the artist. She called me and demanded the number of *The Cleveland Press* so she could complain. Obviously, I would not allow that. I liked the caricature so much that I used it as the heading for my personal stationery for quite a long time. To this day the original copy hangs on the wall in my office.

THE SNOWFLAKE THAT CAUSED THE AVALANCHE

John D. Rockefeller once said, "If you want to succeed you should strike out on new paths *rather than travel the worn paths of accepted success.*"

One day in July 1972, minutes before I went on the air at 10 a.m., Norm, Joe Weiss, and Bob Zingale called a staff meeting to announce the sale of the company. Wain, Weiss, and

Zingale, as they were often referred to, had merged their company, Westchester Broadcasting, with Globetrotter Broadcasting seven months earlier. Now Globetrotter was being sold for $14.3 million. That announcement would change my thinking and my future like none before. When I arrived at WIXY that morning I had no idea it was coming. The unexpected jolt forced me to think quickly about my immediate future, and throughout my five-hour show I thought about leaving. I knew things would never be the same without Norm Wain there to maintain the exciting WIXY culture.

I was neither angry nor distraught. I realized nothing is forever. I decided it was time for me to move on, too. After my show, at 3 p.m., I resigned and gave WIXY a thirty-day notice. It had been a long six years at WIXY 1260, and my body and mind were tired of eight-day weeks and twenty-hour days of continuous record hops and personal appearances, as well as weekly travel for my jingle-writing and commercial business.

I could not help but think of how much I loved the owners and staff. I was brought to WIXY by Norm, introduced to important adverting agencies by Joe, and made several presentations to local clients with Bob. The three of them were close friends, and I had come to know their wives and their children well. Our families spent time together at their homes on several occasions throughout the year, as well as at big circus events, rock shows, and significant WIXY promotions. I would miss them all.

I had grown up at WIXY. I had come a long way from "you'll never make it." This incredible radio station had made me a solid "rock jock" broadcaster. I had reached number one in the ratings. I had been voted "king of the disc jockeys" by fans in a local newspaper contest. I had appeared on the cover of a national publication as one of the Top 12 Radio Personalities in America. I had taken that terrific, humbling trip to Vietnam. A lot had happened to a very private guy in an extremely public business. But I knew WIXY couldn't last.

In fact, the station was already changing. I had seen almost sixty DJs go through the doors during my six years at WIXY. Out of the original group of WIXY Supermen, I stayed the longest.

WIXY had owned morning radio. That would change with the arrival of Don Imus ("Imus in the Morning") on 1220 WGAR. WGAR had a much bigger signal (50,000 watts) than WIXY (5,000 watts). Imus was extremely funny, and Cleveland began listening. It would not be long before Don would overtake Mike Reineri. As successful, unique, and funny as Mike was, Imus was a different kind of funny, and Cleveland was ready for a change.

Part Three

More Adventures in Cleveland Radio

CHAPTER 15

Going It Alone

Everything I had accomplished to this point was now in the rearview mirror. I knew my life would be vastly different after leaving WIXY. I would have my mornings and evenings free. The business of making five to eight record hops a week, appearing at radio station promotions, and doing my six-day-a-week radio show took a lot out of me. I had become mentally and physically tired. I had been riding the wave of success in radio for more than a decade while personally experiencing jaw-dropping ratings. WIXY was responsible for literally and figuratively "cranking up the music" for my career to this point.

During this time I was motivated by the loyalty among the advertising agency relationships I formed at WIXY. From those relationships I was running from city to city, selling and recording jingles for my company, Morrow's Music Machine, while performing on television and radio commercials. All of this was beginning to spawn new energy. My creative juices, now flowing nonstop, were fulfilling the part of my life that had been somewhat dormant while working so many long hours at WIXY. I was a young man, just into my thirties, when all of this was happening. I had also been single for three years, and when the frenzy of travel became a major part of my life, I gave up dating. For me, that was some kind of task.

After leaving WIXY, I decided I needed a little break, so I went to visit my brother Jim and his wife Madelyn in Virginia Beach. While there I could also visit some of the advertising agencies. My sister-in-law asked if I would like a date for the evening and suggested we all go out to dinner. I declined at first, but then she told me of their very close friend, Rosary, who was a single mom with three young daughters. My first thought was, why not? If she has three children, I would be safe. (In my mind, "safe" meant that I would never be interested in anyone who already had children.) My brother liked Rosary so much that he made sure I understood what he expected of my behavior for the evening, "Mess with her and I'll kill you." God has a natural order of things, and I was about to fall in order.

My sister-in-law called Rosary, and we spoke briefly on the phone and agreed to an early dinner. It was not love at first sight but close to it. She greeted me as I walked up the steps to her apartment, and I thought she could not have been more lovely. Her three young daughters—fourteen-year-old twins Diana and Donna, and eleven-year-old Cynthia—were also there to greet me. After a few pleasantries, the girls asked me what I did for a living. I spotted a piano and said, "Here, I'll show you what I do." First I sang a few jingles I had written, and then I created one or two for them. To this day my daughters poke fun at me for the way I walked in their apartment and immediately began playing the piano. I thought they were as cute as buttons, and they seemed to be just as excited as I was about the meeting.

The most important part of meeting Rosary was the respect I had for her as a single mom. We went to dinner, danced the night away, and called it an evening at around 10 p.m. Although Rosary and I met on September 23, 1972, five months would pass before I saw her again.

Shortly after returning from my visit to Virginia Beach, I received a package from Rosary, who was returning the suede jacket that I had inadvertently left behind. She enclosed a note that told me to look in the right pocket. The right pocket contained a second note: *If you go somewhere and leave something behind, that means you would like to return.* After reading that note I got such a tingle inside I couldn't believe it. We began to speak often on the phone, almost every evening, and my phone bill climbed to over $300 a month. Mark McCormick's International Management Group (IMG), who managed my professional life and finances, saw the phone bill and said, "Marry this woman. It'll be cheaper than your monthly phone bill." Soon after that conversation, Rosary and I decided I would come and see her again on her birthday in February 1973.

The very moment I laid my eyes on Rosary for the second time, I was in love. We were engaged the following month and married July 22, 1973. Our three daughters and one granddaughter live within five minutes of us, and our honeymoon continues to this day. As an aside, when we married on July 22, it was Cleveland's 177th birthday. So I get to celebrate my anniversary with the woman I love and the family I cherish in Moses Cleaveland's favorite city, both on the same date.

CHAPTER 16

Nick Mileti Brings Me On

Nick Mileti bought the old Cleveland Arena, the historic site of the Alan Freed Moondog Coronation Ball, now recognized as the world's first rock and roll concert on March 21, 1952. As part of the transaction, Nick would also own the American Hockey League (AHL) Cleveland Barons. In a head-spinning five years, Nick would sell the Arena and the Barons, acquire an NBA franchise and crown them the Cleveland Cavaliers, and buy the Cleveland Indians. His next purchase was in 1972: WKYC AM and FM radio, changing the AM call letters from WKYC to 3WE and the FM to FM 105.

As an aside, Nick asked Tom Embrescia, who worked at WIXY in sales, to help him put all these transactions together. Tom initially became vice president of sales for the Arena and then ultimately president and general manager of 3WE. He asked his brother Jim, who had had a stellar career in sales at WIXY and later in television, to become sales manger, and his dear friend, Joe Restifo, to become operations manager. The 3WE management team was in place.

BLIND-SIDED BY A LOVABLE SICILIAN CONSPIRACY

While relaxing and enjoying my new life away from WIXY, I received a few "How are you doing?" phone calls from Tom Embrescia. Tom and I were close friends (I had taken him on his very first sales call at WIXY), and I detected a sense of urgency in his message. The reason for Tom's call was to talk about me coming back to radio. Of course the answer was *no*; I was building my jingle company while promoting my voice at the same time. He then asked me who I thought might be a good candidate to replace legendary morning man Jim Runyon, who had been diagnosed with leukemia. Because of his illness and frequent hospital stays, he was unable to perform his morning show on 3WE. He told Tom to look for his replacement since he didn't think he would be able to return to radio.

In my conversation with Tom and Joe regarding the ideal replacement for Jim Runyon, I recommended searching for a person whom the community knew and loved, similar to the legendary JP McCarthy on WJR in Detroit. Because of his deep connection with Detroiters, JP McCarthy had a reputation as the finest and most talented morning personality in America. JP was one to be admired, and I aspired to be like him.

Wittingly or unwittingly, Tom and Joe hatched a plan. They never intended to pursue anyone else but me. Since I continued to let them know I was not available, I went on to describe their ideal candidate, "Someone with a warm and ingratiating personality, and one who would use the morning show to drive and unite a great community. And by the way, you'll have to pay this person at least $60,000 a year. Then you will have a winner." They responded with, "Great, that's who we'll go looking for." He and Joe thanked me, and we left it at that. Little did I know that I was their top choice. Their perfect plan was one small Sicilian step away from being fulfilled.

A week passed. Rosary was visiting me from Virginia Beach; we were looking for a home for our new family after our wedding in July. It was at this time that I received another call from Tom Embrescia. Once again, he asked if I would come and visit with him and Joe. I said, "The timing is great because you can meet my fiancée, Rosary, whom I will marry in July. You'll love Rosary because, like you, Tom, her family is from the same part of the world, Sicily."

When Tom heard that Rosary was Sicilian, the enormously successful sales side of Tom Embrescia emerged; he knew he had just closed the deal. Their common ancestry meant there would be an immediate, subliminal connection. In other words, there was no doubt that he had secured his new morning man.

When Rosary and I arrived at the station, we sat down to talk to Tom and Joe. The two of them looked at me and proudly proclaimed: "We took your suggestion on the kind of morning man we should hire. And thanks to you, we have found him."

"Wow, that's great," I replied. "Who is he, and do I know him?"

Tom and Joe replied in unison, "Yes, you do. As a matter of fact, we're looking at him."

"Oooh no," I said. "I'm not coming back to radio! I'm going to be married soon. I'll have three new children, and I promised Rosary I would be there with her to raise them." At that moment, the Sicilian Conspiracy sprang into action. Tom excused himself and asked Rosary if she would like a tour of the radio station. First of all, he knew she had never seen one before, and it would be a perfect opportunity for him to launch into his ever-so-persuasive Sicilian sales pitch. Tom intuitively knew that after she had heard his convincing but sensitive thoughts, the future Rosary Morrow would ultimately win Larry over to come back to radio at 3WE. While the tour was going on, I sat with Joe and we chatted about his position at 3WE. We spoke briefly of this new opportunity they had presented me with, but it didn't matter because I held firm and remained uninterested.

TOM CLOSES THE DEAL

When Tom was with Rosary, he brought up the fact that I was traveling quite a bit during the week doing commercials and jingles. Being a new husband and father would keep me away from our home. Tom was speaking to Rosary's heart. He knew she would want me home with her and the children on a full-time basis. If I were to come back to radio, that would be the case.

I was unaware of that conversation until later when Rosary and I were alone. She brought it up, saying this might be a great opportunity for me to get back into radio and at the same time be home with her and the girls every night, rather than in some hotel room, alone, in another city. Talk about crossing barriers. At that moment, I didn't see any reason for alarm, but I was beginning to sow seeds of confusion. It had taken me ten years to build my business locally and nationally. I had become a well-known name at advertising agencies at home in Cleveland, as well as in Detroit, Boston, Chicago, Los Angeles, and New York. If I were to go back on the air, for the most part, I would have to give it all up. Those two thoughts would plague me, if only for a short time.

The next day I put Rosary on the plane back to Virginia Beach. The moment I said goodbye to her, it hit me: She was right. While driving back to my apartment in Shaker Heights, I knew I wanted to be home every night at the dinner table with her and my new daughters. I wanted to be there to help them with their homework and take nightly drives to the ice cream parlor. I saw myself taking them on bike rides in the summer and sled rides in the winter. I wanted to be there for them at school functions and take them shopping. The desire to please Rosary and the driving impulse to compete again at a higher level not only urged me on but cleared up the uncertainty.

With all those thoughts rolling through my mind, I picked up the phone the moment I returned home and called Tom Embrescia to say, "Let's go." According to Tom, just as he had internally predicted, it was Rosary who actually inspired me to come back to radio. It was the brotherhood of the Sicilian Conspiracy that brought me back, though it doesn't matter why, really, because it was a decision I would never regret.

I was turned on by the thought of working at one of the most powerful radio stations in America. There are only twenty-five

50,000-watt clear channel stations in the country, and 1100 3WE was one of them. I was also encouraged by Nick Mileti's comment, "I want 3WE to be the WJR of Cleveland, and you the JP McCarthy of Cleveland." He could not have stirred my heart more. WJR and JP were the talk of radio in America, and I wanted that for Nick, Tom, 3WE, and Cleveland.

Nick had invested $5.5 million to buy 3WE radio, but what was more important to me was that he had invested in my ability to carry the most prestigious time slot at the radio station.

It would begin a long, academic journey. I wanted to be more sophisticated, and I know longed to be on a much bigger stage, not because of popularity but to move our community forward. I no longer wanted the label of "rock jock." My desire was now to share things with my audience that mattered most: spouses, children, close relationships, their God, their jobs, and their community.

I never doubted for a minute that 3WE would be anything but a positive experience for me. After all, it had so many weapons in its arsenal that ranged from well-known personalities to blockbuster sports teams and well-attended venues, such as the Coliseum and Cleveland Stadium, that it would be difficult, if not impossible, to beat.

My first day on 3WE radio was April 1, 1973. Just twelve days later, at approximately 6:45 a.m. on April 13, Tom Embrescia called me on our private studio phone to tell me that Jim Runyon had passed away late Friday evening. I immediately announced to the audience that Jim had lost his fight with leukemia. Jim was very popular nationally and was held in high regard by broadcasters across America. A few days later I would record a tribute to Jim written and produced by the American Cancer Society. At Nick Mileti's request, that tribute was played the following evening before the start of the Cleveland Indians baseball game.

CHAPTER 17

A Hunger to Improve

3WE had the most prestigious and powerful radio signal in this part of the country. It carried with it a long history of successful radio programming. Almost all of the 50,000-watt radio stations across the forty-eight contiguous states were well known for having the most talented and popular morning personalities in America. Each one of these radio personalities, like JP McCarthy in Detroit and Wally Phillips in Chicago, were not only popular, they were the adopted favorite sons of their communities. Neither one of these radio pioneers was born in the city he became successful in, yet each made himself a permanent implant to move the community forward. They talked about the town they loved, the people who lived there, and its sports teams.

Even though I was the next generation of these radio icons, I wanted to be one of them. Like Wally and JP, I too was a transplant and desired the same things for my community and for the people who lived here.

At 3WE, I would be working with the following well-known and highly regarded Cleveland personalities: Hugh Daneceau, Tom Carson, Paul Sciria, Jack Reynolds, Phil McLean, Pete Franklin, and the much-respected and dearly loved Rena Blumberg. Each of these legendary radio stars would serve as admirable examples of what would be expected of my new morning show.

I had to deliver because Nick, Tom, Joe, and Jimmy depended on it. We all wanted to achieve excellence, and our 3WE team would be a step up on the ladder of broadcast eloquence for Cleveland. Nick would call his new radio station *3WE, Home of the Superstars.*

Joe Restifo was my PD and offered insights on every aspect of what he desired for the morning show. He taught me that you never flirt with chance. As a broadcaster you need to know where you are going every minute, every time you pause for commercials, every interview, and every moment you open the microphone. My morning show would be peppered with high-profile national and local newsmakers from all walks of life, ranging from politicians to sports stars to religious leaders to showbiz celebrities.

Over the next ten years, Joe would be my mentor, my confidant, and my close friend. He refined my broadcast technique. I met with him every day after my show. The only time I can ever remember him critiquing me was the day I used the phrase, "Boy, did he get screwed," of course, meaning taken advantage of. That day, during our daily meeting, Joe said to me, "Duker, never use the word *screwed* again; it's unbefitting of you." He was absolutely right. As a result, there was never a collision of ideas; Joe and I were always in sync. In fewer than two years, Joe would craft what would turn out to be Cleveland's number one rated morning show.

A COMPELLING METAMORPHOSIS

Joe was also solely responsible for changing my up-tempo, WIXY style to something a little less energetic, while at the same time not losing any of my personality. He had progressively moved me, day by day, to a more refined and engaging Larry. One day, several months after being on 3WE, Joe and I were listening to an air check of my morning show, which is simply a recording of your show. I could not believe the change. As I looked over my shoulder at the recent past, I found myself uniquely transformed from a high-energy rock jock to a multi-dimensional communicator. So subtle was the change that, in reality, I was the same guy my audience had listened to in Cleveland radio for the past six years. Joe had not only knowingly and carefully sculptured a morning show that would showcase me, but he refined the other personalities on 3WE as well.

When I joined 3WE, I inherited the argument that the morning show was so far behind in the ratings (number 12) that reaching number one was not achievable. 3WE 1100 would truly be the challenge of my life. I was also personally aware that I had only been on the air for ten years, which included working evenings at CKLW and middays at WIXY. My last morning job was WTRX in Flint, Michigan, in 1963, and that was a long way from major-market radio in Cleveland.

There was one lingering memory that I carried with me from my first morning job in Flint: Radio morning hosts are a different breed. They get up at 3 a.m. and hit the sack at 8 p.m. This would be my new version of "normal."

As a morning man, I had a deep need to connect with my audience and a sincere desire to awaken them to the dawn of a new day. It's a delicate balance because many in your audience begin their day with hopes and dreams while others are confronted with fears and failures. If they have children, the entire house is a beehive of activity, with everyone heading in different directions. Above all the chaos and turmoil was me, 3WE's new morning man, bringing an invigorating sense of comfort and positive energy to help my audience start their day.

I understood that when the clock radio went off, my voice was often the very first voice the audience would hear, and immediately there were subliminal concerns on how their day would go:

It's 6 a.m. already?

Oh no, Larry said it's snowing again!

I'm headed for the airport and there's an accident blocking the interchange?

Yeah, the Browns won another game!

I had an unwritten partnership with my audience. It was intimate, informative, and exciting!

FORMIDABLE COMPETITION: DEE AND LANIGAN

I knew my approach to the audience would be vastly different from my two biggest competitors: Gary Dee / WERE, and John Lanigan / WGAR, both of whom were established front-runners in Greater Cleveland's morning drive slot. Gary had a stinging personality and was sharp-tongued. His on-air persona was witty and could be extremely intimidating. Paradoxically, Lanigan was smart and had a funny remark about everything and everyone. In those days, John was known more for his comedic style, which is vastly different to his well-rounded, intellectual approach today.

Although my success at WIXY made me well known, I was still the new kid on the block, and I would still have to prove myself in the morning race against these two giants. Although their styles were diametrically different—Gary was very combative, while John was mildly controversial—both were immensely successful. Suffice it to say, John and Gary had settled in, and Cleveland loved them both. There were doubters about my being able to find a hole in the market and garner ratings that would unseat them. I had a different opinion, as well as a new framework for success.

THE GAME PLAN

As I mentioned earlier, I believed 3WE had a unique advantage in the market because 1100 broadcasted the games of the most prestigious names in local sports: the Cleveland Indians, Cleveland Cavaliers, and the Cleveland Crusaders of the World Hockey Association. The heavyweight announcers for these games were employed at 3WE. This worked very well for me because all the evening games were taped. I would play highlights the next morning with live analysis from Pete Franklin, Joe Tait, Nev Chandler, Herb Score, and Steve Albert. If my listeners missed any part of the previous game or simply wanted to hear the highlights again, I would have it for them.

SINCERE INSPIRATION

I recently read a book titled *What Got You Here Won't Get You There* by Marshall Goldsmith. I would not have been able to articulate that title back in 1973, but that's exactly the way I felt. I knew instinctively that focusing on my earlier success at WIXY would prevent me from achieving success at 3WE. While I wanted to use the celebrity I had gained earlier as a springboard to my new show at 3WE, I had to be extremely careful. Celebrity is a double-edged sword. If you continue to believe it, you'll be living off the perfume from an empty bottle. Everyone wants to get better at his or her craft, and I was no different. I knew there was a direct correlation between *what was* at WIXY to *what is now* at 3WE.

There's an old axiom in psychology that says, in essence, w*hat drives people's motivation can be reduced to four items: money, power, status, and popularity.* That may be true for most, but it did not fit me very well. I wanted to leave a legacy for Nick Mileti and my community, one instilled in me by my parents, one of high moral standards and good, clean fun. So, among the laughter, comedy, and interviews on my morning show would be the thread of caring for my city, my audience, and their families. It was also my desire that all would be inspired by it the quality of my morning show. This would be my philosophy at 3WE.

THE INIMITABLE PETE FRANKLIN

All the 3WE personalities loved to joke around with each other, and Pete Franklin was no exception. His show followed mine, starting at 10 a.m. on Saturdays. One Saturday morning, as I was leaving my show and Pete was starting his, he began ribbing me that I had never invited him to my home. I responded, "Of course I have invited you to my home. As a matter of fact, several times."

When we interacted on the air, Pete's personality was characteristically obnoxious, yet playfully fun and arrogant. His comeback was, "Sure you did. When I arrived at your gated driveway, I had to ask your guard for permission to enter. When the foot gates swung open, my wife Pat and I began driving up the winding road decorated with split-rail fences on each side to what we knew would be a mansion. After ten minutes of driving on your private road, we got bored and exhausted, so we turned around and came home." In other words, Pete lightheartedly made me out to be an extremely wealthy man who lived an opulent lifestyle, which was far removed from reality. And Pete was somewhat of a recluse who enjoyed staying home.

There was another funny incident when Herb Score, Nev Chandler, Joe Tait, and I shamed Pete into inviting us to his apartment for brunch since none of us had ever been there. When we showed up, we all broke into laughter at the sight of the welcome mat, which welcomed us in typical Pete Franklin language: *Bug Off!* The soft, lovable, talented *chef du jour* side of Pete made us a very tasty brunch: pancakes with bacon, scrambled eggs, coffee, and orange juice.

Phil McLean was another personality with whom I traded "manly" quips from time to time when he replaced me weekdays at 10 a.m. Phil had been blessed with uncanny intelligence and a voice so low it would rattle the windows. One day, early on in our relationship, I asked Phil where in the world he got such a low voice. He said, "Unlike you, Larry, I have three testicles." He was obviously responding to the adage that men who have low voices have large testicles. Sorry, ladies, it's a guy thing!

THE MORNING SHOW BECOMES # 1

My morning show was moving at Mach 2 speed because we wanted to fly higher and faster than our competition. My daily routine had me waking up at 2:45 a.m., arriving at the station by 4:30 a.m., and reading four newspapers before I went on the air: *The Plain Dealer*, *New York Times*, *USA Today*, and the *Akron Beacon Journal*. Remember, these were pre-Internet days.

I would then meet with my producer, Jim Stunek. We were on constant overload, always discussing the latest news, sports, and entertainment stories. Once we had a consensus of who and what we wanted on the air, Jim would begin waking people up and preparing them for an interview. If a person of interest was in town, we would pursue him or her. After all, we had leverage, not only because Nick Mileti owned the station, but because he knew everyone from Frank Sinatra to Howard Cosell.

Every major entertainer from Andy Williams to Ray Charles to Paul Anka appeared on my morning show. In politics, it was Vice President Spiro Agnew to Secretary of Defense Caspar Weinberger, and in sports, Muhammad Ali to Frank Robinson. In many cases we made it our business to know the scheduled appearances a day ahead of time, which meant I could plan and record the interview for the next day's show after I got off the air. There was always the far-reaching desire to have my morning show be a reflection of the biggest stars in entertainment, sports, and newsmakers in America.

Every once in awhile, Jim would go into a mild panic when I would tell him something like, "Here's Art Modell's home phone. I know it's early, but wake him up anyway and tell him I'd like to talk with him on the air." Jim would then nervously say, "Oh, man, it's 6:15 a.m. I don't know about that, Lar. I'd feel a whole lot better if you called him." Jim usually got his way.

On top of that, Jim was born a funny man. Throughout the morning show he sat directly in front of me. We only played about four songs an hour, so most of the morning was spent on the phone conducting interviews or talking with listeners. Whenever Jim had one of his humorous comments, he would write it on a note and slide it over to me so I would sound like the funny guy. As soon as I hung up the phone after talking to someone a bit strange, Jim would say, "Lar, they're all out there." To this day, I continue to quote Jim's original, quick-witted one-liners.

THE HEART OF THE MATTER

Arbitron (ARB) is a media and marketing research firm serving radio and television, as well as advertisers and advertising agencies in the United States. It measures local market radio audiences. The ratings are released to radio stations four times a year. The Arbitron rating system is a radio station's lifeblood. There may be a range of possible outcomes associated with ARB ratings, but for the most part, they are critically relevant, and your profession lives and dies by the results.

Radio station managers, sales staff, and DJs get very nervous around the release of the Arbitron ratings because they determine your amount of revenue, or lack of it, over a period of time. Although I was aware that the winter Arbitron ratings were about to come in, I was not told they had already arrived.

HAWAII, HERE WE COME

It was January '75, a chilly Monday morning, when Tom Embrescia called me into his office. He was sitting behind his desk. There were three chairs in the front of his desk, and seated in the two outside chairs were his brother Jim, our sales manager, and my immediate boss, Joe Restifo. It would not have been unusual to be in their presence because, as I mentioned earlier, we were all close friends. So I just thought it was business as usual. I sat down in the middle chair. Tom began the conversation by asking whether Rosary had ever been to Hawaii. I said it was her dream to go there one day, and related a story about Rosary and her sister, Angi, as little girls. A favorite play routine included pinning towels around their waists and pretending they were sarongs. They would then put a Hawaiian song on the turntable and dance around their living room like wahinis (Hawaiian women).

Tom held up two United Airlines tickets. With a giant smile on his face, he asked, "Do you know what these are?"

"Of course," I replied. "They're airline tickets."

"These tickets are first-class tickets to Hawaii, and they are for you and Rosary." Tom then went on to give me the explosive news and the true meaning of the airline tickets. "Congratulations, Duker! The October–November '74 ARB ratings are in, and your morning show is the highest-rated morning show in Cleveland. And you, Larry Morrow, are now Cleveland's number one Morning Man."

After the shock wore off, I choked back the joyful tears, smiled from ear to ear, and thanked him profusely. We all hugged because we knew what this meant to our 3WE family. We had taken a giant leap into Nick Mileti's dream of making his radio station one of the most distinctive, respected, and successful in America.

While walking out of Tom's office, I said to myself, "Larry, you did it. You have finally arrived." All those years of wanting the same relationship with my community that JP McCarthy had with Detroit and Wally Phillips had in Chicago was now a reality. I never struggled with feelings of worthlessness, but I did not feel worthy of being mentioned in the same context as JP and Wally. But that had all changed now.

When we finally reached our goal to become the number one morning show in Cleveland, we had successfully transformed and awakened a sleeping, 50,000-watt giant. We were on our way. Becoming number one resulted from eighteen months of hard work on everyone's behalf, from sales to programming. When we began, sales manager Jim Embrescia had to constantly keep his staff motivated. He was dealing with the significant pressure of generating revenue for a radio station that wasn't even ranked among the top ten. Joe Restifo managed to hold his on-air team members together while he analyzed and measured the growth of every 3WE on-air talent. But most important was the evidence of 3WE's leader at the top, Tom Embrescia. Tom continued to emphasize the shared needs of his entire staff. He encouraged everyone at the station and equipped them to reach their full potential, especially me. 3WE had now silenced the over-arching fodder of the skeptics.

After all the excitement, I excused myself and headed for the phone to call Rosary. As I gave her the great news, you could hear Rosary's uncontainable loud scream of excitement. Yes, she was thrilled to be going to a place we both considered paradise, but more important, she was so happy for me. "Honey, you've worked so hard for this. Congratulations and enjoy every minute of your celebration with your team at the radio station. We'll celebrate when you come home." Up to this point, my only other trip to Hawaii had been during my layover on my way to Vietnam for WIXY's "Bring the Boys Home for Thanksgiving" promotion, so this trip was going to be very special for both Rosary and me.

THE CLEVELAND CAVALIERS' FIGHT SONG:
"C'MON CAVS! GOTTA MAKE IT HAPPEN"

Cavaliers owner Nick Mileti came to me in the early fall of 1975 and asked me to write and produce a fight song for the Cavs. He wanted the song to be as memorable and as good as the Harlem Globetrotters' signature song, "Sweet Georgia Brown." No pressure there! I could hardly wait to get home to sit at my piano and begin working on the song.

The moment I sat down, the melody, "C'mon Cavs! Gotta Make It Happen," flowed onto my lead sheet. I also wrote a handful of lyrics. Although I had written the national, award-winning jingle for Smucker's, I had never fancied myself a lyricist, so I asked for assistance from our production director, Dick Fraser, who had a way with words, loved sports, and was a huge fan of the Cavaliers. Dick and I sat down, and for the most part, Dick completed the lyrics.

In addition to being my morning show producer, Jim Stunek was the music director at 3WE. Jim was multitalented and, in this case, a gifted musician and arranger. Jim knew of Nick's request and said to me, "Lar, I would like to arrange the song." For nonmusic people, an arranger is one who writes all the musical charts for the singers and each instrument.

I was very close to Jim and did not want to disappoint him, but in this case, this would be the biggest and most important challenge of my musical career. In my mind there would be no one other than a New York or Los Angeles arranger/producer for this job. After all, this was the NBA. The song would be heard everywhere, including national radio and television. In my opinion, it had to be the equivalent of a Top 10 chartbuster. Anything else was not an option.

Jim had never done anything of this magnitude. However, he and I had worked together since WIXY, and everything that we had done up to this point had been successful, including writing and producing the number one radio commercial in America for American Commodore Tuxedo.

I went to Jim and said very seriously, "Are you *sure* you can write these charts for the quality of the musicians and singers we will be using in New York? Our futures are on the line. You know what I'm up against."

"I can do it," responded Jim. "Just give me the chance." Once Dick Fraser and I finished writing the lyrics, I gave Jim the completed song. He immediately started on the charts, working day and night on them, for twenty-three instruments in all. Jim traveled to New York a few days ahead of me to finalize the arrangements for the recording session.

When I arrived at National Recording Studios in the Big Apple, Jim was very nervous and a bit intimidated as he indicated to me that the musicians for the Cavaliers' session were the best in America. It was Jim's first exposure to this caliber of talent. He explained that the head musician had just produced the latest John Lennon album, and the guitarist had played on recording sessions with Paul McCartney. Many of the other musicians had played with some of the biggest and most popular bands in America. Jim was so nervous that his stomach got the better of him, and he continued to run back and forth to the restroom. My final words to Jim were, "Jim, you told me you could *do it,* so get in there with the best musicians in the world and *do it.*"

When the session was completed, Jim was masterful and received a standing ovation from all of the New York musicians. We recorded the Cavaliers' fight song in New York City on October 17, 1975. The outcome could not have been better. Yes, the writing of the song was good, but Jim's arrangement made the Cavaliers' fight song great. He had taken it to another level.

When we arrived back in Cleveland, I played the finished product for Nick Mileti and Tom Embrescia. Both were visibly pleased. Nick told me he was going to play it on the following week for the board of directors at their annual meeting scheduled at the Coliseum. After the meeting, Steve Zayac, Nick's close friend and president of the Cavaliers, called and told me that when Nick played the song, you could hear a pin drop, meaning that no one on the board liked it. It didn't matter, though, because Nick loved it, and his vote was the only one that counted.

When the new fight song was released at the Coliseum, the fans and the players went wild. Now, thirty years later, it remains the signature fight song for the Cavaliers. When the Cavs appeared in the 2006-7 finals, I received calls from the radio and television networks that would be broadcasting the playoff games, requesting use of "C'mon Cavs, Gotta Make It Happen."

After I graduated from high school I thought I was going to join the Navy like my father, but I opted for the Marines instead. On my way to boot camp I scored my first celebrity interview when I met Elvis Presley in an airport bar.

I donned a different uniform for this publicity photo at radio station WTRX in Flint, Michigan. The DJs were called "the Jones Boys," and I was known as John Paul Jones, the Captain of the Ship. It was my second job in radio. I started at $100 a week for my morning drive-time shift.

Photos from the author's collection unless otherwise indicated.

Duke
Windsor

When I started at CKLW in 1965 my all-night show didn't have any sponsors. Soon my entrepreneurial spirit took over and I worked hard to find a series of new advertisers.

At CKLW I met Rock and Roll greats such as Keith Richards (center) and Brian Jones (right) from the Rolling Stones, and introduced The Who and James Taylor at local concerts. I'm on the left; the other CKLW jocks, from left to right, are Joe Van, Dave Shaffer, Tom Shannon.

WIXY on-air personalities, from left to right: Larry "The Duker" Morrow, Dick "Wilde Childe" Kemp, Mike Reineri, Jerry Brooke, and Lou "King" Kirby.

DJ OF THE MONTH

Larry's dedication to his audience extends to risking his very life. Like the time he went to Viet Nam with a tape recorder to record Thanksgiving messages from Cleveland servicemen to their many loved ones awaiting word back home.

Larry Morrow
WIXY Radio Cleveland, Ohio

■ Though he's only been with WIXY for five years, Larry Morrow has so established himself that it seems that there never was a time without Larry Morrow.

Handsome, bearded, and always on the go, Larry, in addition to hosting his own show weekdays from 10 AM to 2 PM, is in great demand as a master of ceremonies, has written a number of songs, has his own music publishing company, is the voice of many commercials, and writes and records his own jingles.

If all that isn't enough, his role as moderator of **Project 1260** has allowed him to interview such celebrities as Mayor Stokes, Dionne Warwick, and Johnny Mathis.

Despite all these accomplishments, the 32 year old bachelor is proudest of his **What's Cooking** innovation on his regular show. Every item is taste tested in Larry's own, self-decorated apartment, and the listener response has been outstanding.

And Larry Morrow, once known as Duke Windsor on Ontario's CKLW, is most interested in girls and the planets; but his real goal in life is "to live in a castle." ●

When I started at WIXY 1260 in July 1966 I had to use my real name because CKLW owned the name Duke Windsor. My new boss, Norm Wain, heard me on the air and asked, "Who in the hell is Larry Morrow?" A few years later the station was number one and our listeners not only knew my name, they voted me their favorite DJ in a *Cleveland Press* competition. I was also proud to be selected as DJ of the month in *Radio TV News* magazine.

To help bring our DJs and fans together, and to raise money for charity, I formed the WIXY All Stars. We sometimes had some help from members of Cleveland pro sports teams. After each game, we all stayed and signed autographs until the last person went home. From left to right: Bill Clark, Chuck Knapp, Lou Kirby, Mike Reineri.

The WIXY Supermen didn't just play high school teams, we paired up against some of Cleveland's favorite TV personalities, such as Dick Goddard, "Big Chuck" Schodowski and Bob "Hoolihan" Wells from WJW TV-8.

WIXY
BRINGS THE BOYS HOME

WIXY 1260
BRINGS THE BOYS HOME FROM VIET NAM FOR THANKSGIVING

That's WIXY's Larry Morrow (right above) interviewing Sergeant Don Sommers of Parma, currently on duty in Vietnam. Larry recently spent two weeks interviewing Cleveland-area troops in the combat zone. You'll hear their personal Thanksgiving greetings to friends and relatives beginning tomorrow and throughout the Thanksgiving weekend. Another Thanksgiving service to you from Cleveland's Number One Radio Station . . .

WIXY 1260

In the fall of 1969 I traveled to Vietnam, where I interviewed dozens of troops from Cleveland and brought recordings of their voices home in time to broadcast on WIXY at Thanksgiving. This was one of the most rewarding things I've ever done.

Over the years I've had the chance to interview many of Cleveland's most influential leaders, including Mayor Carl Stokes.

There are some guests who appeared on my morning show that I had a special connection with. Paul Anka was someone I really enjoyed interviewing and bringing to the listeners. *(Photo by Janet Macoska)*

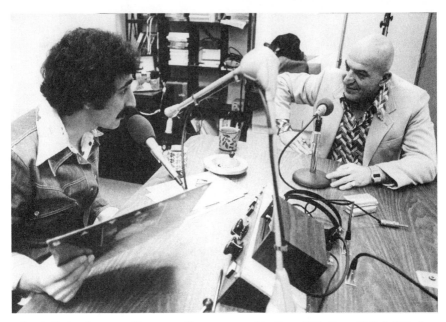

When Telly Savalas stopped by our studios to promote his album "Who Loves Ya Baby," I had our staff waiting for him in the lobby with suckers in their mouths. Small surprises like that helped break the ice with my guests.

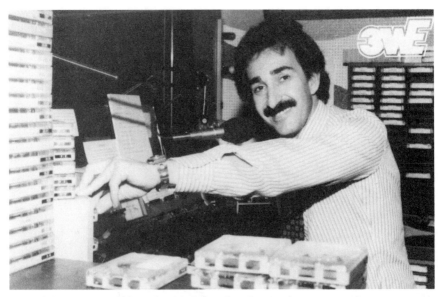

After I left WIXY I decided to take a break from broadcasting, but soon enough a new opportunity at 3WE presented itself and I was back on the air at the 50,000 watt station.

LISTEN TO MORROW

TOMORROW

Tomorrow morning
from 6-9 a.m.,
you have a chance to take part
in Cleveland radio history
on WQAL Easy 104.
Larry Morrow,
the voice of tasteful
Cleveland radio for almost
twenty years is moving to WQAL
FM 104 on your dial. Every
weekday from 6 a.m. to 9 a.m.
he'll play *the music that makes
you feel good* so your mornings
can start out right. Tune in to
Morrow — it's only a day away.

WQAL
EASY 104

A Win Communications statio

I moved to WQAL in 1985 to work with my friends Walt Tiburski and Tony Ocepek. Together we built the station into a Cleveland media powerhouse, until they made a big announcement just four years later that changed it all.

President Jimmy Carter was the first U.S. president I had the opportunity to interview as well as introduce at a special appearance at the Front Row Theater.

As mayor, George Voinovich asked me to help him turn the attitude of our city around. I spoke to business leaders, civic leaders and politicians and brought them on the air to share positive stories about Cleveland and bring a sense of pride back to our citizens. During an interview several years later Mayor Voinovich gave me the name "Mr. Cleveland."

I've always been happy to promote my stations, but this TV ad that "co-starred Madonna" is one that I will never live down.

Meeting golf legend Arnold Palmer was a dream come true. I not only interviewed him, but he gave me a golf lesson, which unfortunately never made it on the air.

To show my love of our city on its 188th anniversary I dressed as its founder, Moses Cleaveland, to reenact his first appearance on our shores at Settler's Landing. I got off to a bumpy start when the rowboat I was planning to use blew off the roof of my car on I-480 while I was driving downtown. Luckily, the Cleveland Fire Department let me borrow theirs. To my surprise, about 300 people showed up to watch.

The Fourth of July free concerts on public square were a very powerful occasions, particularly on stage with the Cleveland Orchestra and conductor Jahja Ling.

Cleveland Indians mascot Slider and I hang out after taking the stage at the Cleveland Bicentennial celebration. We shared a dressing room. (Co-host Debra Winger had her own.)

The first time I met Neil Diamond was at a WIXY Appreciation Day concert we hosted for our listeners. We expected 25,000 people, but were shocked when 100,000 showed up to hear Neil sing "Solitary Man" at Chippewa Lake. I picked up Neil and his band at the airport in my stylish Chevy station wagon. We became friends after that. This photo is from a later show.

To celebrate the 100th episode of his show, Drew Carey invited several members of Cleveland media to make cameos. Here I am on the set with *Plain Dealer* writer Jane Scott and Drew.

Cleveland attorney Avery Friedman (left) introduced me to radio legend Casey Kasem (center) before the opening of the Rock and Roll Hall of Fame on September 1, 1995. During a one-hour radio interview Casey and I became good friends. (It probably helped that we're both from Detroit and both of Middle Eastern ancestry.) He and Avery were instrumental in getting me nominated to the National Radio Hall of Fame.

Another radio legend and hero of mine, Paul Harvey, who I had the opportunity to sit with at the 1995 Radio Hall of Fame inductions.

I've been master of ceremonies for many special events, including the official opening of the new Browns stadium. Here, I'm flanked by U.S. senator George Voinovich and Cleveland mayor Mike White. Next to the mayor is Bernie Kosar.

When I married my wife Rosary I didn't just have a new spouse, I was blessed with three daughters. From left to right: Donna, Larry, Rosary, Diana, Synthia.

Part Four

"Mr. Cleveland"

CHAPTER 18

Turning Cleveland Right Side Up

I wanted Clevelanders to believe that the city they lived in was on its way up. I also wanted them to believe in the 3WE team whose heart, soul, and investments were working diligently to turn our town into one of the most respected cities in America.

I wanted my morning audience to feel a closeness with everything they heard on my show— from information to entertainment. When they came to the radio in the morning I wanted them to have a positive experience. No one endeavors to embark on a journey such as this alone. So I needed Greater Cleveland to join hands with me so that we could reach our destination together. The political turmoil and the riots of the '60s had devastated our beloved city politically and mentally. So we not only needed to rebuild the city, but we desperately needed to build new attitudes about how we would do it. In addition to being on Cleveland's turnaround team, I was building my own team as well. My head and my heart said it would pay big dividends for our community and my radio station.

After six years in Cleveland radio and a gazillion appearances, I had become deeply fond of the city I now called home and the people who lived here. I couldn't help but peek in the rearview mirror and reflect on just how bad it was when I arrived on July 18, 1966. Cleveland burned for five straight days during the infamous Hough riots. Also, during this time there appeared a terrible sign that rested near the mouth of the Cuyahoga River that read, "Help Me, I'm Dying." Cleveland just couldn't get out of the way of itself, and America was laughing. At the center of all of the unrest was the deep racial issue of white versus black. It was sad listening to all the news programs and the reports of the negativity coming out of City Hall. There was constant infighting between politicians, few of whom had answers to the pressing question of how to fix a dying city. Instead, they were personally motivated to suit their own desires, and confrontational politics had become fashionable behavior. The national press was having a field day making fun of Cleveland, and I personally felt a deep hurt for our city. I didn't see the humor in bashing. Worst of all, the overwhelming amount of negative publicity made Clevelanders introverted. I wanted to do something about it.

It was this dirty laundry that inspired me to take action from my lofty position on the largest and most powerful radio station in this part of America. First of all, I wanted to make a visible statement, so I hung a sign on the door to my office that read *Cleveland, Ohio, is the greatest city in America to live, work, play, and raise a family.* This became my mantra, and I was dedicated to making sure every single person, both on and off the air, felt that commitment.

I began seeking out and accepting speaking engagements where I spoke about our community—the *only* subject I would speak on. I had just completed a whole year of schooling as a member of the prestigious 1979–1980 Leadership Cleveland class. To enter the program, a group of community leaders are individually nominated by past graduates. Fifty are then approved by the steering committee and entered into the program. I was proud to have been chosen and approved. Their mission statement says it all: "Leadership Cleveland is a program designed to develop informed, committed, and qualified community individuals, capable of providing dynamic and progressive leadership for Cleveland."

My Leadership Cleveland experience further fueled my commitment to tell the best side of Cleveland's story and have my audience drink from a cup that was half full. Because of the negative press, many Clevelanders believed they lived in a community that was upside down. That was false. I was driven by a secondary need to convince everyone that Cleveland was right side up.

CLEVELAND'S LONG, SLOW CLIMB TO RECOVERY

In 1979, George Voinovich was elected mayor. On a personal and professional basis, I liked George very much. He was committed to turning Cleveland around, restoring its bond rating in New York, and forming public and private partnerships with the city's companies and constituents. His goal was to make Clevelanders feel worthy again. Under his leadership, the city started to respond.

I joined George's team as unofficial spokesperson for Cleveland. My job was twofold: first, to empower a group of introverted and disenfranchised group of people to get involved; and second, to make sure no one, locally or nationally, made fun of Cleveland. As a result of George's initiatives, Cleveland became known nationally as the "The Comeback City."

One specific incident got a tremendous amount of local publicity. Actor John Davidson was to appear at the Front Row Theater, and I was asked to introduce him. I had just seen him on *The Tonight Show;* during his interview, Johnny Carson asked him where he was performing next. John responded that he would be appearing at the Front Row Theater in Cleveland. Johnny then took a negative shot at Cleveland and said, "Isn't Cleveland the end of the world?"

John replied, "No, but you can see the end of the world from Cleveland." How ironic. John was to appear on my morning show the next day to promote his upcoming appearance.

The next morning my producer, Jim Stunek, said, "Lar, I've got John Davidson on the line." I welcomed him, and we spoke for a few minutes about him coming here the following week. I told him that I had watched him on *The Tonight Show* last evening. His response was, "Oh, no!" I forcibly but kindly brought up both his and Johnny's comments about Cleveland. He profusely expressed regret and said he got caught up in the moment. He surely did not intend to demean Cleveland or its people. John went on to say he was very sorry and apologized to the entire city. That next week, when John arrived at the Front Row, he apologized again to the sold-out theater. Message sent, message received.

CHRISTMAS IS FOR CHILDREN

As my 3WE morning show evolved, our Cleveland audience continued to respond to several requests. When Jim Runyon was the morning man on 3WE, he created a very compelling holiday program called *Christmas Is For Children*. When I arrived to replace Jim, Tom Embrescia and Joe Restifo wanted to continue the program and make it even more gripping. The plan was to contact as many foster home agencies in town as possible, including the Metzenbaum Center for Children and the Jones Home. Over four thousand foster children between the ages of six and twelve lived in those homes.

Part of my responsibility was to work with our promotions department and arrange to have all of our radio personalities interview these children over a three-month period, beginning in September. During the interviews, we would ask the children what one special gift they would like to have under the tree for Christmas. When they responded, we would then say, "Okay, Karen, grab my hand. Let's ask Santa to bring you this very special gift and prove once again that *Christmas Is For Children*." Beginning the day after Thanksgiving, 3WE would begin airing these heart-wrenching interviews; when the short conversation was over, we would ask our audience to buy the gift. The phones would ring off the hook. No child went without the gift he or she had requested.

You would think that trying to match up four thousand gifts would be a nightmare. The opposite was true. Everyone who purchased the on-air gift brought it to the radio station in time. The gifts were then transported to the foster homes for the holidays. It didn't matter whether the gift was the newest, high-tech wheelchair or a Cabbage Patch doll. If the child wanted it, he or she received it from our 3WE audience. That particular promotion lasted throughout my ten years at 3WE.

CLEVELAND AND THUNDER THORNTON COME THROUGH

One day, while visiting the Jones Home, I asked the director what they do for these children during the summer. He indicated that it was difficult. You could never do enough. I was disturbed by the thought of them not having enough activities for the summer. After all, these were children without a permanent home. I told him I would try to come up with an idea to do something special for them. As I mentioned earlier, in addition to owning 3WE, Nick Mileti also owned the Cleveland Indians. I went to my boss, Joe Restifo, and asked if he thought it would be a good idea to take four thousand kids to an Indians game. Joe responded with, "Duker, it would be a better idea if you asked your morning audience to pay for it rather than go to Nick and ask him to give them the free tickets." I thought, *What a great idea.* 3WE 1100 was a powerful radio signal in town, and from sunset to sunrise, no radio station east of the Mississippi was on our frequency. That meant that when I came on the air at 5:30 a.m. until around 6:30 a.m., when the sun came up, I had an audience that consisted of thirty-eight states and half of Canada.

I wondered how long it would take to raise enough money from our 3WE audience to buy four thousand tickets. The Indians gave me a discount at roughly fifteen dollars a ticket for bleacher seats. The next morning I presented the idea to my morning audience. Within a ten-day period, Greater Cleveland and the surrounding states gave me over $40,000 for the kids. Cleveland Indians superstar Andre "Thunder" Thornton heard my request and arranged a behind-the-fence party where he met with the kids and signed autographs. Second baseman Duane Kuiper, the captain of the Tribe and a friend of mine, also showed up. Every kid received an autograph, a Cleveland Indians pennant, a baseball, and as many hot dogs, sodas, and bags of popcorn as they could eat. There was enough money left over to buy brand new pool tables for some of the homes. An incredible event that, to this day, warms my heart.

SUPERSTARS ARRIVE ONE BY ONE

One of the benefits of doing a morning show in a major city is that many national television, movie, and record industry stars as well as famous authors want to be on your show. So, one by one they came calling, and I was thrilled to have them on the air. All were popular, but some were very distinguished. I had the pleasure of sitting with numerous American icons, from Telly Savalas to Christy Hefner to Muhammad Ali.

Pete Gidion, the district promotion manager of the north-central division of Decca, Coral, and Brunswick Records, called me to ask, "How would you like to have Telly Savalas on your 3WE morning show?" After I picked myself up off the floor, of course the answer was a prompt *yes*. At that time, Telly was the star of the number-one police show on television, *Kojak*.

Pete indicated that Telly was only going to do one radio and one television interview in Cleveland, and I had him for radio. Pete was also promoting Telly's newly released album on Decca records, *Who Loves Ya, Baby*, which was his most popular phrase from *Kojak*.

Pete warned me that I had better do my homework because Telly was very smart and had at one time worked for the government. "Telly can be impatient," Pete said, "and when Telly feels the interviewer is not interesting, he'll bail out."

"Don't worry," I said. "I'll brush up on everything about him."

When Telly's limousine arrived at our studios at Park Centre, the entire 3WE staff looked out our second-story window at this bald actor who played a tough New York City cop with a fiery, righteous attitude. From his television and movie persona, I believed Telly to be well over six feet tall. When looking at him from up above he looked just like the giant I thought he was.

Telly's character also sucked on a lollipop to help him quit smoking. This prop had become as popular as the phrase "Who loves ya, baby?" I thought it would be very cool if Telly walked into our lobby and was greeted by over thirty members of our staff, each one sucking on a lollipop. I was quite nervous about meeting and interviewing him. I wanted it to go well for several reasons, not the least of which was that my close friend, Pete Gidion, would not be disappointed with the radio exclusive. I also didn't want Telly to get bored and walk out on the interview.

Within a few minutes, the front doors of our lobby opened and there he was, Detective Theo Kojak, looking like he had just stepped out of our television screens. When he saw all thirty of us standing there sucking on lollipops, he broke into laughter and thanked me several times for the unusual and thoughtful welcome. I was also struck by his appearance. Telly was my size. I'm just a little under five-feet-ten.

Before we sat down for our interview, I mentioned to Telly that we had a mutual friend in Paul Anka, and that the three of us had a deep connection. Our mothers had all come from the same geographical area of the world, just a few miles of each other, in the Middle East. He then gave me a hug and said, "Larry, this is going to be a great interview."

As we were discussing Telly's movie career, he would mention a movie and I immediately knew his character. The first movie we talked about was *The Greatest Story Ever Told*, a Warner Brothers epic that had received five Academy Award nominations. I quickly mentioned his Pontius Pilate character. He talked about *Birdman of Alcatraz*. I said, "I loved your portrayal of Feto Gomez." I could see the smile on his face because he knew how much I had seriously prepared for our time together.

We concluded the interview with me asking him when he went bald. He said he actually could grow hair, but he had shaved his head for the character of Pontius Pilate and decided to remain bald for his signature look. He later indicated to me that this was one of his best interviews because it felt to him more like a couple of friends getting together.

What electrified me most about being on the air was forming personal relationships with celebrities such as Neil Diamond, Bob Seger, and Paul Anka. The outpouring of warmth that was communicated from these interviews was rooted in our special relationship. Through our on-air conversations, I was able to convey those feelings to my listeners, who then connected with the personalities and felt they knew them as well as I did. For as far back as I can remember, even as a young boy, I always had a keen interest in people. Getting to know them, hearing their life stories, and discovering what mattered most to them came very natural to me.

Unfortunately, what came with this kind of fame was the loss of my personal and private lives. You try to deal with all the familiar platitudes. I fought all the trappings of success. However, limousines picked me up. I could go to the front of the line, and many times someone offered to pick up my tab at restaurants. I was a private guy in a public business who didn't enjoy the fuss people made over me. While I loved being around listeners and taking time for conversation and autographs, which to me was real, being around and introducing international and national superstars at Musicarnival, Public Hall, and thirteen Cleveland Indians home openers was business.

I knew I led a privileged life as an insider, but I wanted most of all to be the guy people saw on stage and on television, listened to on the radio, but still felt they could invite over to their house for pizza and a beer. I received many invitations and enjoyed every experience.

THE BLIZZARD OF 1978

Iconic meteorologist Dick Goddard had been issuing warnings about a winter storm that would have serious consequences for the Northeast Ohio region. It would arrive during the week of January 23, 1978. Dick also warned that this storm had the potential to be one of the worst we had seen in some time.

I live in Geauga County, just east of Chagrin Falls, which is east of Cleveland. Because of its elevation and location in relation to the lake, Chardon, Ohio, receives the brunt of the snowstorms and wind, with Chagrin Falls next in line. It's called the eastern snow belt.

Dick was right. The storm struck just before dawn on Thursday, January 26. I had been following television weather reports carefully on Wednesday evening as the snow began to fall quite heavily. Neither the U.S. Route 422 exchange nor I-480 existed at that time, so the only way for me to get to the radio station in downtown Cleveland was to travel through Chagrin Falls, through Shaker Heights, then to Cleveland, which was my normal forty-five-minute ride to work.

Thursday morning, the storm was in full swing. I don't believe I had ever seen a combination of snow that deep and wind that fierce. I spoke by phone with Joe Restifo on Wednesday evening and assured him that I would be on the air by 5:30 a.m.

Just before going to bed right after dinner at 6 p.m., I called my snowplow guy and told him I wanted to leave my house no later than 2 a.m. because of the severity of the storm. He guaranteed that my driveway would be cleared by 1:45 a.m.

I woke at 1 a.m., looked outside, and couldn't believe my eyes. The snow on my front porch was at least three feet deep. I bundled up and headed for work. This was also before cell phones, so there would be no one to call if I got stranded. The snow on my driveway was cleared just enough for me to get out. But the constant battering of snow and wind had covered our street to the extent that boundaries were not visible.

There were snowplows everywhere, but the roads were so heavily snow-covered that you couldn't move any faster than ten miles an hour. I also knew that trying to get out of Chagrin Falls would be trouble because of steep hills, which were now closed. It took me two hours, taking side roads out of Chagrin Falls, just to get to Shaker Heights. Once I was in Shaker, I knew I would make it to the station.

After the longest and scariest three-and-a-half hour drive that I could ever remember, I arrived in our parking garage at 5:15 a.m. and hit the air at 5:30 a.m. I knew it was going to be a long day. What I didn't know was that when all was said and done, Ol' Man Winter had sent us the worst winter storm in Ohio history. It became known as the Blizzard of '78. The storm continued to batter Northeast Ohio all day Thursday and Friday. I received calls all morning long from police, passing on their emergency requests to my audience to please stay in their homes, because it was too dangerous to drive in that terrible weather.

I also took calls from transportation companies, businesses, industries, and schools that were closed for the day. Dick Goddard announced that the atmospheric pressure had fallen to 28.28 inches in Cleveland, the lowest ever recorded in Ohio. Winds were being clocked at 50 to 70 mph.

I stayed on the phone all morning, taking calls from listeners and those in authority stating that enormous snow drifts had covered cars and houses, blocked all of our expressways and railways, and closed our two airports. I received a call that the Ohio National Guard was going out to assist with heavy equipment to clear roads, assist electric utility crews, rescue stranded persons, and transport doctors and nurses to local hospitals. At the request of the police in several cities, I put out a call to those who owned snowmobiles and four-wheel-drive vehicles to help deliver medicine and assist in transporting doctors to hospitals.

My phone never stopped ringing. When my shift was over at 10 a.m., my replacement, Phil McLean, couldn't get in to work, so I took a thirty-minute break while Joe Dannery continued with news and information updates. I went back on the air at 10:30 a.m. and worked until 3 p.m. I took another short break and returned for the afternoon show from 4–6 p.m. Pete Franklin, who hosted his Sports Line show from 7–midnight, also couldn't get in, so I remained on the air until 8 p.m.

Joe Dannery and I, along with a skeleton crew of engineers and management, were the only ones who could make it in that day. I spent over sixteen hours giving informational updates on that unforgettable day.

Now that all the roads and expressways were shut down, Joe and I stayed at the Cleveland Statler Hotel, just down the street from the radio station. The hotel was packed, but Joe and I were able to share a room and return to the station the next morning at 5 a.m.

The Blizzard of '78 lasted through Friday, and the death toll of fifty-one made this one of the deadliest winter storms in Ohio history. The following week, when life returned to normal for our city and state, our general manager Tom Embrescia made available to our audience coffee cups that had our 3WE call letters on them and an inscription that read, "I survived the Blizzard of '78." I don't recall how many hundreds of cups we gave out, but it was significant. To this day, Clevelanders will stop me somewhere and say, "Thank you for getting me home safe and sound during the Blizzard of '78. And by the way, I still have my 3WE coffee cup."

RONALD MCDONALD HOUSE

In the spring of 1978, I was having lunch with Dudley "Bun" Blossom, then part owner of the Cleveland Indians. After our lunch, we were walking down East 9th Street when Bun bumped into his good friend Mike Clegg, and we were introduced. The friendly chatter among the three of us had been going on for a while when Mike spoke of his association with the Ronald Mc- Donald House, a cause he was deeply and personally involved with. At this point in my life I had never heard of a Ronald Mc- Donald House, and I was certain Cleveland hadn't either. Be- cause Mike's passion for the cause was so infectious, I asked him if he and his wife Sue would join me on my 3WE morning show to share their story.

The Cleggs's story began when Mike and Sue's third child, Scotty, was born with Down Syndrome. Two years after his birth, the Cleggs were given the heartbreaking news that Scotty had leukemia. They selected Dr. Sam Gross as the best person to handle their son's cancer treatment. At the time, Sam was chief of pediatric oncology at Cleveland's Rainbow Babies and Children's Hospital. He had recently formed a group for the parents of children diagnosed with cancer and invited Mike and Sue to join.

While at the meeting, Mike and Sue listened intently as Dr. Gross spoke of a special house in Philadelphia called Ronald McDonald House, where the parents of sick children could stay for little or no cost. This embracing house was designed to be a home away from home for parents in the midst of the combined emotional trauma of having to deal with their child's long-term medical treatment and being miles and miles away from the comfort of their own home and familiar surroundings. In addition, the Philadelphia house provided a haven for fami- lies who couldn't afford hotel rooms—those who were all too fa- miliar with the experience of having to camp out on hard, cold, hospital benches or wait for hours on end in cramped waiting rooms. Ray Kroc, founder of McDonald's, funded the house in Philadelphia and gave them $20,000 for the naming rights. He agreed to do the same for Cleveland.

After their meeting with Sam Gross, Mike and Sue Clegg,

along with the rest of the group, decided they wanted to move the idea forward. Mike became the group's leader, and the plan was either to build a new house or to find a building that they could renovate for the Ronald McDonald House of Cleveland.

The group's next step was to form a nonprofit organization called Children's Oncology Services for Northeast Ohio (COSNO). It wasn't long before COSNO found the perfect location for the new house: the old College Motel, a building close to all of the hospitals in downtown Cleveland, located on the corner of Cornell and Euclid Avenue in University Circle. Once the purchase of the building was secured, COSNO hired an architect to handle the renovation issues. Like many old buildings, the former hotel was a mess. To make it ready for the grand opening, tentatively slated for September 1979, the inside of the structure had to be completely gutted and rebuilt and a new façade applied.

Quickly, I grew close with Mike and Sue and the cause they were so passionate about. I offered to lend a helping hand by volunteering to become their voice to let Greater Cleveland know how important a Ronald McDonald House would be not only to our city but to the communities located in our seven-county area as well. Mike liked the idea so much that he agreed for me to take charge of public awareness. The campaign was officially launched on a Saturday morning during my 3WE weekend show, when I asked Clevelanders to help me with some of the needs for our house.

One of my initial goals was to secure lamps for the twenty-eight rooms, so while on the air, I put out a request to my listeners: "If anyone listening has new or almost new lamps to donate for our rooms, please call me. If you do, I'll come and pick them up." My close friends Barry and Susie Levett, owners of the House of Lights on Mayfield Road, heard my plea. Barry called me and said, "Following your show today, come over to my house and let's talk about what you need." When I arrived at his house, I described for him the lighting needs that ranged from the guest rooms to the common areas. Within minutes he was on the phone with one of his vendors.

Now, you can imagine how excited I was when I heard his conversation. "Hi, Charlie, this is Barry Levett. Would you please deliver twenty-eight brand new lamps to the Ronald McDonald House on Euclid Avenue and Cornell in Cleveland, Ohio? Make sure the bill comes directly to me." When he got off the phone, he had a huge smile on his face as he said, "I'm also going to send my guys down there on Monday morning to put up giant lights in your parking lot so all the families who stay at the house will feel safe."

Over a period of two weeks, each time I asked my audience for important materials for the house, they responded quickly. Landscape companies offered to cut our lawn for free. Mass merchandisers called me and said, "We're sending over barbecue grills for the house. How many would you like?" Painting companies responded with, "Tell me what you need and we'll get it done." Needless to say, Clevelanders responded with free equipment and services that helped us dramatically reduce our cost of operation.

We opened Ronald McDonald House on September 25, 1979. What made the opening so memorable was the presence of Jim Murray, general manager of the Philadelphia Eagles, who was Ray Kroc's inspiration for the first Ronald McDonald House. Also present was Thom Darden of the Cleveland Browns. The guest of honor for the opening was Ray Kroc, the famous owner of McDonald's. I was touched and honored to act as master of ceremonies for the grand opening.

Besides spearheading the efforts for our own Ronald McDonald House, Mike Clegg is also responsible for the creation of the Ronald McDonald House PRO-AM golf tournament. This prestigious golf outing, held every June, is one of the most renowned charitable golf outings in America. Joining the 144 amateurs and 18 resident pros are PGA Tour professionals ranging from Arnold Palmer to Jack Nicklaus, Kent State's own Ben Curtis, and LPGA superstars such as Annika Sorenstam. I joined Mike on the very first Ronald McDonald House PRO-AM golf committee in 1979 and we're still going strong. To date, the tournament has generated just under $3 million for the house.

Having been part of both of these organizations from the beginning, I am proud to say that the Ronald McDonald House was the house that love built, and the Ronald McDonald House Pro-Am Golf Tournament contributes to the house that Mike Clegg built.

CLEVELAND HITS THE RESET BUTTON

We had come a long way from the riots of '66, '68, and the 1969 burning river debacle, all of which caught the attention of the nation. For those of us who lived and worked in Cleveland, we had heard enough. We had put up with negative publicity far too long, and it was now time for it to end. For me and many others who loved our city, the national media was the elephant in the room. To mix a metaphor, they had heaped on us just enough negative publicity to poison the well.

When George Voinovich became mayor of Cleveland in 1979, he challenged the business community to help him transform the city. After all, George had been born here, graduated from Collinwood High School, and received his undergraduate degree and doctorate of law from Ohio universities. George encouraged corporate and political leaders to put aside their differences and to begin to build bridges. In 1989, nine years into his tenure as mayor, *Fortune* magazine applauded the new trajectory in "How Business Bosses Saved a City."

Our Cleveland skyline was changing. The George Voinovich team had an encouraging and dramatic effect on Cleveland and its people. Pride mattered, and with the rebuilding of Cleveland came a new downtown and a new attitude. There was this tremendous feeling of accomplishment. *We did it!* Bipartisanship was now the rule of the day. You could sense that individual agendas had been eliminated. Politicians were working together. Community leaders were giving selflessly of their time, financial resources, and finally, positive support from the local media. We had found a new prosperity and had won the respect of the doomsayers. Nationally, we had become the new template of a dying city's rebirth. We're a nation of second chances, and Cleveland had just been blessed with one.

Yes, the buzz of activity was happening all around the city, but where the uplifting change really mattered was in the discussions in boardrooms, bars, family kitchens, at water coolers, and on local and national television. Everyone was beginning to take notice of Cleveland's tremendous turnaround. As a member of the Voinovich team, I called the presidents of local companies so they could tell their encouraging stories on my morning show.

The momentum, both visually and mentally, was building. New buildings were popping up everywhere. To complement the new construction, my thought was to contact the owners of older buildings that had become dirty from years of soot build-up, and ask them to sandblast or power-wash them so they would look new again.

UNION CLUB BUILDING RESTORED TO RADIANCE

The Union Club in Cleveland has a reputation as the most unique and prestigious club in the city. Most of Cleveland's CEOs and presidents are members. One afternoon as I drove by it on my way home, I thought an organization with an august membership like that should surely have a clean building and be a shining example of what our city should look like. After all, many of its members were on the Voinovich turnaround team.

At that time, the Union Club building may have been one of the dirtiest in town and needed a good scrubbing. The next morning on 3WE, I got on the air and said, "If anyone knows the president of the Union Club, will you please have him call me?

I'd like to talk to him about getting the building sandblasted and cleaned."

What I didn't know was the president of the Union Club was one of Cleveland's most respected businessmen who ran a Fortune 500 company. While listening, Mike Clegg, a major player in Cleveland, one of my closest friends, and senior vice president at Ostendorf-Morris, called and said, "Larry, my friend, you may have bitten off more than you can chew. The person you're looking for is Brad Jones, the chairman of Republic Steel."

Needless to say, I was petrified to pick up the phone and call him. Once we connected, he began our conversation by saying, "Larry, I've had at least twenty people tell me you were looking for me." After sharing a laugh, we talked briefly, and he graciously agreed to come on my morning show the very next day. I was thrilled when he said that plans were in the making to have the Union Club building sandblasted and cleaned up. Some months later, the historic building was restored to its original radiance and took its rightful place as one of the cleanest and most beautiful buildings in downtown Cleveland.

LIKE-MINDED PEOPLE, LIKE-MINDED PASSION

We all know that failure is a fact of life. Cleveland not only bought into that adage, it parked there and wore it out. But for me, the city that was given up for dead in the mid-to-late '60s was coming back to life. Under Voinovich, the leaders in Cleveland had unbridled imagination and a plan that kept a frenetic pace on the turnaround. The wind was now at our backs, and we were picking up speed all along the way.

SEVEN YEARS OF SUNDAYS

Just as I was leaving for a family vacation in the summer of 1979, the station's sales manager, Tom Wilson, asked me if I would like to host a Sunday morning brunch from Stouffer's Inn on the Square (now the Renaissance Hotel) with the general manager, Pete Dangerfield.

When I met Pete, I liked him immediately. But during our conversation I told him I was concerned about now working seven days a week. Pete replied, "I came to Cleveland from Dayton, and was thrilled to hear you talk about the city you love. Our city is in trouble, Larry, and downtown is a ghost town. I want you to bring your vast audience of Greater Cleveland listeners and community leaders into the heart of our city by broadcasting the brunch over the radio while interviewing community leaders. The combination is a win-win for all of us, and I need you to deliver. We'll rebuild this city one person at a time."

How could I say no? On our first Sunday broadcast, we drew only fifty people; the following Sunday, one hundred. Then it hit. On our third Sunday over six hundred people showed up for a delicious Sunday brunch in "Cleveland's living room," as Pete would describe it. Pete talked about mouth-watering scrambled eggs, crispy bacon, strawberries Devonshire, steaming coffee, and chilled orange juice. Pete's vivid description of the irresistible food tantalized the audience so much that they hopped in their cars and headed for downtown Cleveland.

Pete and I had long meetings with the heads of Cleveland venues: Playhouse Square, the Cleveland Play House, other entertainment venues, and local charities in Cleveland. Our goal was to have my audience come downtown for brunch, attend a Cleveland function, and head home. The experience was wonderful.

Over a period of six years, our Stouffer's brunch grew to over sixteen hundred people on any given Sunday. During football season I brought in local high school bands to play fight songs to energize our audience before they went to see the Browns. Pete was correct; looking back, it was a touchdown for us. We made people feel good again about their city.

The show was two hours long, and each interview had the thread of why Cleveland was the greatest city in America in which to live, work, play, and raise a family. I hosted that show for almost seven years until Pete was transferred to Atlanta. Afterward, I happily went back to spending Sundays with my family. I had become acutely aware of the precious value of family and my time.

That downtown experience caused my equity to spike. My penchant for promoting Cleveland and the people who live here had a profound impact on my personal and professional persona. My pulse still quickens when I think back to how much fun it was watching thousands come into our city to celebrate those beautiful Sundays. It was another little piece to add to our turnaround puzzle.

EVIDENCE OF OUR COMEBACK

With the flurry of robust spending on new construction, we looked around and suddenly found we were living in a new city. When the forty-five-story Sohio Building (later to be the BP Building, and now 200 Public Square) broke ground on Public Square, buttons were popping off our chests faster than Cleveland's own Jerry Siegel and Joe Shuster's Superman flying through the air at warp speed.

I was called on to host the Sohio opening just two years later. During the ceremony, Rosary and I were taken to the roof of the building by the main custodian. When the doors opened and we walked out, the view was breathtaking. We felt as though we could reach out and touch the Terminal Tower. For me, this represented the marriage of the old and the new Cleveland. It was a stunning panoramic view of our city from its newest neighbor. At that moment, it dawned on me that we might be one of only a few who would ever enjoy this view.

Upon returning to the celebration in the lobby, I became emotional. As I looked out at this entire group of caring individuals, it struck me that not only had we addressed the earlier failures of our city, we had won. Almost every business in Cleveland was there for the Sohio Building grand opening. The disharmony and gloomy fog that had hung over Cleveland for so long had finally lifted, and in its place was a new American city.

A LOST AND LAST OPPORTUNITY WITH WOODY HAYES

It was early 1987 and Woody Hayes was being honored at a sold-out celebration dinner in the main ballroom at Stouffer's Inn on the Square. The downtown Cleveland event was being held to celebrate Hayes's twenty-seven-year reign as head football coach of the Ohio State University Buckeyes.

There were so many popular OSU football alumni seated on the dais, such as two-time Heisman Trophy winner Archie Griffin, that the event organizers had to build up the stage to accommodate the head table—three levels of risers and a podium for the speakers. It was a privilege for me to act as master of ceremonies for this grand affair. The dais would include several of Woody's present and former players, many of whom played in the National Football League.

When the evening had concluded and as Woody was preparing to leave, I had a brief opportunity to sit quietly with him and ask a few questions. It was obvious that Woody knew that I hailed from "that state up north," meaning Michigan, because my opening statement was, "I cannot believe that those of you who wear the scarlet and gray have asked me, whose blood pours maize and blue once a year, to emcee this evening for such a distinguished man." Everyone in the audience knew that I loved Ohio State and the man being honored that evening.

For my first question I asked Woody, "When you were returning from a recruiting trip in southern Michigan and were running low on gas, did you actually say, 'We'll push this damn car all the way to the Ohio state line before I contribute one penny to any business in the state of Michigan'?"

With a friendly smirk on his face and looking directly into my eyes, he promptly answered, "You're damn right I did!" When

I burst out laughing, the expression on Woody's face communicated, *What's so funny about that?* He then asked, "Larry, next question?" I knew that what I was about to ask would be much more heartfelt than the first question. With a sensitive and softer tone in my voice, I asked, "Woody, in your illustrious career at Ohio State, what was the one thread of coaching these men, other than football, that you wanted them to remember?" His answer was quite profound. Woody explained that only one percent of college football players ever make it into the pros, so his utmost and fundamental goal was to make sure they received an education and got their degree so they could lay a solid foundation and support themselves and their families in the future.

On my way home, I turned on my tape recorder only to realize that I had not hit the record button on my cassette player. One of Woody's famous quotes was, "One thing you cannot ever afford to do is to feel sorry for yourself." That may be true, but that night I couldn't have felt sorrier for myself. My audience would never hear him speak from his heart about the men he coached at Ohio State. What made losing the discussion with Woody so long-lasting and painful was that this celebration of his life was his last Cleveland appearance. Wayne Woodrow "Woody" Hayes passed away on March 12, 1987, at the young age of seventy-four.

BARRY MANILOW & BETTE MIDLER SING MY JINGLES

One of the advertising agencies I was working closely with on voice and local jingles was Griswold Advertising, then Cleveland's largest ad agency. My contact there was Dave Walters, who was producing many of their national campaigns. Although Dave very much liked the Smucker's jingle I had written and produced, he was a little suspect of my ability to produce another winner. Dave insisted that if I were going to work with him, I would have to record in New York and use the Steve Carmin Singers, whom he had used in the past and with whom he had great success.

I had met Steve on the phone when he helped me negotiate a creative fee for writing the Smucker's jingle. Originally from Cleveland, Steve moved his family to New York so he could write and produce jingles. His claim to fame was the very familiar Budweiser campaign, "When you say Bud, you've said a lot about a beer." His Budweiser campaign lasted for years. He was America's jingle sweetheart.

I agreed with Dave that if he used me for his next campaign, I would travel to New York and use the Steve Carmin Singers. At the time, I was the on-air radio and television spokesperson for BF Goodrich tires. Dave wanted a new jingle for them. I called Steve, who helped me set up his singers for my recording session. When I arrived in New York for the session, the singers were the then-unknown Barry Manilow, Bette Midler, Melissa Manchester, and Ron Dante, who became Barry's lifelong producer.

Following my session, Barry called me in Cleveland to tell me he had a song originally called "Brandy," but he didn't like the way it was structured. He said he had changed it around and renamed it "Mandy." Barry asked if I would give it a spin. He was hoping to sell the song to a recording company. With 3WE's massive coverage, this would be a good measurement of potential interest. I agreed and told Barry I would get back to him. I spoke to Joe Restifo and Tom Embrescia about the song. They not only loved it, they gave me permission to play it.

As promised, I played "Mandy," and my audience loved it. When "Mandy" took the nation by storm, I called Mike and Jules Belkin and mentioned that 3WE would like to get involved in bringing Barry Manilow to Playhouse Square. They agreed. Believe it or not, we had to call the concert off for lack of sales. Despite the song being so popular, not many knew about Barry. One year later, after continuous exposure, Barry would sell out the Coliseum.

ERIC CARMEN AND THE RASPBERRIES

The very next jingle I wrote and produced for Dave Walters and Griswold was for one of their largest clients, Bryant Air Conditioning. After writing the jingle, I told Dave I was friendly with Eric Carmen of the Raspberries. At the time they had catapulted onto the national scene with "Go All the Way" and "I Wanna Be With You." I asked if it would be okay to get the band for the jingle and record it here in Cleveland. I told Dave that I truly believed the Raspberries would one day have legendary status. If they agreed to do the jingle, it would serve a dual purpose: It would make for a great local story due to the Raspberries being local fan favorites, and because of that, Bryant would receive added free publicity.

When I spoke to Eric Carmen, he thought it would be fun for the group. I then called Dave Walters and told him I had a commitment from Eric and the Raspberries. Dave agreed, and this time we recorded the jingle right here in Cleveland. The original group was Eric Carmen, Wally Bryson, Dave Smalley, and Jim Bonfanti. We all had fun recording the jingle, and they did not charge me more than if I had I used local talent.

TRYING TO BALANCE BAD NEWS

I had been working at 3WE for almost ten years when the rumors started to circulate that the station might be sold. Initially I did not take the rumors seriously, but suddenly, the present began to look a lot like the past. Tom called the staff together in our lobby and announced that Nick had sold 3WE to the Gannett Company, owners of *USA Today*. Just as at WIXY, those who brought me here were moving on. Also, as at WIXY, the steep climb from almost nothing to enjoying the view from the top was about to become a distant memory. I couldn't believe it had happened again.

Once the new owners arrived, things began to change rather

quickly. They had a plan in place, and that plan was about to take the right-side-up 3WE and turn it upside down. Over the next few years there were several changes at the station, but none like the one that was about to happen. Following my Friday morning show, the new program director, Oogie Pringle, called me into his office and said, "Look, Larry, beginning this Monday morning, 3WE will be known as Country 11. As of Monday, we have a new morning team, and we are moving you to afternoon drive, 3–7 p.m."

Although this format had been successful throughout America, I felt that it was now on the wane. To me, the music was now outdated—the sound of twangy country. I told Oogie that they were late in putting this type of format on the air and that it would destroy the radio station. He told me it didn't matter how I felt.

I was rendered powerless. I intuitively knew Clevelanders would bail out faster than you can say *"goodbye, ratings."* Worse yet, I had to stay. I had just signed a three-year contract and had nowhere to go. My only option was to stand by and watch my respected radio station come tumbling down. I had been around long enough to know that radio is transitory. The sustainability of a radio performer's career depends not only on strong ratings but on strong leadership as well. The departure of the Mileti and Embrescia team spelled doom for me. By all accounts, I knew my career was in jeopardy.

While I recoiled at the thought of this type of format change, I was a team player and agreed to show up on Monday for my new shift. I tried to deal with the idea that my radio station, where I had joyfully parked for ten years, was about to implode. It took me all weekend to deal with the disorder in my life, and I was deeply angered as I tried to prepare myself for the onslaught of changes: the abrasive new morning team and the sound of hoedown country music. The new Country 11 was ill-equipped for battle; they didn't understand the Cleveland audience.

On my first day with the new format, I did my very best to act as if I had been playing this kind of music forever. I could not have been more relieved when 7 p.m. rolled around and my on-air shift was over. As I suspected, our phones rang off the hook all day long. The loyal 3WE listeners were in shock. As I left the broadcast studio, I had to walk by Oogie's office. He asked if I would step into his office. He then told me, "I heard your show today, and to be honest with you, Larry, you're not good enough to work afternoon drive." At the moment, I felt rudderless and was drifting backwards. "So, beginning tomorrow morning, I've decided to move you to middays, 10 a.m.–3 p.m."

Oogie's comment was a hard pill for me to swallow. It was hurtful and unnecessary, causing me to immediately sever my relationship with the radio station. For just a moment I was disengaged. One side of my brain heard, "You're not good enough." The other side said, "Weren't you just singled out as one of the Top 12 radio personalities in America?" That paradox made it very difficult to accept Oogie's opinion. We were now on a collision course. I am hardly ever aroused by anger, but this time, I was. I wanted my response to be professional but firm because it was going to be a career-altering discussion.

I stood and addressed Oogie: "First, as I mentioned earlier, you're late with this format change. Clevelanders will never buy into it. Second, our listeners feel embittered and betrayed by what you've done to their radio station. And finally, I don't recall anyone ever speaking to me with such a disrespectful tone. I will not be in tomorrow; I have done my last show for this radio station."

The illogicality of the past seventy-two hours had a devastating effect on me. I was under contract; my daughter, Donna, was about to be married; and leaving the radio station meant I would have no income. Throughout my discouragement, it was my faith in God that allowed me to focus on the happy and positive side of the ledger. I knew the Lord had a plan for my life. His plans and His timing are perfect.

TELEVISION?

The three-year, noncompete clause in my 3WE contract prohibited me from working in radio within a fifty-mile radius of the Terminal Tower building. Luckily for me, my contract did not forbid me to work in television.

I received a call from Aaron Fox, founder and chairman of Fox & Associates, a local advertising and marketing agency with offices in several other cities, including New York. One of their largest local accounts was Pick 'n' Pay, then the top grocery chain in Greater Cleveland. Aaron asked me to audition as host for a new television show called *Let's Go To The Races*. I really didn't think I had a chance because they had brought in talent from New York, Chicago, and Cleveland for what is commonly referred to as a "cattle call," an industry term for many talents coming together for an audition. Auditions went on all day at WUAB TV 43, and I was the last one at 4:30 p.m. Following my audition, Aaron asked if I could stay over and have dinner with Richard (Dick) Bogomolny, the chairman of Pick 'n' Pay, who had been there all day to observe the auditions.

We sat down in the conference room with Aaron, Dick, and a few members from the agency. They informed me that I would be the host for this new half-hour show, which would be taped on Wednesday mornings and played back that same evening following *M*A*S*H*, then the number-one rated show in its time slot. We had an incredible lead in.

Let's Go To The Races turned out to be a monster success, both from a ratings standpoint and at the grocery level. First and foremost, the exposure from the Wednesday evening television show, where they announced their weekly specials, gave Pick 'n' Pay a twelve-hour head start over their competition. Second, the following morning, Pick 'n' Pay ran a full-page ad, with my picture holding up a race card, noting the winning numbers from the prior evening's horse races. Pick 'n' Pay's weekly specials were also in that ad.

Let's Go To The Races ran in 1983. At the end of the run in December, both Fox and Pick 'n' Pay agreed to take a four-week hiatus to study the effect the television commercials had on Clevelanders. Their findings indicated that the appearance of the meat that consumers saw in the store did not match the color of the meat on television. I was told Pick 'n' Pay blamed Fox, and Fox blamed Pick 'n' Pay for the discrepancy. Fox may have won the argument, but they lost the account. When the new advertising agency took over the account, we could not come to terms on a contract.

The show went back on the air in early 1984 with another host and did not last long. I could not have been more appreciative to Aaron Fox and Pick 'n' Pay for the career-saving television exposure, which also paid for my daughter's wedding!

BECOMING "MR. CLEVELAND"

At the end of *Let's Go To The Races*, my 3WE radio contract was renegotiated. I was released from my three-year noncompete. I was now able to return to radio. I was contacted by Kim Colebrook, a close friend and general manager of WERE 1300. At that time, WERE was highly regarded as Cleveland's news/talk station with well-known and widely respected journalists. Kim had asked me to host a one-hour talk show from 9–10 a.m. I gladly accepted.

I wanted my first day to be very special, so I invited our celebrated mayor to be my guest. Cleveland was still working on its turnaround, and I thought it would be wonderful to have George Voinovich spend an hour with me talking about our city.

During the interview, George referred to me with three distinct honors: Mr. Cleveland, the Voice of Cleveland, and Cleveland's Number One Civic Booster. I could not have been more pleased with that reference. Only three other people in Cleveland's history had ever been bestowed with that title, so to this day, it is a moniker I am proud to wear.

RADIO OR TELEVISION?

During this time I received a call from Jane Hirz, producer of the *Dave Patterson Show* on WKYC TV 3 that competed with the TV 5 *Morning Exchange*, hosted by Fred Griffith. Dave was working part-time in television in Philadelphia while continuing to honor his contract as host of the show. Due to Dave's hectic travel schedule, I covered for him, on and off, for over a year while he was deciding whether to move to Philadelphia. I knew that when Dave left I would be asked to be the permanent host of the show. But one problem remained: I was now hosting a show on WERE. In time, one or the other would have to go, and I wasn't sure where I would end up. Until now radio had been my life, but I had just come off of a hit television show on WUAB, and Channel 3 wanted me as soon as Dave left for Philadelphia.

While the uncertainty of radio versus television was plaguing me, I continued my live radio show on WERE at 9 a.m. and then ran over to WKYC and taped the television show at 10:30 a.m. It was at this time Kim Colebrook was about to end the indecision. Kim offered me a management position in addition to my radio show. I did my best to avoid Kim because I was pressing Jane Hirz for resolution. Jane said, "We are very close. Hang in there with me. I'm sure Dave will be leaving soon, but we can't press him." That caused me to steer away from Kim, who obviously wanted an answer. He walked into my office on a Monday and asked if I had reached a decision. I told him, not yet. "Larry, I need to know your answer by the end of your show on Wednesday."

As paradoxical as it may sound, part of me wanted to move permanently to television, but I was moved by the nature of staying in radio and continuing to hone my craft. Wednesday came and I had to make a choice. I called Jane and asked if Dave was still on board. "Yes," was her response. I said, "Jane, I have to accept WERE's offer. It is not fair to keep Kim waiting." Jane then said, "Larry, you have to do what you have to do."

I went downstairs to Kim's office and signed a one-year contact as vice president of operations and communications for WERE. I then walked up to my second-floor office and the phone rang. It was Jane. "Larry, I have great news. Dave just resigned and we are now ready to sign you to host the new TV 3 morning show." Timing is everything. Sadly, I had to tell Jane, she was a minute too late.

Once I became the permanent host for the 9 a.m. talk show, I committed to immersing myself in the process of making WERE a serious contender in the market. I was also extremely excited about the opportunity to work with golfing friend, news director Bob Price, and newsman Bob Tayek. They were arguably the most popular and highly regarded names in radio news in Northeast Ohio.

Following the announcement of my promotion, I went to chat with each member of the news staff and get their creative input for our new approach of the *Good News, Good People* format, which was mixing hard news and soft entertainment together. My first stop was with Bob Price to explain my concept. After all, I was grounded in entertainment and news at WIXY and 3WE and, for the most part, I had implemented some of that concept. The ratings indicated that a combination of hard and soft news was a viable format.

FORK IN THE ROAD

Sitting in Bob's office, I anticipated a response like, *Congratulations, Larry, I'm excited we're going to be working together.*

What I got was, "Larry, I just told my news staff to not listen to a word you have to say."

There's an unspoken fear when someone speaks to you like that, and he sensed that in me. I asked him to repeat himself because I couldn't believe what I had just heard. Again, he said, "I just told my news staff to not listen to a word you have to say."

I had been in the Marines, so I was aware of how to gain a strategic advantage over an enemy. But this was not an enemy;

it was a friend who had just launched a preemptive strike. Generally, people admire and respect candor, but this threat paralyzed me. In that dreadful moment, our relationship had turned toxic. Where I came in looking for feedback on my ideas, Bob had poked a hole in my balloon, and all channels of communication were immediately shut down. I had seen this movie before with Oogie Pringle.

We both knew there would be no solution to this problem; it was a simple disagreement over programming policy. Bob took the higher road and resigned a short time later. Bob Tayek replaced him as news director.

Kim Colebrook hired a consultant I had previously worked with in Flint, Michigan, to find an afternoon-drive talent. He found a Cleveland transplant, Vivian Goodman, working in our nation's capital. She had a great voice and authority in her on-air news style. Vivian was a journalist with an uncompromising style. She was an intellectual and brought prominence to our show. They believed mixing Vivian's voice and mine, along with our playful styles, would be an afternoon drive-time hit. Vivian did the hard news and I did the soft. It was exactly what Kim and I had talked about when I accepted my new position.

What made the new approach work so well was that this ear-catching format represented a perfect balance of our playful and entertaining styles, in combination with a news delivery that gave our listeners precisely what they tuned in to hear.

Under Kim's leadership, WERE started to hum. Kim was a highly skilled and intelligent leader. Legendary General Douglas MacArthur, chief of staff for the United States Army, said, "A general is just as good or just as bad as the troops under his command make him." WERE's staff had lined up whole-heartedly behind Kim, and Bob Tayek was also a powerful entity. As new director, Bob was wired to the political and community newsmakers in Cleveland. And now that Vivian was in place, there was consensus within the ranks and we all knew the good ratings would follow.

The combination of news and entertainment spiked the ratings, and Vivian and I were able to acquire a very strong listener base of Clevelanders searching for hard news, mixed with a little entertainment, as they drove home for the evening.

MOSES CLEAVELAND / MR. CLEVELAND

I had felt for many years that the founder of our city, Moses Cleaveland, had been overlooked. Because I was making so many speeches on Cleveland's turnaround, I wanted Clevelanders to know more about the history of their city. The 188th anniversary was just days away when I received permission from the Cleveland Police Department to reenact the landing of Moses Cleaveland on the east bank of the Cuyahoga River. I asked my audience to join me for the celebration on Sunday, July 22, 1984. For the festivities, I planned to dress up in a period costume resembling something Moses Cleaveland might have worn.

As I mentioned before, Rosary and I were married on July 22nd. When we woke on our ninth wedding anniversary, we went downstairs and I made breakfast for Rosary. Following breakfast, we exchanged cards and gifts, and I went directly upstairs to shower, shave, and get dressed as Moses Cleaveland. After getting dressed, I took one look in the mirror and had a flashback. *Oh, no, the last time I was in a costume, I was nearly laughed off stage at Cleveland's Public Hall when I introduced Gary Puckett and the Union Gap.*

But this time would be radically different, and a life-changing moment for me and my career.

When I came downstairs, Rosary stared. "You're not driving downtown dressed like that, are you? What if someone recognizes you? I can't believe I'm married to Moses Cleaveland." Then she looked out and saw our car in the driveway with our neighbor's aluminum boat tied to the roof, and her nonverbal communication was deafening: *I can't believe my husband is doing this on our anniversary.*"

I was planning to use the boat for the reenactment of the landing. The evening before, I had tied the rowboat to the roof. Anyone with Boy Scout training would have known you never tie a boat to a car top with the bottom facing down: the wind can get underneath and lift it off the car.

When I left my driveway, all seemed well as I left Chagrin Falls driving at 35 mph. As I merged onto I-480, things continued to go well as I slowly increased my speed to 55 mph. I now felt confident to maintain my speed at 55 mph. At this point, the wind gusts got under the boat and ripped it from my car, causing deep gouges in my front hood and roof. The boat was blown twenty feet off to the side of the highway.

I soon found myself, dressed like a Pilgrim, wrestling with a rowboat on the side of the highway, unsure what to do next. One guy, who must have heard about the reenactment, actually recognized me. He pulled his car off to the side, rolled down his window and with a giant smile on his face, shouted, "Hey Moses, do you need any help?" We then joked and agreed that Moses Cleaveland didn't have it this hard when he landed in the Western Reserve 188 years earlier. I ended up leaving the boat by the side of the highway and later came back to pick it up when the momentous event was over.

The plans for the event included my driving to the Cleveland fire department station in the Flats to have them escort me to Settler's Landing. When I arrived with my Honda looking like it had been through a demolition derby and explained that I no longer had a boat for the landing, they suggested using their rowboat. They then tied a long rope from the rowboat to their celebrated fire boat, used for lake parades, to escort me to the landing. The fire boat was equipped with three hoses on each side that could spray water up to twenty feet. It was the kind of boat that captured everyone's attention. They towed me to the location where Moses Cleaveland had landed. It was also the site where Lorenzo Carter, the first permanent settler in Cleveland, had settled.

About three hundred people showed, including a *Plain Dealer* photographer and four members of the Cleveland Grays, who were founded in 1836 as a private militia as the first company of uniformed troops. I then began my short walk up to Public Square and the crowd followed. I carried the famous William Ganson Rose book, *Cleveland, the Making of a City,* and the Cleveland flag, which to my knowledge had never been flown on Public Square. Earlier in the week I had spoken to Mayor Voinovich and he arranged for me to have the Cleveland flag hoisted on the Moses Cleaveland quadrant just in front of the Terminal Tower. It would fly right alongside the American flag and the state flag of Ohio. Following a brief speech and dedication, I went inside the Stouffer hotel, where I hosted my weekly two-hour talk show and continued the celebration with honored guests.

CHAPTER 19

The President's Man

One day, while sitting at my desk at WERE, I received a call from Robert Bennett, then vice-chairman of the Cuyahoga County republican party and later chairman of the Ohio republican party. Bob and I knew each other. We had both served in the Marines and enjoyed sharing stories about our time in the corps. Following a few minutes of small talk, Bob presented me with a once-in-a-lifetime opportunity that I never dreamed would come my way. "Larry, how would you like to introduce the president of the United States? President Reagan is coming to Cleveland next month."

My jaw dropped. "Bob, tell me you're not kidding."

"I'm serious," he said. "Our presidential welcoming committee got together and came up with a list of names who we thought would be the perfect choice to introduce the president. It was unanimous: Larry Morrow."

I told Bob what an honor it was to have been chosen and what a thrill it would be to introduce President Reagan. The only fly in the ointment for me was the certain disapproval of my father, who was a staunch democrat. When I got home that evening, I shared the good news with Rosary and my three daughters. After that, I called my mom and dad.

When Dad came to the phone, I said, "Dad, your son will be on stage with the president of the United States. I have been asked to introduce him next month. That means I will meet him and shake hands with him."

Dad replied, "You introduce that man and you will not be allowed to come back into this house. Do you understand?"

I never argued with my dad, but this time I did, gently, with all the conviction I could muster. Yet he still wouldn't listen. With my father, if you wanted to win you had to do it with logic or reason, not argument.

"After all, Dad, Ronald Reagan *is* the president of the United States."

He then, with mild repugnance in his voice, called out to my mother; "Katherine, your son is on the phone and he's going to introduce a republican."

Unlike my father, my mother could not have been more excited for me because she knew what this meant for me and my career. Remember, I was raised in a very simple home with five siblings. Not only was it a simple home, but in our small, quiet neighborhood in Pontiac, all the neighbors knew and talked with one another.

My mom knew this kind of news would light up our neighborhood and be the talk of her little gatherings with friends and relatives. "Honey," Mom said, "Make sure you get his autograph and get a picture with the two of you so we can show all our friends that my son was with the president of the United States." Up to this point, it was the highlight of my broadcast career.

INTRODUCING THE PRESIDENT OF THE UNITED STATES

It was a typically dry, cloudy, and somewhat chilly day in October when President Reagan came to Cleveland. His schedule had him speaking from the podium on the stage that had been erected on the steps of the county court house at precisely 10:30 a.m. I was told to be at Stouffer's Inn on the Square at 8:30 a.m. to be cleared for security.

I arrived precisely on time to meet with the Secret Service and to be cleared. These agents are equipped with the latest military weapons, ranging from pistols to machine guns, and are trained in close combat. They wear radios and surveillance kits to maintain constant communication with a central command post and other personnel.

This was my first encounter with a special agent and obtaining a high-level security clearance. First of all, I had to show my driver's license to identify myself. Then I was inspected with a metal detector wand over every inch of my body. After that, I was given a special badge to wear on my trench coat to signal to all special agents that I was cleared to be close to the president. As soon as I pinned my badge to my coat, I was sent to city hall to await the his arrival.

When I arrived at Lakeside Avenue, the entire four-square-block area had been cordoned off with metal detectors. They were performing a bomb sweep, so I had to wait an additional fifteen minutes before being allowed to continue to city hall. As I waited for the bomb sweep to conclude, I glanced up at the surrounding buildings and took special notice of the windows. Before that day, I had never thought much about those windows, but now I was keenly aware that each building with a view of the court house stage had been checked out by the frontline of the Secret Service a few days earlier.

On the day of President Reagan's appearance, I found it amazing that each of those windows now had a Secret Service agent assigned to it. In all, there were five hundred agents guarding the windows. If a building office, or window could not be guarded, it had to be either evacuated while the president spoke or shut down for the day. For example, the BP building was under construction at that time, which meant the site was evacuated and shut down. In addition to the five hundred agents posted in the windows and at the top of the buildings, three hundred armed agents dressed as civilians mixed in among the thirty thousand spectators who would be standing to hear the president. So, for those of you who were in attendance that day, the person standing next to you, in front of you, or behind you might have been a fully armed Secret Service agent.

Following the bomb sweep, I arrived on the stage at court

house an hour before the president was to arrive. Good thing, because I needed a bathroom break. I had already consumed two cups of coffee. As I opened the front door to the court house, immediately in front of me was a Secret Service agent who told me I was not allowed in because all the rooms had been secured. I then told the agent that I desperately needed to visit the men's room.

Assuming that he would flag me through, I quickly started to move past him, only to be met with a massive hand pushing against my chest. This time, he said with even greater emphasis, "I told you this place is secured and no one, including you, is allowed to come in." With that, he opened his coat and revealed a weapon that looked like an Uzi machine gun. No further dialogue was necessary.

Air Force One arrived at Hopkins International just a few minutes after 10 a.m. The president had support from the truckers' union, who had lined both sides of I-71 with huge 18-wheelers as the motorcade traveled north, thus eliminating any chance of attack. Two helicopters flew directly above the president's limousine. One was fully equipped with his S.W.A.T. team; the second one carried his medical team. St. Vincent Charity Hospital had an operating room medically staffed and fully equipped with all of his medical records in the unlikely event of an emergency.

The reason for this incredible amount of security was to ensure there would be no repeat of an earlier assassination attempt on President Reagan's life, where he had been shot by John Hinckley, Jr., at the Hilton Hotel in Washington, D.C.

WE WILL BE WATCHING EVERY MOVE YOU MAKE

The crowd passed through the metal detectors just past 9:30 a.m. Within a short period of time, thirty thousand people were standing in front of the stage, waiting to hear the most powerful leader in the free world.

The special agent in charge came to me and gave me my final

instructions. "First and foremost, what are you going to say when you introduce the president?" My response was, "I've been working on the president's introduction for the past few weeks and it's only about four minutes long." He kindly, but bluntly, corrected me and said, "No, Larry. When I instruct you, you will step to the podium and the *only* thing you will say is, *Ladies and gentlemen, please welcome the president of the United States.*" That was very disappointing for me, because I had worked so hard on memorizing the introduction, and I thought Clevelanders would have enjoyed hearing it.

The next question the special agent asked me was, "Will you have your hands in your pockets or out of your pockets?" I was puzzled, so I asked, "Does it make a difference?" His next comment was, "You bet it does. You will be standing directly behind the president; there will be over eight hundred very nervous, armed agents watching every move you make." I knew I was in trouble. I had been born and raised in a family that speaks with its hands. One wrong move and I could be history. We agreed I would use my right hand. I was then told if I had to take my right hand out of my pocket for any reason, I could only proceed after receiving approval from the agent.

Our secret code for me to ask permission was visible only between the two of us. We agreed that I would stare at him for a certain amount of time and that was our signal that I was about to take my hand out of my pocket. He would then inform the command of my hand movement. After Mr. Reagan departed, I asked an agent what would have happened had I taken my left hand, or both hands, out at the same time. He answered, "You don't want to know."

We have almost seven billion human beings living on the Earth, yet only a handful will ever know the overwhelming thrill of standing next to the most important man on the planet and saying, "Ladies and gentlemen, please welcome the president of the United States."

Part Five

WQAL

CHAPTER 20

Dad, You'd Better Get Your Fanny Over to FM

I had now been working at WERE for a little over two years and longed to get back to a format of music and talk. I knew intuitively that my talents were better-matched to my success of the past. The interviewing process had begun to take on a feeling of confrontation that never suited my personality. I was also prodded by a series of conversations with broadcast pals who encouraged me to make the move to FM radio, which had already become fully entrenched in the ratings battle.

WMMS owned contemporary radio in Cleveland and the ratings confirmed it. My daughters' comments also rang true: "Dad, if you're going to remain on the air and be part of mainstream radio, you'd better get your fanny over to FM; that's what all our friends are listening to." The experience of doing talk radio and being a member of the management team at WERE would prove to be invaluable tools down the road.

My friend Rick Coan, who spent much of his early career with Stouffer restaurants and hotels, once told me, "In the restaurant business, your shelf life is one meal; in the hotel business your shelf life is one night." But I knew in radio your shelf life was your last rating period. Anything with a shelf life comes with an expiration date. I knew if I were going to extend my broadcast shelf life, it had to be FM radio. I met with Kim Colebrook and informed him of my wanting to move on. This decision was something that had been in my heart for a long time.

Although Kim tried to persuade me to stay, he supported my decision. I resigned that day. The parting was bittersweet; I was sad about leaving because Kim had not only encouraged me to try out news talk, he had taught me so much about management principles and guidelines for which I would be forever grateful. He had also stuck with me during a time when I believed radio had gotten the best of me. Upon my leaving he said, "Duker, let me put confidence in your decision. Every experience ushers in another. All the best to you, my friend."

We parted great friends. I will remember Kim Colebrook for helping me find a new path in my life. What I didn't realize was that the future Kim had forecasted was just around the corner.

After resigning from WERE, I walked out of the station wondering, *Now what?*

I had always been interested in exploring new ideas for radio with other people who had been places I had not. I wanted to share my gifts with people who had similar dreams, and help each other grow in business and in our community. *But where?*

The answer was literally around the corner as I continued my walk from Chester Avenue to one of my favorite restaurants on Euclid Avenue. Just before reaching the restaurant, I spotted an old friend walking toward me. It was Walt Tiburski, my one-time intern at WIXY. Walt had left WIXY to become sales manager at a relatively new FM radio station, WMMS, "Home of the Buzzard." Over time, Walt Tiburski's genius would take WMMS from small, insignificant ratings, selling commercials for a dollar each in the beginning, to the highest-rated FM radio station in America. Under Walt's guidance, WMMS would be voted *Rolling Stone* magazine's *Nation's Best Contemporary Radio Station* several times over twelve years. We shook hands and exchanged a few pleasantries. Then I said to Walt, "I hear you recently bought WQAL 104.1 FM."

Walt said, "Yes, Tony Ocepek, and I are just putting the pieces together." Tony was another radio icon who owned radio stations scattered throughout Ohio.

I then said to Walt, "Let me help you; I want to be your new morning man."

Walt appeared to be encouraged and said, "Let's have dinner and talk about it." What I did not know was, just moments before we bumped into each other, his current morning man and operations director on WQAL had demanded a new contract with a huge raise in salary.

WALT AND TONY NEEDED A MORNING MAN–
AND I NEEDED TO BE NEEDED

Walt and Tony felt squeezed because they did not want to make waves internally and wanted to show financial strength with their bank, Ameritrust, which held their financing note. Walt and I agreed to have dinner that evening. Afterward Walt suggested we get together the following morning at the east side Marriott, now called the Cleveland Hilton, so I could meet his partner, Tony Ocepek, and discuss how we might go further in our discussions.

As good fortune would have it, while we were having breakfast at the Marriott, Joe Zingale was seated just a few feet away from our table. We had all remained friends with Joe. When Joe spotted us, he walked over to our table and said, "Walt and Tony, I don't know what you guys are talking about, but if it's about Larry coming to your new radio station, sign him because he will take you to the top of the ratings."

That's all Walt and Tony needed to hear—a vote of confidence from someone who had experienced great radio success in Cleveland. They had invested their life savings and were betting on this morning show and WQAL to carry them the distance.

The three of us individually had all been successful in radio, but this time was vastly different because Walt and Tony were now owner-partners.

For me, I was making a big broadcast jump to FM radio.

Could we all do it again? Time has a way of diminishing the lus-
ter of the past, but we all wanted a second life and were willing
to work hard to get it.

We were all well known in Cleveland radio circles. If a reporter or a member of the media had seen us together again,
they would have assumed that I was talking about a position
for me at WQAL. So, for that reason, our second meeting was at
a secluded restaurant, far away from Cleveland, in Willoughby
Hills. We sat in the back of the restaurant in a corner away from
the restaurant traffic. That evening proved to be one of the most
exciting evenings of my life. As we looked in the rearview mirror
together, we spoke of great times in radio apart from each other
but more important, greater times together at WQAL. We were
all hungry for a greater challenge. We were not individuals any
more; we were a team. We all knew it would be better to row
our boat slower and in unison than to go faster just for the sake
of individualism.

THINKING IN SYNC

You could tell by spending just a few minutes with Tony
Ocepek that he didn't cozy up to a relationship with anyone until he felt he not only liked you but trusted you. At first glance,
his appearance was that of one who had graced the cover of *Fortune* magazine. Or, without knowing, and asked to guess what
he did for a living, you would comfortably say, the president of
Harvard University. He was refined and buttoned down all the
way. He wore a white shirt and tie, smart-looking sport jacket,
and shiny wingtip shoes. He was physically fit.

Yet despite his sharp appearance Tony enjoyed being lost in
the crowd. Where most of his ilk ran exhaustively to get noticed, Tony did not court attention. He was quiet and comfortable with anonymity.

After spending some time with Tony and Walt, I could see
how WQAL would approach business and promotion. Tony

would dominate the inside—including the close relationships with our business partners. Walt's promotional strategy dominated the outside. Neither one overshadowed the other.

For me, Tony was the business symbol of WQAL. You could feel it immediately. Under his leadership, the management team would work in an entrepreneurial environment. Tony wanted all of us to take a leadership role at WQAL and in our community.

You always knew where you stood with him, every step of the way.

Although Tony and Walt shared the same goal, they lived in different worlds.

Tony Ocepek was a realest: no fluff, no hype, but encouraging. He had penetrating insights on how we should approach the market. He was extremely rational and relied on intellect rather than emotions or feelings.

Walt Tiburski was an idealist, a high achiever with extremely sharp edges. He depended mostly on feelings. When you met Walt, you immediately liked him. He wore a big smile that was engaging and had a down-home quality that said social stature and sophistication are commodities of little consequence.

Although extremely friendly, Walt was larger than life and a magnet of attention. After all, he had a national reputation as one of the most successful and admired general managers of radio in America for what he had accomplished at WMMS. His national notoriety made him more colorful and at the same time mysterious. Those who worked closely with him called him a promotional genius. Walt knew and understood the outside world of promotion.

Describing Walt's past is to say we'll not see his like again. He was blessed with one of the most imaginative minds I had ever been exposed to. I was with him for just a few minutes and realized he was one of the best radio Monopoly players I had ever seen—he liked taking everything off the table. Translate that to owning every radio entertainment venue in town, leaving very little for anyone else.

WEAVING MAGIC

In tandem, Walt and Tony were one of a kind. They knew exactly what they wanted, and more important, how to get it. Together they embodied an excitement that shouted, "Wow, I want to be on your team!" Both were born gifted and possessed superior intellects. They also placed a high value on people and relied heavily on commitment. They knew how to leverage people and had the capacity to get them to laugh their way and to work hard their way, which in my mind were marks of insightful and caring leaders. That's what made our first evening together so exciting.

Like Norm Wain and the early days of WIXY, Tony and Walt wanted to get the right people on the bus. Get the wrong people off the bus. Get the right people in the right seats and then determine where you want to drive. We also shared attitudes about the road we would travel. We would create a corporate culture at WQAL that would manifest itself in ways that would make everyone on our staff excited. They also possessed keen insights on people and they intuitively knew only good people would take them there.

What stirred my heart the most that evening was how we all felt love for our community. Cleveland was on the upside of its turnaround that began in 1979. It was also the time Mayor George Voinovich had given me the title "Mr. Cleveland" and I was proud of the moniker. I had always felt it was not enough to defend your community, but you had to be transformed by your commitment. In other words, not only do as I say, but do as I do.

It was now 1985, six years into a new and exciting Cleveland. We were going to position WQAL as the axis around which much of the positive talk about Cleveland would rotate, and a great deal of it would begin on my morning show. Tony and Walt were highly animated as they insisted that everything from important community initiatives, to high-profile entertainment venues, to highly-attended sports events would be launched from the morning show.

For the three of us the evening turned out to be magical. WQAL was going to be this huge apparatus forming behind a city on the move. We had all tapped into each other's minds and could feel the winds of change blowing in our favor. When the evening concluded, I was so grateful for the faith they put in me. I agreed to a one-year contract, and I left for home as WQAL's new morning man and vice president of operations and programming.

JOE ZINGALE'S CRYSTAL BALL

WQAL's morning show was resting in eleventh place in morning-drive ratings, far behind WDOK, our closet competitor. So it would be our first target. WDOK also had long-standing, very funny, popular Ted Hallaman in morning drive. If we were ever going to beat WDOK, it would have to begin in the morning. At that time, "Tall Ted" had been regarded by his peers, and more important, by his audience, as a Cleveland morning fixture for over thirty years. Ted had worked at WQAL for six years with giant morning-drive ratings before departing for WDOK, taking the ratings with him. He was a well-established winner in the "Lite Rock" format. Ted left WQAL for WDOK/102FM in 1980. I can still hear Tony Ocepek's voice asking me that morning at the Marriott, "How long do you think it will take to catch WDOK and beat Ted Hallaman?" My quick response was, "If you promote me and tell Cleveland I'm back on morning radio, less than two years."

That, to be honest, was improbable. But I really wanted to make it happen.

If WQAL was going to become the city's community leader and beat WDOK at the same time, it would take a lot of hard work. I would have to devote twelve-hour days at the radio station and commit to long evening hours for personal appear-

ances. But my instincts assured me I could bring the right people to the table and could help deliver results both in exposure
and revenue. I had accomplished that in the past and felt comfortable in assuring them I could do it again.

CHAPTER 21

Tune in to Morrow Tomorrow

Walt and Tony indicated that their plan was to spend more than $250,000 on television, billboards, and bus boards in our first year, and much of that would be on the new morning show. They kept their word. On New Year's Day, 1985, the day before I went on the air, WQAL ran a full-page ad in *The Plain Dealer* that featured my picture and the line: *Tune in To-Morrow To-morrow, on the all new WQAL 104.1 FM.*

That phrase, along with my picture, appeared on almost every bus billboard throughout the Greater Cleveland area. It was also strategically placed on billboards on the heavily traveled expressways: I-480, I-77, I-271, I-71, and I-90. You couldn't miss the announcements proclaiming that Larry Morrow was now on WQAL.

My first day on WQAL was the first Monday of the New Year, 1985. When you opened your morning *Plain Dealer* that day, there was another full-page ad: *Tune in Today, To-Morrow on the all new WQAL 104.1 FM.* My shift began at 5:30 a.m. Just as I opened the microphone and began to speak, to my surprise, Walt Tiburski greeted me with a hot, steaming cup of coffee and said, on air, "Larry, here I am, all these years removed from WIXY 1260; I was your intern then and brought you coffee every morning just as you hit the air. And now, here I am, the owner of WQAL, still bringing you coffee just before you go on the air." He had also bet me that I would not make it through the first hour without mentioning the call letters of my last radio station, WERE.

Much to my dismay, Walt won the bet. Five minutes into my show, I said, "Good morning Cleveland; I'm Larry Morrow on the all new WQAL. I'll be with you here on WERE until 10 a.m." When you're nervous, and I sure was, you tend to remember your last radio station more than the present one. I owed Walt breakfast, which I bought later that morning as we celebrated our new life together.

UPHOLDING LEGACIES

Had we not known better, we would have thought Joe Zingale was sitting at his table that morning at the Marriott peering into the future.

I have never believed in crystal balls, but in this case Joe was right. His comment to Walt and Tony during our breakfast meeting that morning would be a harbinger of things to come. We started getting ratings that not only supported our vision but brought new energy and idealism. Together we would validate the original design for WQAL.

Within a relatively short span of eighteen months, supported by over a quarter of a million dollars in advertising and very long days and nights, WQAL's morning show had come from relative obscurity to the number two–rated morning show in Cleveland and just three-tenths of a point behind the very popular Jeff and Flash at number one–rated WMMS.

We struck quickly. Beating WDOK's morning show appeared to be an insurmountable hurdle, but thanks to a prolonged advertising blitz and sticking to our game plan, we pulled it off. Rising to the top so quickly had enlarged my thinking and it sparked new excitement at WQAL far beyond anyone's expectations. In response to our ratings, WDOK was forced to make a change in its morning drive.

At this point in my life, I was unsure what was ahead.

Most of my workdays started with relative calm—up at 2:45 a.m., arrive at our beautiful studios on the eighteenth floor of the legendary Keith Building on 17th and Euclid Avenue by 4:30 a.m., read five newspapers, and hit the air at 5:30 a.m. Following my air shift at 10 a.m., the frenzy began: meetings with Walt and Tony about what needed to be done with programming and personal appearances, and special meetings with leaders in the community.

Walt was emphatic about building the identity of WQAL and my association with it. He protected my reputation like a treasure and wanted to use it to WQAL's advantage. It was critical that people no longer associate me with WIXY, 3WE, or WERE radio. When it came time for me to make appearances, Walt wanted to be assured that whenever my name appeared anywhere, WQAL would be right next to it: WQAL's Larry Morrow or Larry Morrow/WQAL. At any and all of my appearances, the two were never to be separated.

I distinctly remember a popular real estate company using my name to promote my appearance at one of its large functions. Walt caught one of the promotional pieces for the event with my name as master of ceremonies without the WQAL call letters. Walt called them immediately and said, "Correct it now or Larry will not be there." They corrected the flyer and I appeared at the event. To ensure that his policy was enforced, Walt designed a contract for every appearance.

Because of the popularity of WQAL, I found myself in demand for commercials, speaking engagements promoting Cleveland as Moses Cleaveland, and charitable events. Occasionally, Mayor Voinovich or one of the leaders in our community would ask me to wear my Moses Cleaveland period costume to special events where they had invited a small group of visiting business people or mayors from around America. Sometimes the dinners were on a small yacht near Shooters night club. Following dinner, I would give the history of our great city while dressed as Moses Cleaveland.

WQAL'S SPLIT PERSONALITY

WQAL was an easy listening ("elevator music") format going nose-to-nose with the rating bell-ringers in Cleveland radio. Soon after we had made our initial impact, WQAL made national headlines in radio publications as a result of its swift rise to the top. From our original meeting, Walt, Tony, and I designed a carefully balanced blend of talk and music in the morning and intuitively knew it would work. We knew we were going against the grain, ignoring some easy-listing rules that had made the format a national success.

Owners, general mangers, and program directors around America marveled at what WQAL had accomplished so quickly. Walt was invited to national easy listening seminars, radio group meetings, and roundtable discussions to speak about our success. He brought me along to talk about our ground-breaking morning show. We spoke about how we had carefully infiltrated our market with our newly designed morning drive template. We also knew we had carefully sculpted something exciting and radically different for our market. In our seminars with major-market radio stations across America, Walt Tiburski issued a warning, "It would be dangerous for other stations to use the WQAL template. What made us different were talented radio people who knew and understood the marketplace."

He also cautioned them that Cleveland was experiencing a turnaround, and that I had been in the center of numerous community activities and popular civic affairs that brought tremendous attention to WQAL: from CEOs of Fortune 500 companies, to heads of entertainment venues, to interviews with the president of the United States. That's what we felt Clevelanders wanted to hear, and we were able to bring it to them. Walt concluded, "Unless you can pull off that kind of community entertainment and commitment, you had better think twice about changing."

We were setting an explosive pace for our new morning

format and rest-of-the-day-programming. To the easy listening national formats, although dangerous, Walt and Tony had not only defeated a contemporary foe in a major market, they climbed the ratings ladder quickly and had championed a new art form.

DR. DIGIT PAVES THE WAY

We were also blessed with men and women from sales, promotions, and programming who would dramatically change the way WQAL was viewed in our community. First and foremost Walt and Tony went after Mark Biviano, who had a fierce reputation as a tough task master and a tremendous sales record. He was currently working for WGAR. The hiring of Mark would guarantee a prolonged shelf life for WQAL. Mark had an unusual approach to sales and programming. He was also an intellectual whose thought patterns paralleled those of people who understood quantum physics, rather than radio. Mark had a solid grasp on the behaviors of salespeople and radio performers. Even more important was his ability to understand how the buyer made decisions and to persuade them to put their faith in commercials on his radio station.

By May 1986, Walt had surrendered his GM title to Mark, whom the entire WQAL staff referred to "The Biv." I grew close to Mark and to this day refer to him as "Brother Biv." We all benefited from Mark's wisdom. He had sayings that to this day I remember and quote from time-to-time:

Trying to make this happen is like trying to nail Jell-O to a tree.

We have only three ways to look at a problem: It's fixable, worth fixing. It's fixable, not worth fixing. It's not fixable. Get it fixed!

You can't un-ring a bell.

I will decipher the Arbitron ratings, then Dr. Digit will make his report to the staff.

This last Biv-ism was a reference to Mark's ability to dissect the possible gains, losses, and flaws in the Arbitron ratings book. If there were any noticeable shortcomings in any day-part of WQAL, he knew the strategy to right the ship. To my knowledge, Mark was seldom wrong. He was also a wordsmith and lexicon expert. If he ever heard an announcer or a salesperson make any kind of grammatical error, he would correct them on the spot. I was his favorite target because he listened on his way in to work in the morning. I was an English major, so I believed I knew as much about the presentation of words and phrases as anyone.

One day Mark walked into my studio and said, "Duker, 10:03 in my office." That phrase, 10:03, was a reference to the two of us getting together immediately following my air shift. We met almost daily. We would then thrash out anything he thought needed discussion. It could be anything from an interview he liked to a discussion with a listener that he didn't like. We rarely disagreed.

There was one occasion when Mark said, "Duker, I'd like to talk about your interview with the owner of the Cleveland Browns, Art Modell, this morning at 7:20 a.m. I'm sure you know a prepositional phrase consists of either a noun or a pronoun and any modifiers of the object." "Yes, I do," I responded. "Well, this morning, you used a noun instead of a pronoun."

I began laughing uncontrollably and said, "Biv, you need to get a life." Even today, some twenty-five years later, when Mark and I get together, we both laugh at those little nuances that made him unique and all of the announcers better. Mark's standards may have appeared overly rigid, but he strongly condemned certain behaviors, and incorrect grammar was one of them.

Mark imposed discipline on all of us as if we were his children, and he made us take responsibility for all of our actions. Additionally, Mark would not stand for any division within its ranks. He respectfully demanded that all departments within the radio station work in sync with each other, like a finely tuned Swiss watch.

During one of our management meetings, which consisted of the sales manager, promotions director, and me, Mark noted something rather serious had fallen through the cracks.

"Look team," he said, "we have more to fear from inside inefficiency than we do from outside competition. Get it fixed." His brand of wisdom kept WQAL razor sharp. Coming from the Marines, the one thing I learned was to trust your leader. So when you were told to do something, you just did it because you knew at one time or another, your leader had experienced it.

Mark made sacrifices many of the staff did not see, but I did. His transparency elevated people's expectations. It was obvious to all that he was driven to excellence and was absorbed in his work. Tony and Walt brought him in for that very reason. For me, it was leadership to be admired. Mark's greatest asset was his influence as a coach to all of us. Moving the ball forward was not good enough. Getting the ball in the end zone was the key. Nothing less, nothing more, nothing else.

Mark's toughest job was acting as intermediary for Walt and Tony, who consistently listened to their radio station. If they ever heard anything they didn't like, Mark got the call, many times on a Saturday evening or Sunday afternoon while he was home with friends or family. Mark was also a carbon copy of Walt and Tony. For the most part, and for me, working for them and with them on the management team was living a fairy tale. There was no room for anything but brilliance from the entire WQAL management staff. We all demanded that from ourselves and, ultimately, from each other.

WALT TIBURSKI FLEXES HIS PROMOTIONAL MUSCLES

It was 1985, and Walt knew he needed to dramatically change the culture in every area of the radio station, from sales, programming, and promotion, to the on-air staff. For the new culture to take hold in the same way as it had at WIXY, 3WE, and WMMS, Walt believed the station needed to own most, if not all, of the community and entertainment venues in Cleveland. Up to this point, there was an existing mindset at WQAL that as long as you could own one or two important venues in town, that was fine. But not according to Walt.

Over lunch one day, Walt explained his theory about owning the radio market. "Look, Larry, most radio stations in town believe that as long as they get their share of these important events, then that's okay. Well, it's not okay! Remember, here at WQAL, we run the table." The term "running the table" is used in the game of eight-ball billiards when a player knocks all the balls in the pockets before his or her opponent ever has a chance to shoot.

Walt explained that it would be critical to form close and trusted relationships with those who controlled the Home and Flower Show, the Front Row Theater, the Boat Show, the Air Show, and the popular Cleveland Grand Prix. Once the ownership of these events was secured, it would mean tremendous exposure for the radio station, and at the same time, be a revenue generator.

After close scrutiny of those who could help us, it became apparent that Walt, Tony, Mark, and I knew most of the decision-makers. We focused on a strategy to bring every one of these events home to WQAL. At the conclusion of my morning show at 10 a.m., Mark and I would hop in the car and head to see another community leader; it was almost a daily occurrence. If we needed Tony or Walt, we called on them. I would get the biggest thrill from Mark after we left a client and brought home the order. Once we were seated in the car, Mark would clinch his fist, alluding to victory, and say, "Cha-ching," referring to having taken an account away from another radio station. To me it was a game of chess. You maneuver your opponent's king into a check from which it cannot escape, thus bringing the game to a victorious conclusion. Checkmate, game over. It was a great feeling when this happened, and it happened often.

WQAL'S FIRST MAJOR PROMOTION: A CHILLY BEGINNING

In January 1985, our first month in business, WQAL had been playing an album by Richard Clayderman, a handsome, twenty-two-year-old French-born pianist. Richard had acquired musical acclaim at only twelve years old when he was accepted into the prestigious Paris Conservatoire de Music. At eighteen he had an international reputation as one of best-known and most successful pianists in the world, and by age twenty, he had six hit albums under his belt. His most recent album, *The Classic Touch*, and an earlier album, *The Music of Richard Clayderman*, had WQAL's audience humming. Walt decided to explore the possibility of bringing Clayderman to Cleveland. He contacted Clayderman's record company and struck a deal to bring him to Cleveland to perform at Larry Dolan's Front Row Theater on January 20, 1985.

Walt and Tony had only owned WQAL for a few weeks when this decision was made. This promotion would be WQAL's debut event, giving exposure to all of its personalities and setting the stage for what you could expect from Walt's and Tony's new radio station. We heavily promoted his appearance and, within a few weeks, half of the three thousand tickets had been sold.

On the day of the concert, Cleveland would experience the coldest day ever recorded. The high that day was -5, and the low reached -17 degrees. I borrowed this expression from Dick Goddard and mentioned on the air that day: "It was colder than the bottom of a beaver's belly."

Because of the weather, both the Front Row and all of us at WQAL had reason to worry. We were understandably afraid that when the concert began that only a handful of people would show up. Wow, were we surprised. When I drove into the Front Row Theater parking lot, only a few spaces were available. The concert was a sell-out. As master of ceremonies, I had the pleasure of introducing our entire WQAL broadcast staff, all smartly dressed in handsome black tuxedos. The evening was framed in such a way that the message sent to the Greater Cleveland mar-

ket was that WQAL's first public appearance was a harbinger
of greater things to come. It was not only our new look but our
new attitude. From that moment on we became broadcast and
entertainment partners with Larry Dolan and his popular Front
Row Theater.

OWNING IT ALL

Within the first two years of working together, we owned every important entertainment and community venue in Greater
Cleveland; 104.1 was a promotional machine. WQAL's call letters were everywhere: on billboards, bus boards, and television.
All of our WQAL personalities were on stage representing our
radio station at almost every venue. Some of the events drew
enormous crowds. The annual Christmas tree lighting ceremony
drew more than 100,000, as did the Cleveland Orchestra's annual fourth of July free concert at Public Square. WQAL did not
sponsor these events, but I was honored to host them for many
years, which brought additional acclaim to WQAL.

In the mid-eighties, Channel 3 began to carry the Annual
Cleveland Christmas Tree-Lighting Ceremony on television. Up
to that point, I had acted alone as master of ceremonies. Now
I would share the responsibilities with Jim Donovan, sports di-
rector of Channel 3. The ceremony is always held at dusk on the
Friday evening following Thanksgiving. Santa Claus shared the
stage with the mayor and, together, they would pull a lever and
magically illuminate the 100,000 lights decorating the trees on
Public Square, down Euclid Avenue, and all the way to East 9th
Street.

Snow can be very pretty, especially around that time of year.
It can also be a curse. On Thanksgiving Day, a countywide winter storm of gargantuan proportions draped a thick blanket of
snow throughout Greater Cleveland. The temperature had also
dipped into the teens. Public Square looked just like the setting of the 1983 holiday hit movie, *A Christmas Story,* for which

several scenes had been filmed at Higbee's department store on Public Square, in addition to the now-historic Ralphie's house in Tremont.

As the evening began, Jim Donovan hosted WKYC's segment on television and asked me to join him on stage at the southwest quadrant of Public Square. Following an on-stage interview with Jim, I had a ten-minute break before joining the weather forecaster, Shane Hollett, for a weather broadcast on the Moses Cleaveland quadrant where the ice rink was located. My young daughter Donna had accompanied me to the event. Since it was so cold, we decided to pass the next ten minutes by joining Shane in the Channel 3 trailer to warm up. We thought this was a perfect choice because the trailer was just outside the skating rink where the weather broadcast would be. When we arrived at the trailer, producers, cameramen, writers, and talent were running around in chaos as though it were rush hour in Hong Kong.

Although there was a security guard positioned outside the door of the trailer, the policy was last person out, make sure the trailer door is locked. At some point while the three of us were inside, the last person out locked the door and inadvertently took the key. In other words, we were now locked in but didn't know it . . . yet. "Shane and Larry, you're on in three minutes," the producer called out for our segment. Shane and I tried to go out the door. It was then that we discovered we were locked in. We pounded on the window and got the attention of the police officer who was guarding the door. We frantically motioned to him that the door was locked. He then tried to open the door and, with a puzzled look on his face, threw his hands up in the air and yelled to us, "It's locked!" Not only could we not get out, he couldn't get in to help us get out.

The only option was to exit through a small window, similar to the size you would find on a school bus. At this point we had no choice, so this was how we made our quick exit. Shane climbed out first so he could help my daughter with her landing.

I climbed out last. The three of us were laughing as we stood in four inches of slush.

Shane was smart; he had galoshes on. Donna was more fashion-conscious and had opted for designer heels. As for me, I was plain stupid. I was wearing Gucci loafers, which meant that on landing, the force created a "slush tsunami" that not only covered my shoes but soaked my pants up above my ankles. My daughter is diminutive and slender, so her feet not only became soaking wet, they were brutally cold. She could barely walk. Shane and I put smiles on our faces, did the weather, and no one knew of my sopping wet, dirty, and very cold feet. Once my part of the program was over, my daughter and I headed for Stouffer's Inn on the Square.

I asked Pete Dangerfield, Stouffer's general manager, if we could use a spare room to thaw out. Seeing the pathetic looks on our faces and our obviously wet feet was all Pete needed to offer a helping hand. He immediately made arrangements where we could thaw out and get warm. We took the elevator to the seventh floor, where Pete had sent up two cups of hot chocolate. As soon as we arrived in our room, we rushed to the tub and filled it with warm water. We rolled up our dripping pant legs and soaked our feet. At this point, our feet were so numb that the warm water created a painful stinging sensation. So there we were, father and daughter, sitting on the edge of the tub, ankle-deep in warm water, sipping hot chocolate, as we waited for the circulation to return to our nearly frost-bitten feet. If we had closed our eyes for a moment, we could have imagined ourselves in a warm palace spa.

CHAPTER 22

Some Memorable Interviews

THE LEGENDARY TONY BENNETT

One day after my morning show at WQAL, Walt called me in
the studio from his office and said, "I have a surprise for you."
When I walked into his office, there was Tony Bennett, American icon and popular singer from the '50s and '60s, sitting with
Walt and Tony Ocepek. Because of WQAL's relationship with
the Front Row Theater, it was not unusual for talented performers to arrive unannounced at our radio station either before or
after their show.

As soon as I was introduced to Tony, I couldn't resist blurting
out, "Tony, many years ago, I, too, left my heart in San Francisco." To this day, "I Left My Heart in San Francisco" remains
Tony's signature song and a sentimental favorite of many.

As a kid growing up in Pontiac, I remember my mother and
father not only loving Tony Bennett's music but playing many
of his albums on our RCA high-fidelity record player. His talent
had a profound influence on my love for music.

Tony's career had suffered a downturn in the rock and roll era,
but he was in the midst of a resurgence in popularity, thanks to
several appearances on *The Tonight Show* with Johnny Carson.
WQAL wanted to be a part of his comeback and had arranged
a promotion around a few of his albums. After all, we were the
leading easy listening station in town and played his style of
music.

Walt had suggested to Tony that if he had time, I would sit down and do an impromptu interview with him. Even though I did not have proper time to plan the interview, Tony had been one of the leading musical entertainers of my youth, and I knew enough about him and his comeback to conduct a fun and informative interview, which I played back on my show the following morning. Tony was extremely engaging, and I discovered that during his downtime when nothing was happening, he had survived a near-fatal cocaine overdose.

He called on his two young sons, Danny and Dae, and told them, "Look, I'm lost here." His sons, who were also in the music business, took hold of their dad's career and began booking him in colleges and small clubs. His new audience of young adults, who had never been exposed to his chic approach to entertainment, had a tremendous appreciation for him and his style of music. At the same time, his new fans helped him shed his Las Vegas image.

During our interview, I discovered that Tony was a gifted painter, and his assortment of paintings was now getting tremendous recognition around the world. Tony released a book called *Tony Bennett in the Studio: a Life of Art and Music*, which became a bestseller among art books.

At the time of our interview, Tony was about to turn sixty years young. My final question to Tony Bennett was, "When do you plan to retire?" His candid response was an inspiration to me for the way I hope to live my life. "Larry, if you study the masters—Picasso, Jack Benny, and Fred Astaire—right up to the day they died, they were still performing."

THE LOVABLE ARNOLD PALMER

It was early 1985 when I received a call from Mark McCormick, founder and chairman of IMG (International Marketing Group), the world's largest sports, entertainment, and media company. Just a few months earlier, I had the privilege of introducing Mark at a function in downtown Cleveland. It was at this time that Mark indicated that Arnold Palmer, IMG's largest client at the time, would be coming to town. Since Mark was going to be out of the country, he asked if I would handle introducing Arnold at two private affairs that would be held near Put-in-Bay on South Bass Island, the potential location for a new golf course and country club. Because I had been an IMG client at one time, Mark knew of my passion for golf. He also knew what a thrill it would be for me to have the opportunity to spend the day with golf's most recognizable face.

On the day of Arnold's arrival, Mark had arranged for me to be picked up at the radio station in a limousine. We then made the trip to the Cuyahoga County airport, where I would meet Arnold and his design team. At the airport, there was a second limousine waiting for Arnold. It was very impressive for me to stand on the tarmac and watch Arnold fly his own private jet and land it perfectly, just like he did with so many wedge shots throughout his illustrious career. I was impressed with the identification on the tail of the plane that read "APN1," which stood for "Arnold Palmer Number One."

There are moments in your life that remain isolated in time and for me, this was one of them. When the plane came to a stop, the stairs came down, and I walked up to greet Arnold as he emerged from his plane. We took a few pictures together before heading out in our separate limousines to the site where the new golf course would be built.

During the day, I asked Arnold if he would give me a short golf lesson, which I would tape for my morning show. Arnold agreed, and everything went perfectly; the golf lesson was helpful and the engaging Arnold Palmer was just as you would imagine—kind and encouraging. That day I had a young, nervous intern shadow me for a college project. He would be responsible for operating the tape recorder for the interview.

At the end of the day, Arnold and his team went one way and I went another. Before we parted, we shook hands and Arnold thanked me for the well-thought-out introductions, and I thanked him for the golf lesson. It had been a long day; I had been up since 2:45 a.m., and it was now after 7 p.m. So, on my way back to the radio station, rather then spending the time listening to the tape of the interview, I slept in the limousine. I knew I would have plenty of time to listen to it the next morning as I prepared for my morning show.

The following morning, as I drove down I-480 to the radio station, I could hardly wait to arrive and listen to my taped golf lesson with Arnold. When I arrived and began preparing my show, I turned on the tape recorder to play back the interview. There are no words to describe the sense of loss and devastation I felt when I discovered a blank tape. I panicked. Regardless of how many times I hit the fast-forward button, the silence was deafening on both sides of the cassette tape. It became painfully obvious that while the intern had turned on the tape recorder, he had not hit the record button. It's an easy mistake to make; that's why you must always verify that both the play and record button have been activated. And, in this once-in-a-lifetime opportunity, they were not.

As I let out a very loud groan that must have sounded as though I were being tortured, I had an immediate flashback to the same sense of emptiness I had felt following my interview with Woody Hayes.

With my arms folded and head down on my desk, all I could think was, *How am I going to explain this to my morning audience, which was obviously waiting to hear about my day with Arnold Palmer?* I did my best to talk extensively about my incredible experience. It may have been sufficient for my audience, but for me, it was equivalent to hitting my drive out of bounds on the last hole of the Masters and missing an opportunity to take home the legendary green jacket. I placed the blame entirely on myself for not pushing down the record button. So the interview with Arnold Palmer was never heard, and the intern's mistake was never mentioned.

MY FIRST INTERVIEW WITH A
PRESIDENT OF THE UNITED STATES

Larry Dolan created the Front Row Speaker Series, which featured a Who's Who in American politics, news, and entertainment. Both Larry and Walt Tiburski felt it would help transform WQAL and put another rung in the staying-out-in-front ladder.

The arrangement had me introducing every speaker, which would not only be a building block for WQAL but another defining role in my broadcast career. The Front Row Speaker Series celebrities had a clause in their contract that called for them to be interviewed by me several weeks before their appearance to promote the event. It was a wonderful arrangement that gave both of us great exposure to the Greater Cleveland audience.

To kick off the Speaker Series, Larry had arranged for the thirty-ninth president of the United States, Jimmy Carter, to come and speak at the Front Row. Not only would I introduce him, but Larry had arranged for me to interview him as well. The former president and I had a friendly conversation that lasted over twenty minutes. When I asked him what he would consider the centerpiece of his time in office, he responded with the Camp David Accord between Israel and Egypt in 1978. The leaders signing the agreement, Israeli prime minister Menachem Begin and Egyptian president Anwar Sadat, would share the Nobel Prize for bringing peace to that part of the world.

I was impressed by his charisma when he lovingly referred to his close relationship with his wife, Rosalyn, and close friend, President Sadat, who had been assassinated on October 6, 1981, while watching a military parade. His ability to sincerely engage in our short conversation made me feel like we were having a fireside chat.

The interview with President Carter was my very first with a U.S. president. While I had introduced President Reagan in Cleveland, I did not interview him. My Carter interview was taped a month ahead of time so I could play short snippets on my Q104 morning show to promote his appearance. At the end of our interview, I asked President Carter if he followed sports. He said, "Yes, I do. I follow the Washington Redskins."

I then said, "Well, Mr. President, our Cleveland Browns are headed for the Super Bowl. If we beat the Denver Broncos on Sunday and Washington beats the New York Giants, it could be the Redskins against the Browns in the Super Bowl. Who do you like, Mr. President?" Acting just like a politician, he broke into a hearty, but friendly, laugh saying, "Larry, if you don't mind, I'm taking the Fifth."

On the morning the speaker was to arrive, I performed my morning show on site from the lobby of the Front Row Theater. I would leave my show at 8:30 a.m. and have breakfast with the speaker in Larry Dolan's office. Also present was the editor of *The Plain Dealer*. Larry's office was adjacent to the green room, which the speaker used as a dressing room. The green room was reminiscent of a classy VIP club, fashioned with plush, shag carpeting, a mirrored wall, and a bar. Featured throughout the room were sleek modern light fixtures highlighted with rich, deep-upholstered pieces. Everything was centered under a beautiful, opulent chandelier.

When we gathered to have breakfast in Larry Dolan's office, Larry would begin with this imperative phrase: "What is privately discussed at this breakfast table stays here at this table. Do we understand that?" In other words, what is talked about here stays here. Imagine that. The editor of the largest newspaper in the state of Ohio agreed to hold a secret rather than leak a story that would sell newspapers, damage the speaker's reputation, and betray Larry's trust. The same held true for me, who worked in an industry where ratings mean everything. We were told stories that, if leaked, would cause irreparable damage to national figures.

While we were having breakfast, many of the speakers would say, "Please don't repeat this, but . . ." I mostly remember Peter

Jennings, then ABC's evening anchor, telling stories about the famous Kennedy family that, to this day, I have not repeated. It was the same with former NBC anchor David Brinkley, then host of the Sunday morning NBC news program *This Week with David Brinkley*. David told us a story that, if it ever got out, would certainly have damaged the reputation of an illustrious and celebrated popular network television news anchor. That story, to this day, has remained in Larry Dolan's office. Sadly, with the communication explosion we all experience today, this kind of "do not tell" integrity would probably not be possible.

MY 20-20 VISION OF ONE OF THE BEST

Of all the speakers, from President Carter, Peter Jennings, Bryant Gumbel, and many others, the most memorable was Barbara Walters.

I was in the green room waiting for Barbara to arrive when, all of the sudden, the door swung open and there she was. She appeared bigger than life to me. Barbara looked more striking than I remember her on her ABC specials. She briskly walked up to me, gave me a firm handshake, and said, "Hi Larry, I'll be with you in a minute, but I have to call my office in New York first." She walked just a few feet away, spoke briefly with her secretary and returned with, "Okay, Larry, tell me everything about yourself, then we can discuss anything you need to know about me in your introductory remarks." Barbara was petite, five-foot-four at best. She was meticulously dressed in a sharp red-and-black two-piece business suit. Her skirt rested at knee length.

The one thing I remembered about Barbara was that she had once played a Playboy bunny in an undercover assignment for ABC. So her shapely figure, her beautiful face, and her engaging smile that would melt any man's heart were part of her Playboy package and were not disappointing on that day. Barbara was all of her trusted and venerable self. Barbara's manner was so captivating that after fifteen minutes together, I felt like we were old friends who had just spent an hour catching up, as opposed to just getting to know each other.

The time had arrived for me to move to the podium, which was in the center of the circular stage of the Front Row. The sold-out crowd was excitedly waiting to see Barbara. After a few introductory remarks, it came time for me say, "Ladies and gentlemen, from ABC News, please give Miss Barbara Walters a warm Cleveland welcome." The spotlight immediately grabbed Barbara as she slowly began walking down the fifty-foot aisle. She stopped often to touch many hands before stepping onto the stage. Of all the celebrities I have had the pleasure of introducing and spending time with, those who stand out the most as being the type of person you could be friends with include President Reagan, President George H. W. Bush, Telly Savalas, David Brinkley, Don Rickles, and Barbara Walters. They all left such a strong, lasting, and favorable impression, that I would hope those whom I've met along the way would feel the same about me.

FUNNY MAN DON RICKLES GOES AFTER ME

I had always been a big fan of Don Rickles. When Larry Dolan asked me to introduce him at the Front Row Theater, I gladly accepted. I not only wanted to meet him, but I was extremely excited to interview him before the show. The evening of the engagement, I took Rosary with me because she liked him as well. She also said, "Whatever you do, do not have us sit in the front row."

The reason for Rosary's concern was that Don loves to walk the stage and destroy everyone in the front row, so I asked Larry if we could sit in the second row. He agreed.

As always, I had deeply prepared for the interview. When I sat across the table from Don Rickles in the Front Row green room to begin the interview, he was exactly like you see him on television or in night clubs. He said, "Okay, Lar', let's do it."

I then laid three pages of notes in front of me on the areas I wanted to cover. I began the interview and said, "I'm sitting here with Don Rickles, one of the funniest men of the planet."

He grabbed all my notes and said, "What's this? Are these your notes for the interview?" Ripping up all my research, he said, "Okay, now we can talk."

Somehow, just the way he said it and did it, to me, was a high form of flattery. I began to laugh. Even if you have listened to me with semi-regularity over the years or have seen me on television or in person, you know I love laughter. There is a huge difference between the words "humble" and "humiliation." This interview exemplified both. I was humbled before him as he totally humiliated me.

It's a well-known fact that I have been blessed with a nose that is more distinctive than most. Well, that's where he started. He said, "What the hell happened to you? When you were born, did the doctor pull you out by the nose? That's the ugliest nose I have ever seen on anyone." He then politely apologized. In his typical demeaning but very funny way, and with his voice slow and apologetic, said, "I'm sorry Larry, that wasn't very nice of me to say that. Actually you would have been better off had you been born without a nose."

Even though I was being hammered with heavy blows from Don Rickles, it was all done in fun. Not for one second was I personally offended. A little embarrassed maybe, but not belittled or put down.

Following my introduction of Don, he went after everyone in the front row. He circled the Front Row stage and hit about fifteen people with insults. Now, before I relate this story, Don Rickles is Jewish and loves to pick on his own and gladly tells you that. He walked right up to a woman sitting in the front row and said, "You're Jewish, aren't you? You know how I know that? It's 85 degrees in here, lady, and you're sitting here with a mink coat on. Take it off." She sheepishly did, and all three thousand in attendance roared with laughter.

LEGENDS: SID CAESAR AND MILTON BERLE

In the early '50s families gathered in their living rooms to watch television network news shows and comedies, such as the very popular Lucille Ball in *I Love Lucy* and Danny Thomas in *Make Room for Daddy*. On the other hand, weekends were reserved for variety shows, such as Ed Sullivan's *Toast of the Town*, Sid Caesar's *Your Show of Shows*, and Milton Berle's *Texico Star Theatre*.

Out of all the television stars in the early '50s, and there were an abundance of them, two distinct figures began to emerge and were given credit for essentially popularizing television in America. I was just barely into my teens when my parents bought their first RCA black-and-white television set. I can still remember hearing my mother say, "Uncle Miltie's on tonight." We couldn't wait to take our places on the floor, sitting in front of the television, waiting for Milton Berle and his cast of characters. At one time during the '50s, Milton was the highest paid performer in America. He was often called "Mr. Television."

You can imagine the thrill I had when Walt Tiburski informed me that Milton Berle, Sid Caesar, and Danny Thomas were coming to the Front Row Theater to perform for one night and I would have exclusive rights to interview them on my morning show. The tour was called "Legends." A day before the Legends' Cleveland appearance, Larry Dolan gave me their flight information, which included the time of their arrival at Cleveland Hopkins International Airport. With that information in hand, I asked my audience to go to the airport and give them a warm and exciting Cleveland welcome.

The following morning, Milton Berle and Sid Caesar arrived at my WQAL studio at 8 a.m. for our live, one-hour interview. The two legendary giants had me so excited that I could hardly wait for the interview to begin. When I shook hands with the two of them, I can remember having sweaty palms. I asked where Danny Thomas was, and they said he was otherwise engaged and not coming. Milton and Sid went on to say how profoundly grateful they were for the affectionate reception by one thousand people who greeted them at the airport. They were sincerely touched.

As we sat down for the interview, Milton complained that our air conditioner was a little too cold and asked that I turn it off. That mild demand turned out to be a defining moment in our get together. A few minutes later, as we were getting levels on their voices, Milton broke into an imperative demand, raised his voice a little, looked me straight in the eyes and said, "Didn't I ask you to turn off the air conditioner?"

I was puzzled by the tone of his voice. It was almost as if a switch had gone off, but it surely wasn't the one that operated the air conditioner. I immediately responded, "Yes, and I'm sure the engineer is going to turn it off." Milton then said, "Now I'm telling you to go turn off the *#"&@<% air conditioner!"

Like anyone, you tend to withdraw when people talk to you like that, but in this case, I quickly got up, hurried to the engineer's office and asked him where the air conditioner switch was located. He said, "You can't touch that Larry, because it will shut off the air through out the entire radio station and we'll roast."

I said, "If it doesn't get turned off, my interview with Milton Berle and Sid Caesar will go up in smoke. At this moment, nothing in this radio station is more important than that switch being turned off." He took me to the electrical box, showed me the lever, and I promptly turned it off. When I returned to my studio, Milton graciously thanked me.

During the interview, I asked the two of them, "What's the main difference between a comic and a comedian?"

Sid Caesar responded first. "Larry, comedians, like Bill Cosby, write their material and make jokes throughout their performances." Milton then explained the comic piece. "Sid Caesar and I are comics, meaning we are just plain funny. We find everything funny and can respond to anything with a funny remark."

So I quickly challenged Milton Berle by saying, "Okay, Uncle Miltie, make me laugh."

He retorted with, "How old are you?"

"I just turned fifty."

"I have ties older than you," he replied. Just like all the early years of watching him in my living room, I nearly fell off my chair in laughter. The rest of the interview was filled with listener calls and a preview of their upcoming evening performance at the Front Row.

I thanked the two of them for serving a cause greater than themselves, meaning television. They had created a mosaic of a great life. I concluded the interview by saying, "Milton Berle and Sid Caesar, I am speaking for our entire Greater Cleveland community. We will be eternally grateful for the thousands of hours you have filled our lives with your humor that enabled us to leave our daily struggles behind. It is so good to laugh, and the two of you made us laugh often for over forty years."

By the end of our hour together, the temperature in the studio, and the rest of the eighteenth floor of the Keith Building, had to be in the 90s. No sweat though, because that one hour with Milton Berle and Sid Caesar, who happened to be two of the funniest men on the planet, turned out to be one of the most rewarding times in my broadcast career.

GEORGE VOINOVICH

One morning in 1987, seven years into the Voinovich administration, I had Bill Reidy, Cleveland's finance director and a Leadership Cleveland classmate, on my morning show to announce that Cleveland had emerged from default and our bond rating had been restored.

Due to my close relationships with the Cleveland turnaround team, including Mayor Voinovich, whenever major announcements came along, many times they were announced on my WQAL morning show. Mayor Voinovich listened to my show every morning, and whenever something was going on in our market that needed clarification or promotion, I would call him at home. I also knew his wife, Janet, well because we had both volunteered at our Ronald McDonald House and had seen each other on many occasions.

One memorable and very funny moment came when I needed to speak to George on the air. I called him at home, and when Janet picked up the phone, she said while on the air, "Larry, George is in the shower."

I found Janet's comment rather comical and I responded, "Well, when he gets out, please have him call me."

Janet said, "No, let me get him because he won't want to miss your call."

The next thing I heard was, "Good Morning, Mr. Cleveland. How are you?"

"George, are you in the shower, because I can hear the water running?"

With laughter in his voice, he responded with, "Yes, I am!" George and I continued our conversation with him covered in a wet towel. I don't remember the content of our short conversation, but I do remember telling my audience with tongue firmly in cheek as I chuckled, "Shame on all of you for the visible picture you have of our celebrated mayor."

CHAPTER 23

From the Cleveland Orchestra to Madonna

THE BEGINNING OF A CLEVELAND ORCHESTRA TRADITION

In the summer of 1985, I received a call from Ruth Miller, a major player in Cleveland's turnaround. Ruth was also the sister of Al Ratner, the co-chairman of Forest City Enterprises, who owned the Terminal Tower. Ruth had come up with a brilliant, innovative idea to promote the Terminal Tower, the City of Cleveland, and the world-renowned Cleveland Orchestra. Ruth's idea was to hold a free concert in front of the Terminal Tower. She wanted to promote not only Cleveland as an entertainment mecca but to give the citizens of the seven-county area an opportunity to see the orchestra perform live over the most popular holiday weekend of the summer. This free concert would be a brand new cultural event for downtown Cleveland and the Cleveland Orchestra. I was thrilled and honored when Ruth asked me if I would act as master of ceremonies for what would soon become a legendary event. The magnitude of this occasion not only stirred my heart, but once again would put me in the center of an event that further propelled Cleveland's turnaround.

Our first concert was a smashing success. Christoph von Dohnányi was the Cleveland Orchestra's sixth conductor in the history of the orchestra. Under Dohnányi, the orchestra was lovingly called "The Best Band in the Land." That title was given to them because the experts felt no other American orchestra could compete with them. His name was tricky to pronounce. His last name actually sounded like "Dock-nyanni." It took me a few days of practice to make sure I got it right. Our first concert drew over 100,000 people on the square. The following nine concerts would be led by resident conductor, Jahja Ling (pronounced Yak Yah), who had a tremendous national reputation. In addition to acting as master of ceremonies for the event, I became close friends with Jahja Ling, which added to the thrill of being part of the Cleveland Orchestra.

CLEVELAND'S CHRISTMAS PARADE

The Friday following Thanksgiving Day always turned out to be my longest work day of the year: rise at 2:45 a.m.; off to my WQAL morning show from 5:30 to 10 a.m.; then get in position for the annual Christmas Day Parade by 1 p.m. I always rode on the Higbee's float with Mr. Jing-a-Ling, a popular local Christmas character. Following the three-hour parade, I would hurry home, take a nap, and get back downtown by 5 p.m. to act as master of ceremonies for Cleveland's annual Christmas tree lighting ceremony, which I had proudly hosted for over twenty-five years.

WQAL was so visible, we even sponsored a Concorde fly-over at Burke Lakefront Airport during the National Air Show and gave away a home free at the popular Home and Flower Show.

All these well-attended events were so community-targeted for WQAL that the exposure not only influenced ratings, it helped to extend our community presence with those who mattered most: advertising agencies, the political base in Cleveland, and the Cleveland listeners. WQAL had become a reliable and powerful force in Greater Cleveland. We had so tipped the scales in our favor that the radio playing field in Greater Cleveland was no longer level. It was as if Tony and Walt had sneaked into a laboratory, mixed up a concoction of their successful radio past, blended it all together, and produced a chemical reaction that would cause a paradigm shift in the market, not seen since WIXY and WMMS.

MARY, MARY

Mary Strassmeyer was Cleveland's much-loved gossip columnist for *The Plain Dealer* for thirty-seven years. Her column was called "Mary, Mary," in which she peeked into our private and public lives on a daily basis. I truly believed that when Clevelanders woke to the beginning of a new day, many would head for their mailbox and grab their early morning *Plain Dealer*. Even before looking at the front page headlines, they would go directly to Mary's column to see *who* was doing what to whom and where; she was that interesting and powerful.

Like many business and media people in Cleveland, I had a very special relationship with Mary Strassmeyer. There were a significant number of people in Mary's trusted network to whom she would go to for a scoop. After all, Mary only printed exclusive stories. When it came to radio, I was one of her confidants. She always protected her sources and would never divulge where the scoop came from. When I signed my contact with WQAL, we wanted to give Mary Strassmeyer the exclusive, but did not want the story released until a certain date. In lieu of the exclusive scoop, Mary honored our request and released the story just before Christmas, which was also timed perfectly for our advertising campaign that announced my return to radio. Not only had I made the move to FM radio, I would be the new morning man at WQAL.

Mary was also a humorist. She loved to laugh, often at herself. One very memorable outing with Mary took place at Cleveland's annual Grand Prix weekend.

On the Saturday before the nationally televised event from Burke Lakefront airport, Jim Foster, the owner and promoter of the event, featured an annual celebrity version of the Cleveland Grand Prix race. I was thrilled and honored each year to be chosen as one of the celebrities.

The cars used for the celebrity race were smaller and lighter versions of the actual Grand Prix cars and they had governors on them, meaning they were held to under 20 mph. Each competing team was made up of two celebrities sharing a car in a relay race. At the sound of the starting gun, the first person on each team drove the car once around the track, completing one leg of the relay route. The exchange point, as it is called, was located back at the starting line, where the first driver would stop and jump out of the car as quickly as possible to allow the second driver to hop in, and speed around the track to the finish line.

The key to winning the celebrity Grand Prix race was minimizing the change-over time between the drivers at the exchange point; a very smooth and quick transition from one person to the next is critical to the outcome. As with all relays, the first team to cross the finish line won the bragging rights for the fastest team and car, along with a big trophy. In the 1986 celebrity race, fitness expert, popular TV 3 personality, and close friend Kim Scott and I teamed up and won the race. The following year, Mary Strassmeyer and I decided to partner and became "Team Mary and Larry."

The hot July sun was shining brightly over the track at Burke Lakefront Airport that Saturday afternoon, the day of the race. It was Mary's decision to begin the race for our team. When she climbed into the car, she jokingly commented, "Larry, this is a really tight fit. I hope I'll be able to get out." Could this be an omen? I can still see all the celebrity cars lined up in a row, waiting to hear that familiar phrase, "On your mark; get set . . ." There was Mary, helmet firmly fastened, both hands on the wheel, a big smile on her face and waiting to push the pedal to the metal. The gun sounded, signaling the start of the race, and Mary was off. She did so well, that when she came back to the starting point, she was in the lead. Now for the critical point: Mary out and Larry in. As hard as Mary tried, she couldn't get out of the car. Suffice it to say, the circumference of Mary's girth was a little larger than the cockpit of the car.

The competitive side of me took a quick look around and discovered that not only had Mary's lead quickly eroded, but the transitions of the other teams had gone smoothly. Our team was losing precious moments and needed a rescue plan. At that point, Mary began to laugh uncontrollably and so did I.

We had just been unofficially removed from being a serious competitor to being a very funny side show, drowning in laughter. Several celebrities, who were laughing hysterically with us, and unfortunately, at us, gathered around to help. We joined forces and attempted to pry Mary out of the car by putting our arms around her and lifting her up. At that point, we assumed she would slide right out. Well, that was not the case.

What happened next caused everyone who could see to erupt in laughter. Both Mary and the car came right off the tarmac. So here we were, all holding on to Mary, who was still stuck in the car, both now dangling at least three feet off the ground. Mary was laughing so hard she had been rendered useless in our effort. Within several minutes we got her out. I got in and finished the race for us, in last place.

When I crossed the finish line, I was at least several minutes behind the last car but was greeted with the cheers and tears of laughter by all in attendance. There is an old adage in competition that says there are only two places: first and all the rest. This was one of those races when no one remembered who won, but all had a humorous story about the team who finished last.

THE TITANS MOVE ON

WQAL's corporate name was Win Communications. It had grown from one Cleveland radio station in 1985 to radio stations across America and Puerto Rico. Walt and Tony had built

WQAL into an enormously successful radio station, but the Win Communications conglomerate allowed them tremendous success, and it was time to get out and go their separate ways. Before the official announcement was released to the press, Walt and Tony called me into Walt's office and told me they had sold the company and would be leaving by the end of the year. One item that had to be in place before their leaving was my contract, which would expire at the end of 1989. Walt, Tony, and Mark Biviano negotiated a new, three-year contract to leave me in good stead with the new company, which was headquartered in New York City.

The announcement of their leaving was not welcome news for me. This would be the third time in my twenty-six-year career in Cleveland radio that I had joined a new radio station, watched it grow to great success only to have the owners sell and move on. This one wounded me, not because I would be left behind with another ownership change, but because together, we had built a community giant. Without their ownership guidance it might never be the same. There's an old feeling in radio that when a radio station is locally owned, it seldom loses.

For me WIXY, 3WE, and WQAL had all grown from a tender shoot to a giant oak in our community. All had been locally owned and operated, rising from almost nothingness to greatness. WQAL's new ownership would now come from a distance outside the area, rather than from within the Cleveland community. At each one of these radio stations, I had formed very close relationships with the owners and it pained me greatly when they moved on. Every time it happened, I too, picked up and left. I wanted this to be different. I loved WQAL and wanted to end my radio career at this radio station.

The new Win Communications brought new thinking to WQAL that started with the decision that the easy listening format was now outdated. There was also another inherent problem confronting WQAL from reaching its financial goals. Despite the fact we had great ratings, much of our audience was over fifty, and WQAL owned that segment of the audience. National advertising agencies had recently taken on a new approach to those in that older demographic. It's called the "McDonald's Theory."

The agencies believed that when you turn fifty, you no longer have to be told where to get a Big Mac, what car to buy, nor where to get the best deal on a new set of clothes. You have been doing this for so long you automatically go to where you have been before. So, in the final analysis, the agencies turned their clients' dollars away from stations across America who had an older demographic. What was so sad about that theory was that nothing could have been further from the truth; the over-fifty generation was a $7-billion group of people with more expendable income than any other. The winning formula we had established from 1985–90 was about to become a thing of the past.

As hard as we tried to convince the ad agencies their assessment of the over-fifty segment of our audience was incorrect, their decision had been made. Trying to persuade them otherwise was like trying to sell someone a new car with faulty brakes; it didn't work and we were forced out of the easy listening format. Even with the huge demographic WQAL possessed, there was no way to sugarcoat the existing problem. The new company believed extraordinary measures needed to be taken and the new WQAL would now be best suited by a Top 40 music format that would ultimately draw a younger audience.

The new goal at WQAL was to attract an eighteen- to fifty-four-year-old audience, with a straight-up focus on the thirty-four-year-old female. National program director Rick Torcasso was brought on to make the change in January 1990. Rick was more than a brilliant PD; he was an insightful vestige from a different era who understood how to reach the core audience.

Just a few years earlier, Rick had successfully launched the new Majic 105.7 and the return of John Lanigan from Florida. He had agreed that once the new contemporary sound was in place, he would move on. Since we had to keep any discussion of a change in format quiet and unobserved, there would be a swift, coordinated effort to put all elements of the music, commercials and promotional announcements on my computer at my home. When this clandestine effort was completed, we would copy everything from my computer and install it at the radio station.

The new Top 40 format was launched on Saturday, April 1, 1990 (April Fool's Day). It was called *WQAL Soft Hits*. What no one could have imagined was the phrase, *Soft Hits*, was about to become a disaster of our own making. The popular Kim Scott was hosting our afternoon drive-time segment and I was hosting mornings. The clever John Lanigan has the ability to drop a verbal bomb that echoes through the city as though it had been shouted from the top of the Terminal Tower. That is exactly what happened when John talked about our new *WQAL Soft Hits* format change.

As well as I can remember, and you're going to have to use your imagination here, John got on the air and said, "I can understand Kim Scott with Soft Hits, but not Larry Morrow." That "foolish" phrase could never be used again without hearing it the wrong way. John's comment got printed in *The Plain Dealer* and the entire radio market was aware of what was happening. Within 24-hours of having been tagged "dubious," our new slogan became *Q-104 plays all the hits from the '70s, '80s and today*.

So, in the final analysis, the popularity of John Lanigan's show brought both good news and bad news. The good news: John promoted our new format, which brought WQAL a tremendous amount of attention. The bad news: in radio circles, we became the laughing stock for a short period of time. Changing our slogan was both costly and embarrassing. Although billboards and advertising materials were printed up and ready to go, they now reside at the bottom of the landfill located at I-480, near I-77. The new format kicked off in the spring of 1990 and was an instant success. Thanks, John!

It was 1991 and changes continued to unravel. Mark Biviano and Kirk Bogus would also leave the station, which left me as the only remaining member of the original management team.

Once again, WQAL was going head-to-head against WDOK, which had already moved into a soft version of Top 40, playing mostly ballads. That meant I would be battling Trapper Jack, who had only been at 102.1 FM for a short time. Q-104's new owners, who purchased Win Communications, also hired Carolyn Carr, who was a well-established and talented female voice in Cleveland, to be my partner. The new partner arrangement was strange for me because, throughout my twenty-five years in Cleveland radio, I had always worked alone. This was an adjustment that was definitely going to take some getting used to. It was the new trend for radio and television that would soon catch on across America and continues to this day.

Following Rick's departure, Win Communications hired another nationally known star in Top 40 music formats, Dave Irvin, who would have complete control over all programming on WQAL. When Dave arrived in the summer of 1991, Carolyn and I had only worked together for a short time. Dave Irvin did not tell me at the time, but he had never liked the two of us together. He not only thought our relationship was bland at best, he felt there was not much in our on-air interaction that stuck to the bone.

At this time, there was a third voice being heard on my show and it belonged to Sally Spitz, who was doing traffic reports four times an hour. Dave firmly believed there was a magical interface between Sally and me during those traffic reports that the audience absolutely embraced. He loved the blend of our voices and believed our personalities mixed well. So, in September 1991, Carolyn left and my new partner became Sally Spitz. The new show was called *Larry and Sally in the Morning*, and it was a grand-slam home run.

On paper, the combination of Larry and Sally would have never worked. I was twenty years older. I was conservative in nature and Sally was liberal. I stayed away from controversy and judgment of music and people. On the other hand, Sally jumped in head first, and, in a friendly way, encouraged battle. After a short time together, Dave's idea of putting us together worked so well, the ratings climbed dramatically and the *Larry and Sally in the Morning* show was on its way.

As paradoxical as it may sound, what I liked most about Sally was her impish way of poking fun at me and all of my conservative habits; from the way I dressed, to the way I thought, to my manners. I was guarded about my family, my faith, and my grammar. Sally broke all the rules and barriers, and our audience loved her for that. And that's what made it work. We were so vastly different in every way that you could think of that our differences became our collective strengths.

CASEY KASEM: A ROCK LEGEND ENTERS MY STUDIO

September 1, 1995, was one the more memorable moments in Cleveland history because it was the opening of the Rock and Roll Hall of Fame. Almost every large media market had their popular radio stations represented and would be broadcasting their music and talk shows from the Rock Hall all day long. Also present for the opening ceremony were well-known rock and roll icons Dick Clark and Casey Kasem. Sally and I had decided that she would take her tape recorder, interview several of the well-known celebrities who were attending the opening, and bring the interviews back to the radio station for us to play on the air.

While Sally was chasing down celebrities, I had received a call from nationally known and highly regarded Cleveland civil rights lawyer Avery Friedman. I had not met Avery but had obviously known who he was. Avery was a very close friend of Casey Kasem's and asked me if I would like to interview him on my morning show. I told Avery we were just watching Casey on our television monitor, and I would love to have him in for an interview. In honor of the Rock Hall opening, Avery was taking Casey around to the radio and television stations for interviews. When Avery asked how much time I could dedicate to my interview with Casey, I replied, "One hour."

I was very excited about the opportunity to spend time with Casey Kasem because we shared several commonalities. Our line of ancestry was Middle Eastern. We both had been raised around the Detroit area and began our radio careers in the Motor City. I had been listening to Casey for over thirty years on his *American Top 40 Countdown* show. I had also seen him, as an actor, many times on *Quincy, Colombo,* and *Charlie's Angels,* as well as his annual appearance on the *Jerry Lewis Labor Day Telethon for Muscular Dystrophy.*

Ten minutes after Avery and I had spoken on the phone, he walked through my studio door with Casey. Although Casey was short in stature, he was a giant of a man. When our one-hour interview began, it was magic. Over a short period of sixty minutes, we had become friends and to this day are still close. I concluded the interview by congratulating Casey on his recent induction into the National Radio Hall of Fame in Chicago. Casey then said, "One day, you too, Larry, shall be inducted into the Radio Hall of Fame."

"From your lips to God's ears," I said. We chuckled, shook hands, and Casey was on his way.

A few weeks had passed and my daughter Diana and I were picking up a gift for my wife in the Citizens Building on the corner of East 9th Street and Euclid Avenue. As we were walking through the lobby, Avery and I ran into each other. I thanked him again for bringing Casey to my studio. I told Avery the interview with Casey was my most enjoyable radio interview ever. Avery went on to say that Casey felt the same. Avery also mentioned that our chance meeting must be destiny because, following my interview with Casey on the day of the Rock Hall Grand Opening, both he and Casey put the wheels in motion to get me nominated into the Radio Hall of Fame.

The following week I met Avery in his office, and he showed me the letter he had written to Bruce Dumont, executive director of the Radio Hall of Fame. The first sentence of his letter said how proud he was to submit my name for consideration and why I deserved nomination. Avery then said, "Larry, we're going to have to work very hard over the next several months to gather all the materials from your career, which have to then be submitted to an eighty-seven-member steering committee for your nomination to the National Radio Hall of Fame. Upon review of your broadcast materials, the steering committee will decide if you are worthy of nomination."

The nomination materials must include letters from Cleveland mayor Michael White, Governor George Voinovich, Cleveland Catholic Diocese bishop Anthony Michael Pilla, Casey Kasem, and several other distinguished members of the Cleveland community explaining why I deserved induction. It took Avery and me five months to pull all of the materials together. The requested materials had to cover my thirty-year body of work. The packet had to include a cassette tape containing a compilation of my radio career, as well as a supportive letter from the president of the Ohio Association of Broadcasters.

On February 29, 1996, just seven months after Avery, Casey, and I had met, Avery called me and asked me if I could stop by his office for a short visit and have lunch. It was not unusual for Avery's request because we had been working on the information for the steering committee for a long time. When I arrived at his office, Avery was sitting in his leather chair. With a big smile on his face, he said, "Larry, please sit down. I'd like to read you a letter.

The letter is dated February 27, 1996. It reads:

Dear Mr. Morrow:
I am pleased to inform you that you have been nominated for induction into the Radio Hall of Fame. You are one of five individuals who have been chosen for your distinguished

career in radio. Please forward your biography and a recent photo to us as soon as possible, for use in our national press release.

Avery got up from his chair, and we happily and gratefully embraced. Avery then mentioned that in Ohio radio history, I would be the *only* broadcaster to have ever been nominated to the Museum of Broadcast Communications, National Radio Hall of Fame. He went on to say that among the inductees are prestigious names like Edward R. Murrow, Paul Harvey, and Orson Welles.

The induction ceremony was scheduled for Sunday evening, October 27, 1996, at the Museum of Broadcast Communications in the Chicago Cultural Center. Avery and I were invited to attend. We flew out of Cleveland in the late afternoon the day of the event. Once we landed in Chicago, our taxi dropped us off at the entrance to the center, where several floodlights beamed upward and lit the sky, signaling an important event.

Other than one trip to England and the other to Vietnam, I had not traveled the world much, but this ninety-nine-year-old building stood out that evening as the *only* building in the nation's third-largest city. When we got out of our cab, a red carpet led to the main entrance to this awe-inspiring five-story building. At one time, the building was Chicago's official reception venue where the mayor welcomed presidents and royalty, diplomats, and community leaders. Looking up, you could see many levels, and each one was fit for a king. For our event, we walked up the grand staircase to the second-level lobby. When we reached the top of the stairs, our jaws dropped. The three-story lobby had arched Romanesque portal, bronze-framed doors and walls decorated with white, Carrara marble mosaics.

When we reached the ballroom, I could sense the excitement of what was going to be an exceptionally rewarding evening and a piece of my radio career that I would never forget. I was like a child on Christmas morning, bursting with anticipation to see what Santa Claus had left. I could hardly wait for the evening to begin because I knew how many important legendary radio broadcasters would be there, and I wanted to meet them.

Sitting at our table was Paul Harvey and his wife, Lynn "Angel" Harvey. Lynn, like her husband, Paul, would be inducted into the Hall of Fame the following year. Next to Paul and Lynn Harvey was a voice I had listened to almost all of my life as a youngster growing up in Detroit, Ernie Harwell, the voice of the Detroit Tigers. Next to Ernie was an old pal of his, Jack Buck, whose son, Joe Buck, is also a famous sports broadcaster. Jack Buck, like Ernie, was a lifetime sportscaster for the St. Louis Cardinals. Rounding off the sports giants at our table was the voice of the Chicago Cubs for thirty-one years, Jack Brickhouse. All these men were legendary in the world of baseball.

Next to Avery was Casey Kasem, who was master of ceremonies for the evening. The broadcast would be heard around America with a huge, live, orchestra-like radio program, something you would see in the 1930s and 1940s.

Seated on my left was a gentleman whose name I didn't recognize, so I introduced myself. "Hi, I'm Larry."

He replied "I'm Johnny. Nice to meet you." I then asked him why he was here. He said he was going to accept the award for Robert Weston Smith, a.k.a., "Wolfman Jack," the gravely voiced disc jockey who was going to be inducted posthumously.

Wolfman Jack broadcasted his shows from Mexico with over 500,000 watts of power, which covered the nation. To give you an idea on just how powerful his radio signal was, the largest radio signal in America is 50,000 watts. I asked Johnny about his association with Wolfman and he said that Wolfman Jack was one of the first DJs in the world to play one of the songs he had written. I said, "I'm a DJ, would I know any of your songs?" He then answered, "Maybe." He was so shy that I had to pull out of him every little tidbit. He said, "I wrote 'Poor Side of Town' and 'Secret Agent Man.'"

"Wait a minute. I've played those songs hundreds of times, but those songs were written by Johnny Rivers."

"That's me, I'm Johnny Rivers."

Without hesitation, I gently hit him on his arm and said, "You're Johnny Rivers, but, the program says John Henry Ramistella."

"That's my real name," Johnny said, "I didn't want to take any glow away from Wolfman Jack when I introduce him."

"How admirable," I said. I spent most of the evening talking with him about his career as a writer and performer.

Following this momentous event, Casey wanted to invite a few of his friends for an after-dinner wind-down. I suggested the Hotel Nikko, where Avery and I were staying. Avery and I thought it would provide an excellent setting for a small group of people to gather and look out over the Chicago River from the Ember Grille. Casey agreed and we all hopped in a few cabs and met at the Grille.

It was 11:30 p.m. when we arrived at the Hotel Nikko. There were seven of us sitting around a few tables. Casey, Avery, and I were sipping coffee and others had an evening cocktail. What made this little gathering so interesting to me was that I felt I was a living a dream. Sitting across from me and talking with Avery and Casey was actress June Allyson. I told her I had watched her in movies while growing up in Pontiac. I also shared with her how much I enjoyed her when she teamed up with James Stewart in *The Glenn Miller Story*. At one time, June was recognized as one of the top two most popular and beautiful women in the world. Grace Kelly was the other.

Seated next to me was another of Casey's friends. He knew I was in the entertainment business and told me he owned an advertising agency in Los Angeles. I asked him how he ended up in California. He began telling me his life story. I learned that, at one time, he had worked for ABC News in New York and was the creator of, as he called it, a little Friday evening television show hosted by Barbara Walters and Hugh Downs. That show was obviously *20/20*.

Seated on my left was another very popular man in the radio business, the current president of 760/WJR in Detroit. I felt as if I had been transported back to the mid-'70s and was starring in the television show *Fantasy Island*. I didn't want it to end. We all talked to the early hours of the morning and then went our separate ways. Lucky for Avery and me, we took the elevator home.

When we met for breakfast the next morning, Avery and I were swimming in reflective memories that only come once in a lifetime. I couldn't believe what had transpired the day and evening before. It was a twenty-four-hour dream I did not want to wake from.

MADONNA NEARLY RUINS MY IMAGE

In the winter of 1995, our new format was beginning to catch hold. Inside WQAL there was a growing concern regarding my label as an "easy listening" morning personality; how then might I be viewed to a relatively new contemporary Top 40 audience? Our general manager had a plan in mind to position Q-104 and me as young, hip, and contemporary. The strategy was to feature me in a television commercial that would be on the soft side of shocking, but remain clean and funny. He came to my office and showed me a television commercial that had been used in several other states to create success. The commercial was designed to draw attention to radio stations, like Q-104, which had changed formats. When I saw the commercial, I personally thought it was funny. My biggest question was, "How would my audience view me in this setting?"

I brought the television commercial home and invited my three daughters over to view it with Rosary and me. No one knew me better than my family, so their opinion would be the basis from which I would make my decision. After viewing the commercial with someone else playing my part, Rosary and one of my twin daughters thought it was humorous. My other two daughters felt the opposite. "Dad, do not do this. The Cleveland audience who knows you might think differently of you. Our biggest fear is they may lose their respect for you."

Since my family's vote was divided, I sought the opinion of a few close and trusted friends, both inside and outside the radio business. Most of my friends felt it would show Clevelanders my sense of humor. In my mind, the decision was now unanimous, and I decided to move forward on doing the television commercial. Ready or not, Cleveland, the explosion you're about to hear is Larry Morrow turning into Madonna!

We live by career choices and this was one I now felt comfortable with. I was not only ready to get back to contemporary radio, I wanted to position the morning show as an exciting ride to work for an adult-contemporary, younger audience.

The filming company was located in Albuquerque, New Mexico, so traveling to the southwestern part of America would be a welcome change in scenery from the cold, blustery Cleveland winter. When I arrived at my hotel, it was comforting for me to be surrounded by Native American décor, because along with being French, my father's heritage was Native American.

The following morning, I was picked up at my hotel in a limousine and taken directly to the studio to film the commercial. On pulling up to the studio, I couldn't believe the beautiful setting. We were snuggled in a quaint little area with New Mexico's mountains as a backdrop. The area is famous for skiing, as well as the annual international hot-air balloon races. Off in the distance was Albuquerque's highest mountain point, snow-covered Sandia Peak.

When I walked into the building, they ushered me directly to where the commercial would be shot. Under several strategically positioned lights was a kitchen, similar to what you would see in a Hollywood studio. The kitchen had a sink, overhead cupboards, an L-shaped countertop where I would stand for the filming, and a blender, which would be an important prop for the commercial. I was dressed in jeans and a blue T-shirt with huge, white Q-104 letters stretched across the front of the shirt.

The commercial began with me saying, "Hi, I'm Larry Morrow from the new Q-104." I announced that we had changed our format and this was the new music you would hear on Q-104. Each time I mentioned an artist's name, like Elton John, I would put their CD in the blender, which was filled with blue water so the viewing audience could see its contents. After mentioning four artists, I said, "We're even playing Madonna." I then added the Madonna CD, turned the blender on, took a sip of the mixture and said, "Here's to ya." I then grabbed my stomach as if I had a severe bellyache and said, "Wow, too much Madonna." An explosion occurred, and in the very next scene you saw me dressed from the waist up like Madonna, which included a white wig, corset, and her famous cone-bullet-bra. The tassels then began spinning out from the tip of the cone to the front of the viewer's television screen to the tune of a jingle singing the Q-104 jingle.

The filming of the thirty-second commercial was shot in two segments. Including the extensive prep, the first segment was actually two hours long.

For the opening twenty-five seconds, there were lighting adjustments for my face and make-up applications. We then broke for lunch.

Following our lunch break, we began prepping for the second segment, which contained the final five seconds. It took the make-up artist an additional two hours to prepare me to look like Madonna. After make-up, the white wig was applied and the final step was for me to climb into the corset. All of this was done with my back to a full-length mirror. When I turned to see myself, I broke out into almost uncontrollable laughter as I said to the film crew, "Madonna gets paid a lot of money to look like this and be taken seriously. I'm not being paid a cent, but people will seriously laugh at me." What made the commercial so very funny was I looked very much like Madonna with a dark, black mustache. These kinds of promotions don't always succeed, but this one did. Our management and program director, Dave Irvin, had produced a winning formula.

Despite the winning formula of the "Madonna" commercial,

not all was well with many to whom I considered to be close and longtime listeners. I began having discussions with many of them, including my family, regarding the commercial. While my family was split on my decision, I mostly offended my church group, who felt the relationship with Madonna and the twirling tassels were unbecoming. Even though it obviously worked for the radio station, it did not work for me or my persona.

When it came time to record another commercial, I decided against it. My personal ambitions were never to go out on the limb and then saw the limb off. God granted me a skill that I tried to use to its fullest. God also gave me a conscience. Ultimately, what mattered most to me was fulfillment, not ratings. Although many of us at Q-104 were striving for the same end, we were not all striving for the same purpose. I never felt ill-advised in doing the commercial because I had wholeheartedly supported it. Nevertheless, there was the issue of how I wanted to be remembered. Aristotle said, "We have a far better chance of hitting the target if we could only see it." My target was never to conquer celebrity; it was always to yield to something more precious than gold: the value of lasting relationships.

In the final analysis, those were the people whom I wanted to please. So in the end, you are either a celebrity devoid of a conscience or a celebrity replete with character. I chose the latter.

The *Boston Transcript* printed this significant poem:

> Here lies the body of William Jay,
> Who died maintaining his right of way—
> He was right, dead right, as he sped along,
> But he's just as dead as if he were wrong.

Q-104 was upset with me, but I promised myself never to do another controversial radio or television commercial.

Part Six

Do All the Good You Can

CHAPTER 24

My Finest Hour

I had hosted hundreds of events in downtown Cleveland, but this event was so grand, it was bigger than of all of them put together. This Monday evening, July 22, 1996, was our city's two hundredth birthday, and I was honored to host a spectacular event as master of ceremonies for Cleveland's bicentennial.

Three participants would share the stage with me that evening: Slider, the Cleveland Indians mascot; Jahja Ling, resident conductor for the Cleveland Orchestra; and Cleveland Heights native and Hollywood film star Debra Winger.

I arrived for the monumental occasion with my tuxedo in hand and was promptly escorted to my dressing room. I shared the dressing room with Slider and Jahja. Debra had her own.

The official bicentennial celebration began as the sun was setting in the west. Long shadows were forming on the east bank of the Flats as people arrived and took their seats. Most brought their own chairs for a good view of the stage, which was to the right of Shooters restaurant, across the Cuyahoga River.

People were everywhere. Thousands were seated directly in front of me. No Cleveland rush hour had ever seen the likes of this many people, seated and standing, all peering down from the Detroit–Superior Bridge. Splitting the east and west banks was a sea of boats, too many to count, gridlocked on the Cuyahoga River. As far as I could see, there wasn't an open spot on land or water. Estimates put the attendees at 450,000, the largest crowd ever assembled in downtown Cleveland. My heart swelled with pride as I looked out over the massive gathering, with my mind drifting back to a day ten years earlier when I posted the sign on my door at the radio station that read: *Cleveland, Ohio, is the greatest city in America to live, work, play, and raise a family.*

I entered stage left to get my final instructions from the producer. By the look on her face and the tone of her voice I sensed a bit of panic. "Larry, we've been following the weather reports closely and there is a rainstorm with heavy winds and lightning on the way. If that happens, I'll give you a sign to cut the Cleveland Orchestra and the fireworks display short. Be prepared for anything." My heart sank at the thought of having to cut any part of the program short.

We were minutes away from starting the program. As I stood behind the curtain, I had a moment alone before walking out on stage. As I heard my final cue from the producer, "Stand by, Larry, we're just moments away," I said in a whisper to myself, "Thank you, Lord, for bringing me *to this place* ... Cleveland's bicentennial; *at this time* ... my thirtieth anniversary in Cleveland radio; *for this reason* ... for my community." Looking out over the massive crowd, I knew a brand new script had been written for the city I loved, worked, and raised my family in.

"Larry, you're on."

I slowly walked to center stage. "Good evening, ladies and gentlemen, I'm Larry Morrow from Q-104, your host for this very special night as we celebrate our two-hundredth anniversary, Cleveland's bicentennial." I have never heard a roar like that—450,000 people cheering their city. The joy from their voices and the applause rolling all around was exciting. When the applause began to subside, I introduced Mayor Michael White, who read a letter from President Clinton congratulating Cleveland on its birthday.

Next up was Slider, who was dressed in a tuxedo and walked across the stage to thunderous cheers from the audience. Then came the centerpiece of the evening, Debra Winger, reading a letter written by Cleveland's Centennial Committee in 1896, addressed to the Cleveland Bicentennial Committee of 1996. One of the questions from the Centennial Committee I found most interesting was the one relating to aircraft. "Have you been able to solve the problem of getting the flying machine to stay in the air?" Debra's reading of the letter was choreographed to music conducted by Cleveland Orchestra. Just as the producer had warned, out of nowhere lightning pierced the sky, followed by a loud crack of thunder, and in an instant the rain began to fall. All of us on stage were protected by a huge overhang, but the enormous crowd was not.

When Debra finished reading the letter, I walked out on stage to announce the conclusion of the celebration: a giant fireworks display, also musically choreographed. As I entered center stage I looked over at the producer, and she gave me the sign to announce to the crowd that the fireworks display would be cut short. The celebrated evening climaxed with the colossal crowd all running for cover from a torrential downpour.

A VIEW FROM THE SUMMIT

Somehow that evening the world around me got smaller. I knew my broadcast career had reached its summit. I could not go any higher. I was now looking down from my highest peak, and I knew there would never be another night like this. It was something a broadcaster could only dream about, but for me, the reality was I was blessed to be able to view it from center stage.

While driving home, I could hardly wait to get home and celebrate my wedding anniversary with Rosary. It had only been thirty minutes since the celebration had ended and I was still feeling the excitement. I couldn't believe the vast number of people stretching as far as the eye could see. I had been in front of large crowds numerous times before as master of ceremonies for downtown events, but nothing could compare to this celebration.

My thoughts also switched back and forth from the present

to the past. As I drove along I-90, my eyes peered over at Lake Erie. I had a flashback to a sign from the early '70s that was perched against the breakwall that stated, *Help Me, I'm Dying.* I sadly recalled all the terrible situations that had hit the national press, creating massive amounts of negative publicity.

It struck me how many in America laughed when they heard the city named Cleveland. Our "Best Location in the Nation" motto had been reduced to the "Mistake on the Lake." Adding to the city's embarrassment was Mayor Ralph Perk's hair catching fire, the famous Dennis Kucinich disputes with the city fathers, and all the infamous sports disasters. Each and every one of these issues was being played out on national television. I also thought back to my first night in Cleveland with the 1966 Hough riots and, two years later, the Glenville riots. Those were lethal and mortal wounds to our beloved city, and I believed at that time recovery was virtually impossible.

A LESSON ON SERIOUS SET-BACKS

What continued to ring in my ears was William A. Ward's famous saying, "Failure is a delay, not a defeat. It is a temporary detour, not a dead end."

Cleveland had victoriously risen from the ashes of defeat and tonight was different. National fame and recognition had now entered the "City on the Hill," a phrase Moses Cleaveland took from the Bible and used in describing *his* Cleaveland two hundred years earlier. We were positively affected by new attitudes, and we embraced them wholeheartedly. Oh, if only Moses Cleaveland could see his city now, all aglow with flames that would burn steadily for many years to come. Our Cleveland bicentennial was not a fleeting, vicarious thrill; you could look all around you and see this was permanent. There was purpose all along the way. The bicentennial has remained one of the greatest moments of my life.

A FITTING END TO AN UGLY ERA

With the bicentennial now in the rearview mirror, there was officially a virtual tombstone marking the grave of an ugly era when Cleveland had nearly imploded. We had risen from the ashes and conquered all the negatives and emerged a winner. We were resilient. The entire turnaround team made sure that their great city had never forgotten its past when, in 1920, Cleveland was the talk of the nation for great things that were blossoming. We had just been named America's fifth-largest city and later, that same year, won baseball's World Series for the first time. Here we were, seventy-six years later, Cleveland restored to its most glorious past.

The negative publicity had narrowed to a trickle. Cleveland had regained its competitive edge and was now the talk of the nation. It was not unusual to go into the flats following a baseball game at Jacobs Field and be among a million people. How appropriate that just a few months after our bicentennial celebration, the Cleveland Indians would win the American League pennant in September and head for the World Series for the first time since 1948. Our beloved Cleveland would once again be on baseball's biggest and most glorious stage. The following year the Rock Hall would host an induction ceremony.

PROMOTING CLEVELAND'S LANDMARKS

In a market the size of Cleveland, what sustains any radio or television personality is how the community relates to him or her. Your audience knows the difference between gold dust and gold, flashy wrapping paper and what's inside. While at WIXY, 3WE, WERE, and Q-104, my aim was to be drawn closer to my audience by fostering a trusting relationship. I did all I could do to get them to know me, but more important, for me to know them and for them to know their community. As an example, early in 1985 when I joined WQAL, I discussed the idea of a

"Landmark Lunch" with Mark Biviano. Mark loved the concept and told me to proceed.

Over the course of a month, I would invite forty people to join me at a Cleveland landmark. At the end of the month, they would join me at a famous Cleveland landmark for lunch. Harlan Diamond, owner of Executive Caterers, gladly joined me in this effort by providing boxed lunches. The event would begin with me giving the history of the landmark. At the conclusion of the luncheon, everyone left the landmark knowing just a little bit more about the city they lived and raised their families in. During the course of my travels, listeners who attended one of my landmark lunches often come up to me and tell me how informative and important it was to them. I did that promotion for fifteen years at WQAL, to great success.

Beneath the surface, people who listen to you in the morning want shared values. Your hope is that your audience is marching in step with you, sharing the same concerns. This WQAL promotion was designed to have my audience build a bond between its radio station, its morning personality, and its community.

A RED-FACED BUT DELICATE REFLECTION

There was one creative promotion that did not sit well with our total audience. Because of my close relationship with the Ronald McDonald House (RMH), I was eager to promote any idea that would benefit the house. Our promotions department contacted RMH and McDonald's restaurants and discussed a promotion that would promote RMH and McDonald's at the same time.

The promotion was called "Breakfast in Bed with Larry and Sally." The idea of the promotion was to raise awareness for the house and serve as a fundraiser. McDonald's would provide breakfast to those who would come and make a contribution to the house.

A very large king-sized bed was delivered to the front of

RMH the morning of the kick-off. Sally and I hopped in the bed at 5:30 a.m. and sat in the bed as far away from each other as we could get. Sally and I both wore pajamas and encouraged those invited to also wear pajamas and join us in bed. It was actually quite uncomfortable to do our 4½-hour morning show sitting on a bed with giant stuffed pillows behind our heads as support.

We invited every politician, community leader, and television and newspaper personality to come and have breakfast in bed with us. When the morning was over, we had accomplished what we had set out to do: have fun, raise money and awareness for Ronald McDonald House, and use the unusual event as a ratings booster for Q-104. "Breakfast in Bed with Larry and Sally" was a giant hit.

What emerged from this promotion was something we were not ready for. Sally and I had an extremely harmonious relationship, but we were not married to each other. Sharing a bed together in front of thousands of listeners during the morning hours when parents were driving their children to school did not sit well. Even though much of the chatter from the promotion was good, there was also large criticism. The simple fact that Sally and I were married to different people did not go over well with our audience. Although it was innocent, we were having breakfast in bed in front of the entire city. There's an old adage that applies to this kind of outcome: Sometimes you get the bear and sometimes the bear gets you. In my opinion, the bear got us!

ON THE SET WITH DREW CAREY

In May 1999, an article in *The Plain Dealer* about the upcoming one-hundredth episode of *The Drew Carey Show* reported that Drew Carey wanted to showcase well-known names and faces from Cleveland who had an impact on his life growing up here. The anniversary show would air in late May.

Avery Friedman, called ABC, which aired the show, and

spoke to the head producer. Avery asked if she would like to have Larry Morrow on the show. As luck would have it, Drew was nearby, and when she asked him, he said, "I grew up listening to the Duker, and I would want him here to help me celebrate this important occasion."

When Avery gave me the news, all I knew was I would appear in several skits with a handful of well-known and respected Clevelanders with whom Drew felt close enough to put on his landmark show.

Following my Q-104 Tuesday show, I flew to Burbank, California. We would film the landmark episode on Wednesday for playback on Thursday. When I arrived at my hotel at 5:30 p.m. in Burbank, I received a surprise call from Casey Kasem saying that Avery had given him the good news.

"Hey, Lar'," he said, "you're going to be on national television with Drew Carey. Let's celebrate. I'm tied up on the Los Angeles freeway, but I'll be over in just about thirty minutes for a bite to eat." When Casey arrived, I was extremely tired, having been up since 2:45 a.m. eastern time. We had dinner, and I finally got to bed at 9:30 p.m. which meant I had been up for nineteen straight hours.

When I woke the next day, Drew had made arrangements to have all of us picked up in limousines and dropped off at the Burbank studios for rehearsal at 11 a.m. Clevelanders appearing on the show were John Lanigan (WMJI), Ted Henry (TV5), Tom Feran (*Plain Dealer*), Jane Scott (*Plain Dealer*), Brian and Joe (106 FM), and me.

I had filmed commercials for national television before but had never seen anything like this. The building was reminiscent of the Quonset huts I lived in while serving my time in the Marines, only this Quonset-like building was twenty times larger. There were four rooms all lined up in a row, each representing a different set of his show: the bar, his kitchen, his office, and the dining room. Each room had two side walls attached to a back wall but no top or front; that's where all the lights and cameras were set. In front of the studios was a large area that seated three hundred people, similar to a football stadium or basketball arena.

Rehearsals began promptly at 11 a.m. None of us from Cleveland had speaking parts. We were wallpaper, a term used for extras who do not have speaking roles but interact with people as if you were talking to them. That was the most difficult part for me—talking to someone without a sound coming out of your mouth, but using eye and hand nonverbal gestures and reactions.

We broke for lunch and Drew interacted with all of us, telling jokes and making a reference to how each of us had played an important role in his boyhood years. During one of the brief breaks, Jane Scott and I sat at Drew's TV desk and took a picture. While we were posing, Drew popped in to join the photo with us.

Rehearsals were now complete, and it was time to break for dinner. The food was set up outside of the studio, and it included an assortment of ribs, hot dogs, hamburgers, salads, and soft drinks. Following dinner, we all returned dressed for the filming of the show and took our places in our designated rooms where each scene would be shot. Filming concluded at 11:30 p.m., and while we were all exuberant, the one hundredth episode of *The Drew Carey Show* was officially over. "Okay, everybody, it's a wrap!" proclaimed the show's head producer.

The three hundred in the audience, which included about a hundred ABC top executives who wanted to be there for this event, all stood around and posed for pictures with Drew Carey and his fellow actors. I interviewed Drew and all of the cast members for my show on Thursday.

After all of the pictures were taken and the interviews were recorded, Drew stood up and said, "The party's at my place!" Limousines, cars, and taxis were waiting for everyone who wanted to be transported to the party. Brian and Joe asked me if I wanted to join them and ride to the party in a limo. I was still extremely tired from the nineteen-hour day on Monday and now another fifteen-hour day on Tuesday, so I told Brian and Joe I was going to pass. I also wanted to get back to Cleveland on Wednesday and play the interviews before the rest of the Cleveland celebrities got a chance to play theirs.

As I was walking out, I spoke with John Lanigan, who asked if I was going to the party. I told John I was too tired. As it turned out, John felt the same way, and we shared a cab back to our respective hotels. We may have missed one of the great Hollywood parties, but as they say in Tinseltown, "That's show biz!"

The following morning John and I flew back to Cleveland together. On Thursday morning, I played back all of the interviews with Drew and his cast members, which was the highlight of my show. I also knew it would be bittersweet.

LEAVING THE CLEVELAND STAGE

It had become obvious to me that the management of WQAL wanted to make a change. It was the first week of May 1999 when they informed me that my contract would not be renewed. It was a pleasant but quick meeting. The management believed I wanted to pursue other avenues. They were planning to move forward and wanted to do it now rather than wait until the end of the year.

I asked when they wanted me to leave. Their answer was the last Friday in May, which would then be my final show at WQAL. They also asked me to please keep our conversation private, including not telling Sally Spitz and the press. I thought not telling Sally would be very difficult since Sally and I had shared everything for the past eight years. I agreed and only passed on the information to members of my immediate family and a few close friends whom I knew I could trust to not say a word.

As the month rolled by and the last week of May was upon us, I had a feeling that whatever the giant send-off was going to be was actually not going to happen. I did *The Drew Carey Show* on Tuesday of my last week and played back the highlights on Thursday. That would leave Friday to do my last show and say a short goodbye to my friend and partner, Sally Spitz, and to our audience.

If WQAL were going to do something special I would surely have heard something through the grapevine. I had too many close relationships in all areas of entertainment, business, and politics to not have caught wind of their plan. Ultimately, it's nearly impossible to keep these kinds of things quiet.

At 10 a.m., following my show on the final Thursday in May, the program director walked into my studio and said, "The general manager would like to see you."

When I walked out of my studio, I knew I would never walk back in.

It would be just a few minutes. During my short walk out of the studio, I couldn't help but think of the past fifteen years and all the happiness, successes, and close relationships I had formed at the station.

I was directed to the financial officer's office, where I was greeted by the general manager, the program director, and the finance director. I was asked to sit down and was promptly told by the GM, "Larry, you just did your last show on WQAL." The finance director, whom I had worked with for almost fifteen years, was directed to tell me of my financial benefits through the end of my contract.

"What would like me to do now?" I asked.

"Larry, clear out your desk and take your pictures off the wall," said the GM. I almost chuckled because I owned my desk and everything in it along with everything in my office. The GM went on to say, "A memo stating you no longer work here at WQAL will arrive to the staff in just a few minutes."

My office was thirty feet away. So I got up without a word from either party, cleared out the personal items in my desk, took my pictures off the wall, said goodbye to no one other than Sally Spitz, who was in mild shock over all of this, and left the building. The time I left my studio at 10 a.m. until I was in my car took no longer than twenty minutes.

That's the way it often goes for radio and television personalities. One day you're sitting in your studio chair with a microphone in front of you, and the next day your replacement is sitting there. There's no explanation given to the audience about why you're gone.

During the filming of *The Drew Carey Show,* my friend Tom Feran, entertainment writer for *The Plain Dealer,* was also a guest. During one of our breaks, I told Tom that I would be leaving WQAL and that Friday would be my last show. Tom asked if he could come by then for an exclusive. When Thursday came along, plans changed. There would be no goodbyes.

After leaving the station offices I called Tom and told him what had happened. We agreed to meet at my friend's office building downtown to do the interview. Following the interview, Tom and I walked back to *The Plain Dealer* to have my picture taken for the article. As we walked, Tom spoke nostalgically and lovingly about the positive impact I had made on WIXY, WERE, 3WE, Q-104, and on our great city. I will be eternally grateful for his words of encouragement. The interview appeared in Saturday morning's *Plain Dealer* entertainment section with the headline, "Morrow Gone, Without a Goodbye."

Like anyone who had spent as much time in Cleveland radio and television and had been as involved as I was, I would have loved to say a few parting words to an audience who had been with me all the way. It was just not to be.

CHAPTER 25

No One Lives a Charmed Life

With radio now behind me, I decided to join a nationally known company as a minority owner. I would be the vice president of operations and new business development. At the same time that I was settling into my new business venture, I put Rosary on a plane to Atlantic City, the town where she was born and raised, so she could celebrate her birthday with her siblings. Little did I know that what lay just around the corner would be a series of life-changing events.

I had made plans to fly out early on Saturday morning to join Rosary, who did not know I was coming. When I arrived in Atlantic City, I was the one who would be surprised. Just before Rosary left for Atlantic City she had come down with, and appeared to recover from, what we thought was a serious bout of the flu. Everyone agreed that the trip would be a good time for her to relax with her family and gain her strength back. That did not happen; she appeared to be much worse than when she left Cleveland. Late Saturday afternoon, the day of her birthday, she was more interested in resting than celebrating, and she thought a short nap would comfort her ailing stomach.

While Rosary was resting with her head on my lap, I received a devastating call from my sister in Michigan. My younger brother, Bob, had passed away from a massive heart attack just one week before his Valentine's Day wedding to his high school sweetheart. The news was overwhelming. I had only been in Atlantic City a few hours when suddenly I was mourning the loss of my brother and making arrangements to return to Cleveland to be closer to my family in Michigan.

When I spoke with Rosary on Sunday, she felt she was getting worse. We decided she would cut her visit short and fly back to Cleveland on Monday so we could get her to our doctor as soon as possible. I was also making plans to go to my brother's funeral in Michigan the following Tuesday.

It was late when Rosary's plane landed at Hopkins. By the time she got off the plane, her pain had increased to the point where she was now delirious. My daughter Donna was with me, and we were both stunned by what we saw. When we got to the car, I immediately called our doctor at home and told him of Rosary's condition. He advised us to go directly to Hillcrest Hospital, where he would have a staff waiting for us.

Suffice it to say, Rosary's condition was much more serious than we could have ever imagined. We discovered her severe abdominal pain was being caused by acute pancreatitis. She had all the symptoms: severe pain, chills, fever, and vomiting. The sad part about the diagnosis was that her father, just a few years back, had passed away from the same illness. My emotions got the better of me as I became engulfed with fear for her and for our family. Watching her in this condition was more than I could bear. It was hard to control myself.

Rosary recovered from that evening, but over a five-month period I would have her back in the emergency room with several new, very painful attacks. Since the attacks kept recurring, doctors at the Cleveland Clinic advised Rosary to have an endoscopy, a relatively routine procedure where you're put to sleep and a camera mounted on a flexible tube is put down your throat to examine the inside of your upper digestive system. The device also allows the doctor to take a biopsy of suspicious tissue. While Rosary was still asleep from the procedure, I was sitting next to her bed praying and waiting for her to awaken. The doctor who performed the procedure entered the room and showed me the results.

"Larry," he said, "we found a tumor in the duct of her pancreas that appears to be highly suspicious. As soon as Rosary wakes, take her over to see Dr. J. Michael Henderson."

At that time, Dr. Henderson's title was chairman of the department of general surgery, but his specialty was pancreatic cancer. That's all I had to hear. I was devastated by the shocking news.

When Rosary awoke, she was in a joyful mood knowing that the procedure was over. I told her we had an appointment to see Dr. Henderson, but I did not share the news I had received.

During our meeting with Dr. Henderson, he could not have been more concerned and loving. As he gently took hold of one of Rosary's hands, he told her, "Rosary, you have pancreatic cancer, and you need emergency surgery." Rosary, still recovering from the anesthesia, was mildly groggy, but upon hearing the horrific diagnosis, she immediately looked at me and said, "Larry, I'm going to heaven." The ongoing sadness for her and me came during our forty-minute drive home. Rosary continued to ask me, "What did Dr. Henderson say again?" Each time she asked the question, I painfully had to repeat what he said.

Rosary's surgery was scheduled for the first week in July. When we woke up the Sunday morning a few days prior to her scheduled surgery, we decided not to go to church but spend the morning talking. Due to the severity of the diagnosis and the fact that we had not known anyone who had survived pancreatic cancer, we truly believed this might be the end. We sat on our couch and cried together for a long time. We talked about how much we loved each other and how our Lord had blessed us with a beautiful marriage and family. We discussed how this might affect our life together and our three daughters, and our young, then four-year-old granddaughter. We also said goodbye to each other.

That conversation was the most painful moment of my life, but at the same time, it was one of the most beautiful. The sheer marvel of stating your undying love for someone whom you have spent half your life with is a deeply painful experience, and at the same time, a life-transforming condition of healing.

Through divine intervention, the love and prayers of family and close friends both here and across America, and a gifted surgeon, Rosary survived the surgery and pancreatic cancer. In March 2010, she was given her ten-year clean bill of health from Dr. Henderson.

In the ensuing years since that awful disease called "cancer" initially invaded our family, I, too, became a survivor, having been diagnosed and successfully treated for prostate cancer. The disease recently reared its ugly head again with our son-in-law, who now battles lung cancer, although he never smoked a day in his life. In the midst of life's battles, our only granddaughter was born deaf and was recently diagnosed with epilepsy.

Throughout the hardships, we haven't felt any different from others who have suffered through difficult times. Like anyone, we pray to the Lord for a happy and healthy life, and that the rest of our family will be protected. Most of all, in spite of the hardships, we have tremendous peace in knowing that the Lord is in control of everything.

COAST-TO-COAST WITH LARRY MORROW

Just when you think the glow has faded from a long and prosperous career, the coach calls and says, "How would you like one more time at bat?" That call came from Avery Friedman. He had traveled to New York and spoken with the national program director at SIRIUS satellite radio and Terry Stewart, president of the Rock and Roll Hall of Fame. Avery and Terry had put together a plan for a new radio show: *Coast-to-Coast with Larry Morrow* would be broadcast from the Rock Hall every Tuesday and Wednesday from 3–6 p.m., featuring classic rock and roll music from the '50s and '60s.

Despite the fact I was spending an inordinate amount of time with my creative company, Larry Morrow Group, I had implicit trust in Avery's idea. He convinced me this would be an opportunity to promote the Rock Hall and Cleveland several times an hour to a national audience. Although a small part of me did not want to go back on the air, the idea of a national stage was enticing. At this point in my life, the questions that haunted me most were: *Did I have one more bullet in my broadcast chamber? Could I make an impact for the Rock Hall and Cleveland? Also, would I have as much fun working alone in front of a live audience, meaning the thousands who visit the Rock Hall?*

Those were all important pieces of a puzzle for me to be happy and successful. After several conversations with Avery and Terry, I decided to go forward in the fall of 2006. After just a few months on the air, I began receiving encouraging e-mails from around America. Terry was thrilled with the response.

Jason Hanley, musicologist and education department manager for the Rock Hall, came to me in late 2006 and wanted to interview me on their famous stage. The event would be called "An Evening With Larry Morrow." The press release read: "Upbeat radio personality and quintessential Clevelander kicks-off the fourth season of the popular series: *From Songwriters to Soundmen.*" I gave Jason all of my broadcast scrapbooks to assist him in his preparation in discussing local radio history, broadcast journalism, and the influence of rock and roll on Cleveland. The intimate interview was slated for Wednesday evening, January 16, 2007, at 7 p.m.

That evening I left my SIRIUS/Rock Hall studio at 6 p.m. to join Jason Hanley with Avery and Terry for dinner in their green room. I had a quiet conversation with Avery concerning how worried I was about the inclement weather and the possibility of my walking out to a sparse crowd. The temperature outside was below zero. The wind was howling, and we had several inches of snow on the ground. In other words, conditions did not bode well for a large crowd. I had good reason to worry, too, because the Rock Hall was using this important event to ring in the New Year.

After dinner, Jason said, "Let's do it." Following his introduction, I walked on to the historic museum's fourth-floor theater. On stage were two chairs with a table between them and two bottles of water on the table. Behind the chairs was a huge 12 x 12-foot screen, which would be the backdrop for the pictures and videos. The lighting was warmly subdued, creating a welcoming and relaxing setting for the interview.

As I entered the stage, to my surprise and relief, there was not one seat without a body in it. All three hundred seats were filled. For me, it was an evening to remember. Jason had put together an entertaining program using several pictures of me with the Rolling Stones, President Reagan, stories of my first meeting with Little Stevie Wonder, and the entire Cleveland connection to rock and roll. Jason used those pictures and stories to thread a pinnacle of achievement in Cleveland radio. People had traveled as far as one hundred miles in the awful Cleveland weather to spend just a little over an hour watching the interview. As apprehensive as I was about the weather, it turned out to be an awe-inspiring evening and one of the most humbling experiences of my broadcast life. The *Evening With Larry Morrow* would turn out to be the capstone of my radio career.

Working on air from the Rock Hall was a pleasure, especially during the summer months. Over one million people visit the Rock Hall each year, as it is one of the top ten entertainment destinations in America; many of those visitors come in the summer months. It was not unusual to have thirty to fifty people peering through the broadcast studio's twelve-foot windows to get a peek at a real live DJ. There were three microphones on the outside of the windows where I could talk with the museum's visitors. The crowds came from as far away as China, England, Japan, Germany, South America, and Australia. Although this communication exchange at the Rock Hall kept me entertained, the intimate relationship with the national audience was vastly missing.

Most of those who listen to SIRIUS radio are in their cars,

and there is no provision made for listeners to call in and speak with the DJ. The format had serious restrictions, which meant that the strategy for long-term listening was to play three songs without any talk, then break, mention the Rock Hall and a quip about Cleveland: "Hi, this is Larry Morrow, broadcasting coast-to-coast on SIRIUS from the beautiful Rock and Roll Hall of Fame studios located on the north coast of Cleveland, Ohio, one of greatest cities in America." So, in a fifteen-second period of time, that short phrase was all the listener heard: who, what, where, and why. Then it was back to more music.

The limitations of the SIRIUS format felt to me like a ball and chain attached to my leg. That was the bad news. But on the other hand, every time I opened my microphone I was speaking to millions.

One evening over dinner I told Avery that the structure of the SIRIUS music format had inhibited me from the kind of radio I wanted to do, and I didn't believe I could continue. I felt I was being dragged down by an undertow of a powerful musical format that had no personality. When working in Cleveland radio, I was speaking to people I knew, in the city I loved, about issues that were part and parcel to their life. That was no longer the case. The SIRIUS format was devoid of connecting the performer to the audience; it was connecting music with the audience. I addressed this issue to Avery with sincere candor. Avery then provided straightforward feedback.

"Larry, the last thing I would want for you is to be unhappy in your work. But if you abandon SIRIUS satellite radio, this most assuredly will be your last radio job. Is that what you want?" I acknowledged his concern. After some discussion, we both agreed it was time to leave.

Avery was present for my last show, and Terry Stewart came to the studio to say goodbye. One lingering concern about leaving was my overarching desire to promote the Rock Hall for Cleveland and for Terry. Despite my deep fondness for both, I left SIRIUS satellite in late 2008.

Departing Cleveland radio was a life-changing event. That evening, as I drove away from the Rock Hall with my headphones resting on the passenger seat next to me, I glanced over at them and thought to myself, "It's over. My forty-year radio career is really over." When you get to the end of something that has brought so much success and happiness to your life, you sometimes say to yourself, "Wow, that went by so fast!" But for me, my forty years in Cleveland radio and television moved slowly. What a ride. *What an incredibly satisfying ride.*

In the book *The Little Prince*, the fox says to the little prince, "It is only with the heart that one can see rightly. What is essential is invisible to the eye." The unseen thread to my audience was them knowing how much I cared for their families and the town they lived in. Inasmuch as I considered my life a very private affair, I shared much of my personal life with my audience. They knew of my deep love for my wife and my three children because I always talked about them. There were also moral and political issues that I knew my audience cared about that drove me to speak out, especially when the contemporary music-of-the-day became suggestive and obscene, and the city I loved was picked on.

In all of these pages, I have tried to recreate the stories with anecdotes to what I considered fascinating inside details. Most of all, I desired to create unforgettable pictures that told stories with profound insights. I sought to tell what it was like to be behind the scenes of major events that affected both Cleveland and me personally. Also, with astonishing frankness, there were times when leaving a certain radio station was painful to me and to my audience. Through all the good, the bad, and the ugly, I don't recall one myth written about me in all of my broadcast life. The people I met on the streets, the backbone of our great city, will never know how much they changed my life. On the other hand, there were those whom I interviewed with globally recognized names who had no effect on my life. There are so many stories to tell, I could fill volumes.

For instance, a few months back I was approached by a woman who told me her husband had won concert tickets on my show. That concert not only was their first date, it was the beginning of a long-lasting relationship. They had just celebrated their twenty-fifth wedding anniversary.

I also recently received an e-mail from a listener in Los Angeles who had heard my voice as the announcer on a program called Truth For Life (TFL) with Senior Pastor Alistair Begg. TFL originates from Parkside Church in Cleveland but is heard around the world. This man heard my voice and sent an e-mail to me to let me know that I had interviewed him when he was a young soldier in Vietnam. The interview that was played back over WIXY 1260 had a profound impact, not only on his life, but for his loved ones back home. As I read his touching letter, my heart swelled with emotion. Here we are, forty years removed from the Vietnam War, but I could sense the tears in his eyes as he wrote it and the tears in mine as I read it.

There was a family with six young children who had met me at an event. The mother said, "I know that you would never come to our house for dinner, but we would love to have you." One of the young children piped up with, "My mom makes the greatest lasagna."

"Well, I *love* lasagna," was my reply, "and I would *love* to come to your house for dinner!" I not only spent the evening with the family, I remained friendly with all of them for most of my career. To this day, their grown children will often write me and tell me what that experience meant to them.

Who could have been more blessed than me by being on stage to introduce the most important men in the world: the presidents of the United States? Regardless of my political affiliation, each of these four men, Presidents Carter, Reagan, Clinton, and Vice President Bush, changed my life. After all, I was only a broadcaster, one who had been told early on in radio school that I would never make it.

Being on the air in Cleveland radio gave me a lifetime of lasting relationships. For all of the above, I am eternally grateful. In theater, depending on what part you play, you leave the stage, quickly change your costume, and return as a new character. For me there would not be a dual role. The character I played in Cleveland radio was not me, it was my audience. I played them as they related to all the things that mattered in their life. You never know how far your voice will carry, but I only wanted mine to carry fourteen inches; the distance from your head to your heart. I will always be eternally grateful for the forty years the Cleveland audience gave me to express how I felt about them and our great community.

Albert Schweitzer once said, "Life becomes harder for us when we live for others, but it also becomes richer and happier." Ralph Waldo Emerson said, "A man is a success if one other life has breathed easier because he has lived." I don't believe that one life has breathed easier because I have lived, but I do believe that my life has become richer and happier. As one national reporter asked me years ago, "Why do you stay in Cleveland rather than move up to New York, Chicago, or Los Angeles?" My response was, "I want to stay here because I have fallen in love with the people of Cleveland and the community they live in."

The only proper way to end my story is the way I always signed off at WIXY 1260:

Do all the good you can . . .

To everyone you can . . .

Every time you can.

Acknowledgments

"The best thing about the future is that it comes only one day at a time."
—Abraham Lincoln

My future in Cleveland radio began over forty years ago, and there are so many along the way who helped me to live it richly and fully—*one day at a time.* My calling in life has led me to places where there was greatness all around me, and I was deeply inspired by it all.

First and foremost, I want to thank my wife of thirty-seven years, Rosary, for her undying patience; over the past two years she has been nothing short of amazing as she endured my complete immersion into the creative process of writing my first book. So, while in bed at night, instead of our little good-night conversations, I would spend the time scribbling on one piece of paper after another, only to find them in the morning all wadded up on my nightstand. During our vacations, when everyone was out having fun on the beach, I sat under an umbrella and typed away on my laptop, which at times almost seemed like the uninvited third person on our trip. At home I locked myself away in my office for countless hours at a time. I would often remark to Amy during editing time, "Poor Rosary. This weekend I spent ten hours working in my office on the book." Now that the book is finally complete, Rosary and I laugh as we think back over the past two years. Her gentle, comical reminders along the way let me know just how much I was consumed by this project:

"You're going to be in your office writing again?"

"You've been working for eighteen months on this book; how much more can you write?"

"What are you doing with all those little pieces of paper you keep scribbling on?"

"Your daughters would like to know when their dad is going to show up again."

I also want to acknowledge my personal attorney, who also happens to be my son-in-law, Charles Alusheff, who constantly reminds me that not everyone will like you, and if they do, something is wrong with you.

I also want to acknowledge my mother and father, who instilled in me a discipline that drove me to express and find kindness in everyone, and taught me there was no gain in dishonesty.

To my older brother, Jim, whose fierce sense of discipline initially encouraged me to follow in his footsteps as an athlete. Whenever I'm faced with the daily challenges that life often brings, I can still hear his words of wisdom: "If you want to achieve greatness in life and as a jock, excuses don't count." Through his spirited attitude and inspiration, I learned how to face weaknesses and turn them into strengths while a football athlete with the 11th Marine Division at Camp Pendleton.

To my younger brother Mickey, whose life has been marked by a passionate unselfishness towards all whom he deeply cherishes, especially our mom and dad, and brothers and sisters.

How I love and look up to my sisters, Sandy and Shari, and the way they exemplified unfailing commitment, love, and devotion to their siblings, spouses, and children.

To my youngest brother Bob, who dedicated his short life to police work and would allow nothing to interfere with his love for his immediate family and the entire Morrow clan. Although he is gone, he will never be forgotten.

Other than my family, no one played a greater role in my life than my dearest friend and spiritual brother Joe Abraham, senior pastor at Scranton Road Bible Church in Cleveland. It was Joe who found me along the way and brought me to a loving relationship with Jesus Christ. Joe dedicated his life to working with the poor, the downtrodden, and the unfortunate. How I love and admire his work. And, as another pastor once said, "May your tribe increase." Through the years, Joe has amassed an impressive collection of stories about how he has patiently endured the frustration of often being mistaken for Larry Morrow. While our similar Middle Eastern looks may have initially brought us together, our strong, spiritual bond has made our friendship eternal.

To my dear, close friend, Avery Friedman, who has not only been an intellectual bloodline of advice over the past fifteen years, but who has kept me hungry for greater challenges in my life, mainly this book.

I also want to thank my neighbor, good friend, and Hall of Fame broadcaster Bill Needle for leaving an inspirational message of encouragement on my cell phone. When the workload of the massive project became overwhelming, and I found myself asking: *Who cares what Larry Morrow has to say?* And when I was plagued by the decision to either go forward or leave the entire project behind, it was Bill's enthusiasm for the book that motivated me to continue writing.

Over lunch one day, novel-writer, movie producer, and friend Scott Lax managed to bring his knowledge and sensitivity to the critiquing process. His insights and commentary encouraged me to continue writing, in his words, a great book.

For the past ten years, my partner and close associate in the Larry Morrow Group has been Amy Lawrence. How could this book have ever been written without her dedication and literary knowledge? Amy and I have sat for hundreds of hours staring at a computer screen, writing and editing. At the outset of the project, two years ago, I informed Amy that I wanted this book to be my words; she was not to change one of them. She has since gone on to change many, including the ones you are currently reading. We have often squabbled over the use of a word, broke for lunch, come back to the office, and continued with our verbal wrestling match. After leaving the office, I would then later call her on the phone to discuss the word again, and eventually give in. Amy taught me to always keep an open mind about how a thought flows and the impact it will have on the reader. Knowing my background as a musician and songwriter, Amy drew the analogy of me writing a musical score. The composer has to understand the instrumentation as well as how certain instruments create memorable affects. The same is true for a writer. The writer has to understand his topic and use words to paint a vivid picture. It's important to have a combination of events that takes people to the edge of their seat, then allows them time to sit back and catch their breath. Thank you, Amy.

A special thank you to Norman Wain, Tom Embrescia, Walt Tiburski, Tony Ocepek, Sam Miller, Richard Pogue, Mike Benz, Marty Zanotti, Mark Biviano, Dale Finley, Jim Brosius, Brian Tucker, Ray Glasser, Frank Tolar, Candy Forest, Linda Scott, and United States senators George Voinovich and Sherrod Brown for their thoughtful and compelling words. Each of you are real life examples in guiding me through an inspiring lifetime of relationships.

My friend, Bill Lubinger, a gifted, award-winning writer for *The Plain Dealer*, was truly an invaluable source of strength in this project. His magnificent ability helped me amplify and chronicle the magic of storytelling. Bill's affection for my story was critical in getting the book done.

Finally, I want to thank my publisher, David Gray, whose words of wisdom were the final inspiration that I needed to put the pedal to the metal and start writing.